# Writing the Research Paper

## A HANDBOOK • SECOND EDITION

# Writing the Research Paper
## A HANDBOOK • SECOND EDITION

## With the 1984 MLA Documentation Style

Anthony C. Winkler

**Jo Ray McCuen**
*Glendale Community College*

**Harcourt Brace Jovanovich, Publishers**

San Diego    New York    Chicago    Atlanta    Washington, D.C.

London    Sydney    Toronto

Cover: HBJ photo by Amy Krammes

ISBN: 0-15-598291-5
Library of Congress Catalog Card Number: 84-81508
Printed in the United States of America

# Preface

This Second Edition of *Writing the Research Paper* retains the handbook format of the first, which makes it possible for students to locate specific topics quickly. Because books on the research paper are consulted but seldom read from cover to cover, we have organized the material into discrete and informative parts that are clearly labeled and indexed; all the information should be easily and instantly accessible in whole or in part.

The primary reason for preparing this new edition is to incorporate the Modern Language Association's new guidelines on writing research papers. The most notable change is the adoption of a parenthetical style of documentation. In our view, this is a sensible change and one that most instructors will happily embrace. Yet there will remain instructors who favor the traditional footnotes or endnotes or who would prefer to teach a single, universal style usable in all academic disciplines.

But such unanimity among disciplines is still a utopian dream. English departments use the author/work style recommended by the MLA. The disciplines of anthropology, biology, linguistics, psychology, sociology, and business, among others, use the author/year style favored by the American Psychological Association (APA). Music, history, philosophy, religion, and theater continue to use traditional footnotes or endnotes, while chemistry, medicine, and computer science use the numbers style. And we writing instructors are responsible for teaching our students how to write research papers not only for us but for other disciplines as well.

What we have done in this edition, then, is to feature the new MLA style in great detail, cover the APA style nearly as comprehensively, give an explanation—with examples—of the traditional footnote and endnote styles, and briefly touch on the numbers style. In Chapter 7, we provide students with a "Guide to Systems of Documentation," a catalog of the styles preferred by the major disciplines. Chapter 11 contains an annotated full-length student paper exemplifying the new MLA style. But the chapter also includes an excerpt from a paper written in the APA style, as well as sample pages from a paper documented in the traditional footnote/endnote style. The result is a book that emphasizes the style favored by the MLA, but that will also be valuable to students writing papers in subjects all across the curriculum.

This edition contains much new material, especially on evaluating sources of evidence and on the use of computers to search databases. We have updated the annotated list of reference sources and moved it to an appendix. We have also added a "calendar" of the various stages in preparing a research paper and have suggested a timetable for completing each stage.

In preparing this new edition, we received indispensable advice and criticism from many colleagues. We are especially grateful to Kathleen A. Hart of Bowling Green State University. Our thanks also to Hazel McCuen, who performed yeoman service in poring over the manuscript and correcting our mistakes.

Anthony C. Winkler
Jo Ray McCuen

# Contents

## Four    Doing the Research    25

## Five    The Thesis and the Outline    43

## Ten   Mechanics   183

## Eleven   Sample Student Papers   199

# Appendix  General and Specialized References  237

# One
# Basic Information About the Research Paper

## 1a Definition of the research paper

## 1b Format of the research paper

## 1c Reasons for the research paper

## 1d Steps and schedule involved in writing a research paper

## 1e The report paper and the thesis paper

# 1a

## Definition of the research paper

The research paper is a typewritten paper in which you present your views and research findings on a chosen topic. Variously known as the "term paper" or the "library paper," the research paper is usually between five and fifteen pages long, with most teachers specifying a minimum length. No matter what the paper is called, your task is essentially the same: to read on a particular topic, evaluate information about it, and report your findings in a paper.

# 1b

## Format of the research paper

The research paper cannot be written according to a random formula but must conform to a specific format such as the one devised by the Modern Language Association, a society of language scholars. The format governs the entire paper from the placing of the title to the width of the margins, and to the notation used in acknowledging material drawn from other sources.

The format of scholarly writing is simply an agreed-upon way of doing things—much like etiquette, table manners, or rules of the road. For instance, in literary articles published recently you are likely to run across passages similar to this one:

> Brashear considers Tennyson to be at his best when his poetry is infused with "that tragic hour when the self fades away into darkness, fulfilling all of the poet's despairing pessimism." (18)

This citation is in the new style of "parenthetical documentation" now being used by the Modern Language Association. The author of a quotation is briefly introduced, the quotation cited, and a page reference supplied in parentheses. In the alphabetized bibliography of the article will appear this listing:

> Brashear, William. *The Living Will*. The Hague: Mouton, 1969.

This sort of standardization is as time-saving to scholars as standardization of pipe fittings is to plumbers. To do research, or even to read articles about it, you must become familiar with the major citation styles used by scholars—all of which are covered in this book.

2

# 1c

## Reasons for the research paper

One obvious reason for writing a research paper is that the experience familiarizes the student with the conventions of scholarly writing. The student learns accepted styles of documentation, the ethics of research, and a great deal about the chosen subject.

A second reason is that students become familiar with the library through the "learn by doing" method. Even the simplest library is an intricate storehouse of information, bristling with indexes, encyclopedias, abstracts, and gazetteers. How to ferret out from this maze of sources a single piece of needed information is a skill that students learn by doing actual research. The ability to use a library is a priceless skill, because sooner or later everyone needs to find out about something: a mother needs to know how to stop her child from biting his fingernails; a physician, how to treat a rare illness; a lawyer, how to successfully argue an unusual case. Everyone can profit from knowing how to do research.

There are other benefits besides. Writing the research paper is an exercise in logic, imagination, and common sense. As students chip away at the mass of data and information available on their chosen topics, they learn

- how to think
- how to organize
- how to discriminate between worthless and useful opinions
- how to summarize the gist of wordy material
- how to budget their time
- how to conceive of a research project from the start, manage it through its intermediary stages, and finally assemble the information uncovered into a useful, coherent paper.

# 1d

## Steps and schedule involved in writing a research paper

Generally, there are seven distinct steps requiring you to produce at least five hand-ins over a period of five weeks. With some variations, many instructors will more or less observe this schedule:

| WHAT YOU MUST DO | WHAT YOU MUST PRODUCE | WHEN IT'S DUE |
|---|---|---|
| 1. A topic must be selected that is complex enough to be researched from a variety of sources, but narrow enough to be covered in ten or so pages. | Two acceptable topics, one of which will be approved by the instructor. | At the end of the first week. |
| 2. Exploratory scanning and in-depth reading must be done on the approved topic. | A bibliography of all titles to be used in the paper. | At the end of the second week. |
| 3. The information gathered must be recorded (usually on note cards) and assembled into a coherent sequence. | | |
| 4. A thesis statement must be drafted, setting forth the major idea of your paper. | Note cards, a thesis statement, and an outline. | At the end of the third week. |
| 5. The paper must be outlined in its major stages. | | |
| 6. The paper must be written in rough draft and the thesis argued, proved, or supported with the information uncovered from the sources. Borrowed ideas, data, and opinions must be acknowledged. | A rough draft of the paper. | At the end of the fourth week. |
| 7. A bibliography must be prepared, listing all sources used in the paper. The final paper must be written. | The final paper, complete with bibliography. | At the end of the fifth week. |

# 1e

## The report paper and the thesis paper

The two kinds of papers usually assigned in colleges are the report paper and the thesis paper. The report paper summarizes and reports a writer's findings on a particular subject. The writer neither judges nor evaluates the findings, but merely catalogs them in a sensible sequence. For instance, a paper that listed the opinions of statesmen during the debate over the Panama Canal treaty would be a report paper. Likewise, a paper that chronologically narrated the final days of Hitler would also be a report paper.

Unlike the report paper, the thesis paper takes a definite stand on an issue. A thesis is a proposition or point of view that a writer or speaker is willing to argue against or defend. A paper that argued for ratification of the Panama Canal treaty would therefore be a thesis paper. So would a paper that attempted to prove that Hitler's political philosophy was influenced by the writings of the philosopher Nietzsche. Here are two more examples of topics as they might conceivably be treated in report papers and thesis papers:

Report paper: A summary of the theories of hypnosis.
Thesis paper: Hypnosis is simply another form of Pavlovian conditioning.

Report paper: The steps involved in passage of federal legislation.
Thesis paper: Lobbyists have a disproportionate amount of influence on federal legislation.

Teachers are more likely to assign a thesis paper than a report paper, for obvious reasons. Writing the thesis paper requires the student to exercise judgment, evaluate evidence, and construct a logical argument, whereas writing the report paper does not.

# Two
# Choosing a Topic

**2a** How to choose a topic

**2b** Topics to avoid

**2c** Narrowing the topic

# 2a

### How to choose a topic

Ideally, you should choose a topic that interests you, that is complex enough to generate several research sources, and that will neither bore nor stultify. We offer the following advice.

- Pick a subject that you're curious about, or that you're either an expert on or are genuinely interested in. For example, if you have always been intrigued by the character of Rasputin, the "mad monk" of Russia, you can learn more about him by using him as the topic of your paper. Similarly, an interest in the career of Elvis Presley might lead to a paper analyzing and evaluating his music.
- If you are utterly at a loss for a subject, have positively no interest in anything at all, and cannot for the life of you imagine what you could write ten whole pages on, then go to the library and browse. Pore over books, magazines, card catalogs. An encyclopedia can be a veritable supermarket of possible topics. Browse through its entries until you find an appealing subject. Even a general idea can be whittled down to a specific topic (see 2c below). But you must first arrive at the general idea.
- Take your time as you search for a topic. Don't latch onto the first workable idea that pops into your head. Mull it over. Ask yourself whether you'd really enjoy spending five weeks on that subject. If you have any qualms, keep browsing until you get an idea that really excites you. All of us are or can be excited about something (thankfully, not the same thing). So whatever you do, don't make the mistake of choosing "any old" topic merely for the sake of getting on with it. Choose carelessly now and you'll pay dearly later. But choose carefully and you'll be rewarded with the age-old excitement of research.

# 2b

### Topics to avoid

Some topics present unusual difficulties; others are simply a waste of time. Here is a summary of topics to avoid.

#### 2b-1　Topics that are too big

The research paper, though it may be the longest writing assignment you will receive during the semester, is still scarcely longer than a short magazine article. Obviously, you can neither review the evolution of man nor completely fathom the mysteries of creation in ten pages. Don't even try. Regrettably, we cannot give you a good rule of thumb for avoiding impossibly broad topics. Use your common sense. Check the card catalog. If you find that numerous books have been written about your topic, then it is probably too big. The signs that you may have bitten off more than you can chew usually come only after you're already deeply mired in the research. Reference sources that multiply like flies; a bibliography that grows like a cancer; opinions, data, and information that come pouring in from hundreds of sources—these signs all indicate a topic that is too big. The solution is to narrow the topic without darting to the sanctuary of the trivial. Here are some examples of hopelessly big topics: "The Influence of Greek Mythology on Poetry"; "The Rise and Fall of Chinese Dynasties"; "The Framing of the U.S. Constitution."

### 2b-2  Topics that can be traced to a single source

Research papers must be documented with a variety of opinions drawn from different authorities and sources. One reason for assigning the research paper in the first place is to expose students to the opinions of different authorities, to a variety of books and articles, and to other reference sources. Consequently, if the topic is so skimpy that all data on it can be culled from a single source, the purpose of the paper is defeated. Choose only topics that are broad enough to be researched from multiple sources.

Biographies are numbered among those subjects that must be chosen with care lest they lead to a one-source paper. If you choose to write about a person, use an approach that allows the use of a variety of sources. For example, you might focus on your subject's contributions, motivation, or development. Avoid becoming so charmed by any single account of your subject's life that you end up merely parroting it.

### 2b-3  Topics that are too technical

A student may have an astonishing expertise in one technical subject, and may be tempted to display this dazzling knowledge in a research paper. Resist the temptation. Technical subjects often require a technical jargon that the teacher might not understand and might even dismiss as an elaborate "snow job." The skills that a research paper should instill in the student are better displayed in a paper on a general subject. Stick to some subject broad enough to be understood by any decently educated reader. The following are examples of overly technical topics: "The Use of Geometry in the Perspective of Paolo Uccelo"; "Heisenberg's Principle of Indeterminacy as It Applies to Subparticle Research"; "Utilitarianism versus Positivism in Legal Rights Cases Involving Minorities."

### 2b-4   Topics that are too trivial

Obviously, your own common sense and judgment must steer you away from such topics, but here are some that teachers would reject as too trivial: "The Use of Orthopedic Braces for Dachshunds Prone to Backaches"; "The Cult of Van Painting in America"; "The History of the Tennis Ball"; "How to Get Dates When You're Divorced."

# 2c

## Narrowing the topic

Big, monster-sized topics are easy enough to think of, probably because big issues such as feminism, civil rights, and human aggression are constantly bandied about in the press and in casual talk. But it is a serious mistake to try to corral one of these monsters in a ten-page paper. First, it is difficult to make sense out of the millions of words in the library on such issues. Deluged with innumerable sources, most of which you simply haven't got the time to go through, you will end up choosing a few random sources out of hundreds, with the attendant risk of making a bad, unrepresentative choice. Second, apart from being more difficult to research, the big topic is also more difficult to write about: one never knows quite where to begin, and one never knows how to end without seeming silly. Third, omissions and oversights are nowhere more crudely obvious than in a small paper on a big topic.

The first step, then, once a general subject area is found, is to narrow it down to a suitably small topic. There is no easy or set way of doing this. One must simply be guided by the available sources and information; again, common sense must come into play. No python knows the exact dimensions of its mouth, but any python instinctively knows that it cannot swallow an elephant. Experiment with your topic: pursue one train of thought and see where it leads, and whether or not it yields an arguable thesis. Pare down and whittle away until you've got something manageable. Bear in mind that ten pages amount to a very modest length—some books have longer prefaces. Here are a few examples of the narrowing that you'll have to do:

| BROAD TOPIC | FIRST NARROWING | FURTHER NARROWING |
|---|---|---|
| Mythology | *Beowulf* | Courtesy codes in *Beowulf* |
| Migrant workers | California migrant workers | Major California labor laws and their impact on Mexican migrant workers |

| BROAD TOPIC | FIRST NARROWING | FURTHER NARROWING |
|---|---|---|
| Theater | Theater of the Absurd | Theater-of-the-Absurd elements in *Who's Afraid of Virginia Woolf?* |
| Jack Kennedy | Jack Kennedy's cabinet | The contribution of Averell Harriman as U.S. Ambassador to Russia |
| Russia | The Bolshevik Revolution of 1917 | The role of Grigory Efimovich Rasputin in pre-revolutionary Russia |
| Indians | Famous Indian fighters | Major Rogers' Rangers during the Indian wars |

The first attempt at narrowing a topic is usually easier than the second, which must yield a specific topic. Use trial and error until you've got a topic you're comfortable with. Further narrowing, if necessary, will suggest itself once you're into the actual research.

Note that whatever topic you choose must be approved by your instructor. So before you become too involved in narrowing the subject, be sure that in its basic outline your teacher approves of it.

# Three
# The Library

**3a** Layout of the library

**3b** Organization of the library

# 3a

## Layout of the library

Most of the research for your paper will be done at a library. Basic architectural design varies from one library to another, but certain facilities are standard. All well-organized libraries include the following:

### 3a-1   Card catalog

The card catalog is an alphabetical index of all books in the library. It consists of $3 \times 5$ cards that are stored in little drawers, usually near the main entrance of the library. The card catalog lists all books under at least three headings: author, subject, and title. The cards are alphabetized by the first important word in the heading. A book that straddles two or more subjects will be listed separately under each subject. If an editor, translator, or illustrator is involved, the book will also be listed under the name of each, in addition to being listed under the name of the author. A jointly authored book is also likely to be listed under the name of each author.

Basic research generally begins with a search of the card catalog, which literally puts a wealth of information at a researcher's fingertips. On pages 15–17 are examples of index cards that list the same book in different ways.

In combing the card catalog for books and sources on a topic, don't overlook the possibility of finding useful material under separate but related headings. For example, if you are looking for sources on "Pablo Picasso," you should also look under such cross-references as "Modern Art," "French Art," "Abstract Art," and "Cubism."

### 3a-2   Microform indexes

Many libraries now use microform indexes for periodicals as well as for their permanent book collections. Systems vary from one library to another. Microfilm systems are used by some libraries to index the articles of major periodicals. Most such systems depend on microfilm readers that allow for a fast scan or slow search. A microfiche storage system is also used to catalog articles published in major national newspapers. Either system (or both) may be available in your own library.

### 3a-3   Stacks

"Stacks" is the name given to the shelves on which the books and periodicals are stored in the library. The stacks may be either *open* or *closed*. If the stacks are open, readers may roam at will among the shelves and handle the books; if the stacks are closed, readers are denied direct

**Figure 3-1** Author card (also called "Main entry")

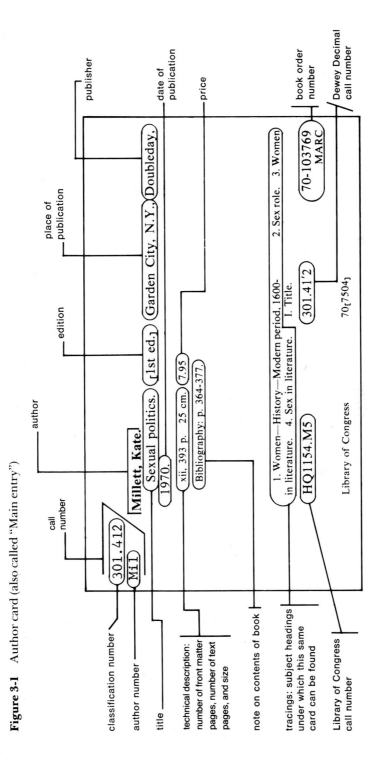

title
(usually
typed in
black ink)

301.412
Mil    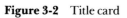 Sexual politics.
       **Millett, Kate.**
              Sexual politics.  ₍1st ed.₎  Garden City, N.Y., Doubleday,
              1970.
                   xii, 393 p.   25 cm.   7.95
                   Bibliography: p. 364-377.




                   1. Women—History—Modern period, 1600-        2. Sex role.   3. Women
              in literature.    4. Sex in literature.      I. Title.
              HQ1154.M5                          301.41'2                    70-103769
                                                                             MARC

              Library of Congress               70₍7504₎

**Figure 3-2**   Title card


**Figure 3-3**   Subject card

subject
heading
(usually
typed in
red ink)

301.412
Mil    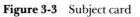 WOMEN--HISTORY
       **Millett, Kate.**
              Sexual politics.   ₍1st ed.₎   Garden City, N.Y., Doubleday,
              1970.
                   xii, 393 p.   25 cm.   7.95
                   Bibliography: p. 364-377.




                   1. Women—History—Modern period, 1600-        2. Sex role.   3. Women
              in literature.    4. Sex in literature.      I. Title.
              HQ1154.M5                          301.41'2                    70-103769
                                                                             MARC

              Library of Congress               70₍7504₎

subject
heading
(usually
typed in
red ink)

301.412   (FEMINISM)
Mil       **Millett, Kate.**
            Sexual politics.   [1st ed.]   Garden City, N.Y., Doubleday,
          1970.

            xii, 393 p.   25 cm.   7.95
            Bibliography: p. 364-377.


            1. Women—History—Modern period, 1600-          2. Sex role.   3. Women
          in literature.   4. Sex in literature.   I. Title.

          HQ1154.M5                    301.41′2                    70-103769
                                                                   MARC


          Library of Congress              70[7504]

**Figure 3-4**   Cross-reference card

access to the shelves, and must obtain books from clerks by listing the title of the book, its author, and its call number on a request slip. Closed stacks are more common at larger libraries; in smaller libraries the stacks are usually open. While inconvenient to a reader, closed stacks reduce the chance of pilferage, misfiling, and defacement of books. Open stacks, on the other hand, allow a reader to browse at leisure.

### 3a-4   Reference room

Encyclopedias, indexes, gazetteers, and other works that are ordinarily consulted for information, rather than read from cover to cover, are stored in a reference room. Usually large and unwieldy, these volumes are generally confined to use within the reference room; they cannot be checked out and taken home.

### 3a-5   Main desk

The main desk functions as an information center as well as a checkout counter for books. Librarians and clerks stationed here are trained to help the researcher find material or track down difficult sources. Library personnel can be of invaluable assistance; if you are confused and lost, don't be afraid to ask them for help.

### 3a-6   Reserve desk

Reserve books are kept at the reserve desk. Books on reserve are available for use only in the library and only for a limited time—generally for an hour or two. Teachers will often place on reserve any book or magazine essential to their lectures or courses. When the demand for a book exceeds the supply, the book will often be placed in the reserve collection, which in many libraries is listed in a separate reserve catalog.

### 3a-7   Audiovisual room

Cassettes, tapes, picture slides, filmstrips, and other nonbook media are stored in an audiovisual room and generally indexed by whatever conventional filing system the library uses (see Dewey Decimal System and Library of Congress System below). The audiovisual librarian will help you locate this kind of material. Often the audiovisual supply room adjoins an equipment area where students can listen to tapes or watch a film. Some libraries, replete with extensive new audiovisual hardware, now call themselves media centers rather than libraries.

### 3a-8   Microform room

Microfilm and microfiche are stored in a microform room. Microfilm is material photographically stored on filmstrips; microfiche is material photographically mounted on frames. For centuries, back issues of journals, magazines, and newspapers were piled up in dusty heaps in the dark, cobwebbed stock rooms of libraries. But with the advent of cameras that can reduce entire pages to a tiny filmstrip, periodical material is now economically stored in this microscopic form and read with magnifying equipment.

### 3a-9   Newspaper racks

Many libraries subscribe to major national and foreign newspapers. Current issues are generally displayed on long wooden clamps, known as newspaper racks, that hold and store the newspapers. Often the newspaper racks are surrounded by comfortable chairs in which a reader can sit for a leisurely assessment of world events. Typical newspapers found in these racks include *The New York Times, The Washington Post, The Los Angeles Times, The Christian Science Monitor, The Wall Street Journal, The London Times, The Manchester Guardian, The Hindustan Times,* and *Die Zeit.*

### 3a-10   Xerox room

Xerox machines are available in most libraries for photocopying. The charge for this service ranges anywhere from a nickel to a quarter.

### 3a-11   Typing room

Typewriters are available in many libraries, either at a reasonable rental rate or without charge. The machines are usually kept in a designated typing room, which is often soundproof.

### 3a-12   Carrels

Carrels are small enclosed desks equipped with bookshelves, and are especially designed to provide students with a quiet, insulated enclosure for reading or research. The carrel section of a library is set aside for students intent on serious scholarship. Some libraries even impose fines on students caught capering in this area. Carrels can generally be reserved by advanced students for either a semester or an entire school year; the remaining carrels are distributed among lower-division students on a first-come, first-served basis.

### 3a-13   The computer

The computer is fast becoming an invaluable research tool in the library. Information is stored in databases and accessed through a terminal. Section 4a-1 discusses the use of a computer to search for sources and information.

# 3b

## Organization of the library

Even the great libraries of antiquity, such as the one in Nineveh in the sixth century B.C., or in Alexandria in the third century B.C., searched constantly for more efficient systems of organizing their collections. Clay tablets were grouped by subject and stored on shelves; papyrus rolls were stacked in labeled jars. The Chinese, whose library tradition dates back to the sixth century B.C., grouped their writings under four primary headings: classics, history, philosophy, and belles lettres. And by 1605 the English philosopher Sir Francis Bacon had independently devised a system of classifying all knowledge into three similar categories of history, poetry, and philosophy, which were then further subdivided to yield specific subjects.

Knowledge has grown so enormously, and classification systems have become so complex, that today librarians are trained extensively in classifying books. The two major classification systems now used by libraries are the Dewey Decimal System and the Library of Congress System.

### 3b-1   The Dewey Decimal System

Devised in 1873 by Melvil Dewey and first put to use in the library of Amherst College, the Dewey Decimal System divides all knowledge (fiction and biography excepted) into ten general categories:

| | |
|---|---|
| 000–099 | General Works |
| 100–199 | Philosophy and Psychology |
| 200–299 | Religion |
| 300–399 | Social Sciences |
| 400–499 | Language |
| 500–599 | Pure Science |
| 600–699 | Technology (Applied Sciences) |
| 700–799 | The Arts |
| 800–899 | Literature |
| 900–999 | History |

Each of these ten general categories is subdivided into ten smaller divisions. For example, the category of Literature (800–899) is further divided into:

| | |
|---|---|
| 800–809 | General Works (about Literature) |
| 810–819 | American Literature |
| 820–829 | English Literature |
| 830–839 | German Literature |
| 840–849 | French Literature |
| 850–859 | Italian Literature |
| 860–869 | Spanish Literature |
| 870–879 | Latin Literature |
| 880–889 | Greek and Classical Literature |
| 890–899 | Literature of Other Languages |

The specific category of English Literature is further divided into narrower groups:

| | |
|---|---|
| 820 | English Literature (General) |
| 821 | Poetry |
| 822 | Drama |
| 823 | Fiction |
| 824 | Essays |
| 825 | Speeches |
| 826 | Letters |
| 827 | Satire and Humor |
| 828 | Miscellany |
| 829 | Minor Related Literature |

An endless number of more specific headings are easily created through the addition of decimal places. For instance, from the category of English Literature—820—the more specific heading of Elizabethan Literature is devised: 822.3. The addition of another decimal place creates an even more specific category for the works of Shakespeare: 822.33.

The obvious advantage of the Dewey Decimal System is the ease with which it yields specific categories to accommodate the rapid proliferation of books. Probably for this reason, the system is currently used in more libraries throughout the world than all other systems combined.

### 3b-2 The Cutter/Sanborn Author Marks

The Dewey Decimal System is generally used in conjunction with the Cutter/Sanborn Author Marks, devised originally by Charles Ammi Cutter and later merged with a similar system independently invented by Kate Sanborn. The Cutter/Sanborn Author Marks distinguish between books filed under an identical Dewey number. In the early days of the Dewey system, books with the same Dewey number were simply shelved alphabetically by author. But as more and more books were published, alphabetical shelving became impossibly difficult, leading eventually to the invention of the Author Marks.

The Author Marks eliminate alphabetical shelving by assigning a number to every conceivable consonant/vowel or vowel/consonant combination that can be used to spell the beginning of an author's surname. These numbers are published in a table that alphabetically lists the various combinations and assigns each a number. For instance, the "G" section of the Cutter/Sanborn Table lists the following combinations and numbers:

| | |
|---|---|
| Garf | 231 |
| Gari | 232 |
| Garl | 233 |
| Garn | 234 |
| Garnet | 235 |
| Garni | 236 |

To assign, for example, an Author Mark to the book, *Double Taxation: A Treatise on the Subject of Double Taxation Relief*, by Charles Edward Garland, a librarian (1) looks up the combination of letters in the Cutter/Sanborn Table closest to the spelling of the author's surname—in this case, "Garl," with the number 233; (2) places the first letter of the author's surname before the number; and (3) places after the number the first letter or letters of the first important word in the title, giving an Author Mark of G233d. The call number of the book is its Dewey Decimal number plus its Author Mark:

336.294
G233d

Similarly, the book *Religion and the Moral Life*, by Arthur Campbell Garnett, has a Dewey Decimal number of 170 and an Author Mark of G235r, giving the following call number:

170
G235r

Under this dual system, a book is shelved first by sequence of its Dewey Decimal number, and then by sequence of its Author Mark. To find any title, a student must therefore first locate the Dewey Decimal category on the shelf, and then identify an individual book by its Author Mark.

Fiction and biography are classified in a special way under the Dewey Decimal System. Fiction is marked with the letter "F" and biography with the letter "B." Fiction is alphabetized by author, biography by subject. For example, F-Pas is the classification of a novel by Boris Pasternak; B-C56 is one of the several biographies about Sir Winston Churchill. If the library has an especially large fiction or biography collection, these books might also be given Author Marks.

### 3b-3  The Library of Congress System

The Library of Congress System is named for the library that invented it. Founded in 1800, the Library of Congress at first simply shelved its books by size. Its earliest catalog, issued in 1802, showed the United States as the owner of 964 books and 9 maps. By 1812 the nation's collection had increased to 3,076 books and 53 maps. By 1897, when the library finally acquired a building of its own, the collection had grown to half a million items and was increasing at the staggering rate of 100,000 per year. The library had acquired such a vast and expansive collection that a new system was necessary for classifying it. Published in 1904, the Library of Congress Classification System has since grown immensely in popularity and is now widely used, especially by larger libraries.

The system represents the main branches of knowledge with twenty-one letters of the alphabet. These branches are further divided by the addition of letters and Arabic numerals up to 9999, allowing for a nearly infinite number of combinations. The system is therefore especially useful for libraries possessing enormous collections. Here is a list of the general categories:

| | |
|---|---|
| A | General Works—Polygraphy |
| B | Philosophy—Religion |
| C | History—Auxiliary Sciences |
| D | History and Topography (except America) |
| E–F | America |
| G | Geography—Anthropology |
| H | Social Sciences |
| J | Political Science |
| K | Law |
| L | Education |
| M | Music |
| N | Fine Arts |
| P | Language and Literature |
| Q | Science |
| R | Medicine |
| S | Agriculture—Plant and Animal Industry |

| T | Technology |
|---|---|
| U | Military Science |
| V | Naval Science |
| Z | Bibliography and Library Science |

These general categories are narrowed by the addition of letters. Numerous minute subdivisions are possible. The Language and Literature category, designated by "P," is further subdivided thus:

| P | Philology and Linguistics: General |
|---|---|
| PA | Greek and Latin Philology and Literature |
| PB | Celtic Languages and Literature |
| PC | Romance Languages (Italian, French, Spanish, and Portuguese) |
| PD | Germanic (Teutonic) Languages |

The addition of numerals makes possible even more minute subdivisions within each letter category. From the general category "P"—Language and Literature—is derived the more specific category of Literary History and Collections, designated by "PN." The call number PN 6511 indicates works dealing with Oriental Proverbs; PN 1993.5 U65, on the other hand, is the call number for a book about the history of motion pictures in Hollywood.

The classification under this system proceeds from the general to the specific, with the longer numbers being assigned to the more specialized books. Like the Dewey Decimal System, the Library of Congress System also uses an author number to differentiate books shelved within a specific category. To locate a book with a Library of Congress classification, the student must first find the subject category on the shelf, and then track down the individual title by its author number.

### 3b-4   Classification of periodicals

Periodicals and newspapers are classified differently from books. Current issues are usually shelved alphabetically by title and are accessible to the public. Back issues, either bound in book form or reproduced on microfilm, are stored elsewhere—usually in a special section of the library to which the public may or may not be admitted, depending on whether the stacks are open or closed.

### 3b-5   Classification of nonbooks

Nonbook materials—films, microfilms, recordings, news clippings, sheet music, reproductions of masterpieces, transparencies, slides, programmed books, and other audiovisual material—may be listed either in the general catalog or as a special collection. No hard-and-fast rule exists for classifying this kind of material; ask your librarian how it is cataloged. (See Figure 3-5, p. 24.)

**Figure 3-5**   Cross-reference sample catalog cards for nonbook materials

Map
974.1
Nat        National Geographic Society
                Maine with the maritime provinces of
            close-up Canada. Washington, D.C., 1975.

SOUND
FILMSTRIP
140        Basic systems of philosophy.
Bas            (SOUND FILM- STRIP).  Westwood
               Educational Productions,

TAPE RECORDING
290        Conger, George P.
Con            Philosophical basis for world religion.
           Cincinnati, Ohio, Sound Seminars, n.d.

FILM LOOP    SCATTERING--EXPERIMENTS.
531.1133  Diffraction and scattering around obstacles.
Dif            Educational Services, 1964.

KIT
327.73   The Making of American foreign policy.  (Kit)
Mak            Newsweek Educational Division.--New York:
               Newsweek, c1977

(SOUND SLIDE)
709.44   Life and arts in the XIII century.
Lif          (SOUND SLIDE).  Harrison, N.Y.,
             Cultural History Research, 1960.
             51 col. slides. 2 x 2 in.
             and tape:

kind of material

(RECORDS)
821.08   The London Library of Recorded English
Lon          XTV 23862 (23863, 23864, 23865)
             Britain Agencies Inc.
             4 s.  12"   33 1/3 rpm

             Album 1, Books I and II.

classification
number

title and
description of
material

1.  English poetry-collections

cross-references

24

# Four
# Doing the Research

# 4a

## Where to look for information

To begin your search, you might consult the appendix of this book. There you will find an annotated listing of many useful reference sources. The annotations give information about sources whose content and scope cannot be deduced from their titles. After that, you might observe the following list of suggestions.

- Check an encyclopedia for general information on the subject. For further sources, check the bibliography at the end of the encyclopedia article.

- For definitions of technical or controversial terms, check the various standard dictionaries.

- Check the card catalog under the subject heading. Also, check any cross-listings noted on the subject cards.

- Check the various periodical indexes for magazine articles on the subject. If the subject is in the social sciences, be sure to check the *Social Science Index*. Likewise, if the subject falls under the heading Humanities or Education, check the *Humanities Index* or the *Education Index* for journal articles on the subject.

- Check the specialized references available on the subject.

- Check the *Book Review Digest* for summaries of the contents of reviewed books.

- Check the various *Who's Who* volumes for information about noteworthy people.

- For information about places and countries, consult gazetteers and atlases.

The search for sources is governed by a kind of domino theory: one source tends to lead to another. A book will suggest an article; an essay will send you flying after a magazine. You will discover at this stage whether your topic is too narrow or too broad. If it is too narrow, you'll hunt and peck for pitifully few sources. If it is too broad, you'll be engulfed by a sea of references. In either case, it isn't too late to change your focus, your direction, or even your topic. Check with your teacher. Better to change now, before you've done the ground work, than later.

Do not be ashamed to make liberal use of the researcher's most powerful tool: the mouth. Ask your library personnel for help. They are trained to find the proverbial needle in the haystack and will prove invaluable in helping you uncover material on your topic.

### 4a-1 Using the computer in your search

The computer has become an indispensable search tool in many modern libraries. Vast quantities of information stored in databases are available to the researcher through a computer terminal.

In a nutshell, a *database* is a computerized collection of information that can be instantly accessed through a terminal. Many database systems are menu driven: the user is shown a variety of choices on the screen, asked to make one, and is in this way gradually led through a series of narrowing options. Some libraries make the computer terminal freely available to students. Others restrict its operation to library personnel to whom all search requests must be submitted. Among the many databases that are available on-line to libraries are the following:

| | |
|---|---|
| DIALOG: | DIALOG consists of over 100 databases cataloging information in a wide range of subjects, including government, health, education, social and physical sciences, humanities, and business. It is operated by Lockheed Information Systems. |
| BRS: | Bibliographic Retrieval Services offers access to over 30 databases. |
| Mead Data Control: | Mead distributes and produces LEXIS and NEXIS. The first is an enormous library of legal information, including millions of court opinions and federal and state statutes. NEXIS is a news retrieval service. |
| New York Times Information Service: | Abstracts over 20 news services along with many special and general interest publications. |
| ERIC: | ERIC is an acronym for the Educational Research Information Center, a network of clearinghouses that gather and produce unpublished materials such as project reports, dissertations, and research findings. The 16 ERIC clearinghouses specialize in one of these subjects: career education; counseling and personnel services; early childhood education; educational management; handicapped and gifted children; higher education; information resources; junior colleges; languages and linguistics; reading and communication skills; rural education and small schools; science, mathematics, and environmental education; social studies and social science education; teacher education; tests, measurement, and evaluation; and urban education. |
| OCLC: | Online Computer Library Center, based in Columbus, Ohio, is a database listing the collections of over 1,000 member libraries. OCLC also includes an on-line listing of all Library of Congress materials in English catalogued |

since 1968. Many member libraries have interlibrary loan arrangements that permit a student to obtain a needed book from the collection of another school.

This list gives you an idea of the kinds of databases available to many libraries. Ask your librarian about the facilities of your own library.

### 4a-2   Assembling a working bibliography

The bibliography is a list of sources on the research topic. These sources will range from encyclopedia entries to magazine articles, from scholarly essays to chapters of books and information stored on microform. At some colleges they may also include computer databases. The *working bibliography* is made up of those sources consulted for information; the *final bibliography* is an alphabetical list of those sources actually used in the paper.

The working bibliography is assembled as the researcher scans the references and card catalog for information on the subject. Promising sources are noted down on $3 \times 5$ bibliography cards (to be distinguished from the $4 \times 6$ note cards). The bibliography card should contain information about the sources to be consulted, along with a brief note on why it is likely to be useful. (See examples on pp. 29–30.)

### 4a-3   The proper form for bibliography cards

Some instructors do not require that students use cards for a working bibliography, merely that they have one, however compiled. Others insist that the cards be used in the form described here.

If you have a choice, use the bibliography cards. Because they are portable and can be easily arranged in alphabetical order, they are generally more useful than a notebook or scraps of paper. Each source actually *used* will be recorded on two kinds of cards: the title will appear on the smaller bibliography card; notes on the source will appear on the larger note card. If the source is merely checked but not used, it will appear only on the working bibliography card. Once the source is eliminated from contention, its card can be placed in an inactive pack.

- Record each source in ink on a separate $3 \times 5$ card.
- Use the same form on the bibliography cards as will be used later in the final bibliography. This makes it possible to prepare the final bibliography by simply transcribing from the cards those titles actually used in writing the paper. The following basic information must be listed on the cards:

> Name of author(s)
> Title of work
> Facts of publication
> Page(s) of information

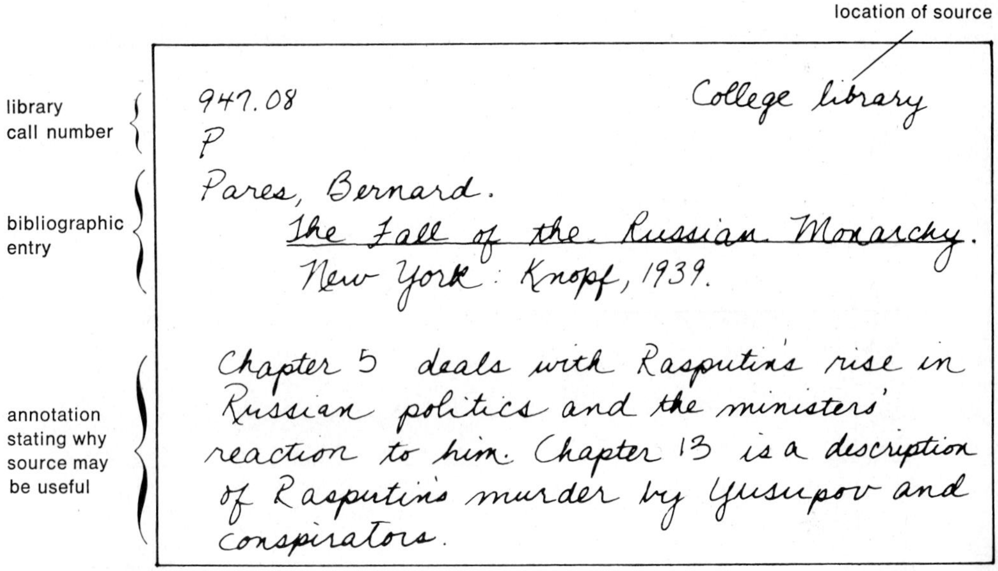

location of source

library
call number

947.08
P

College library

bibliographic
entry

Pares, Bernard.
  The Fall of the Russian Monarchy.
  New York: Knopf, 1939.

annotation
stating why
source may
be useful

Chapter 5 deals with Rasputin's rise in
Russian politics and the ministers'
reaction to him. Chapter 13 is a description
of Rasputin's murder by Yusupov and
conspirators.

**Figure 4-1**  Bibliography card for a book

**Figure 4-2**  Bibliography card for an encyclopedia article

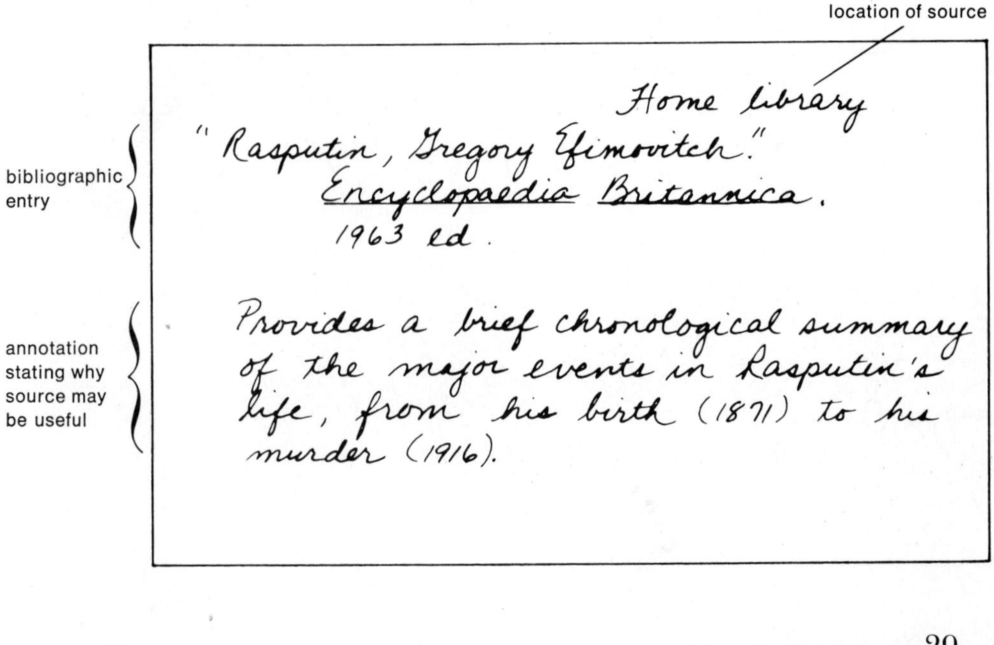

location of source

bibliographic
entry

Home library

"Rasputin, Gregory Efimovitch".
  Encyclopaedia Britannica.
  1963 ed.

annotation
stating why
source may
be useful

Provides a brief chronological summary
of the major events in Rasputin's
life, from his birth (1871) to his
murder (1916).

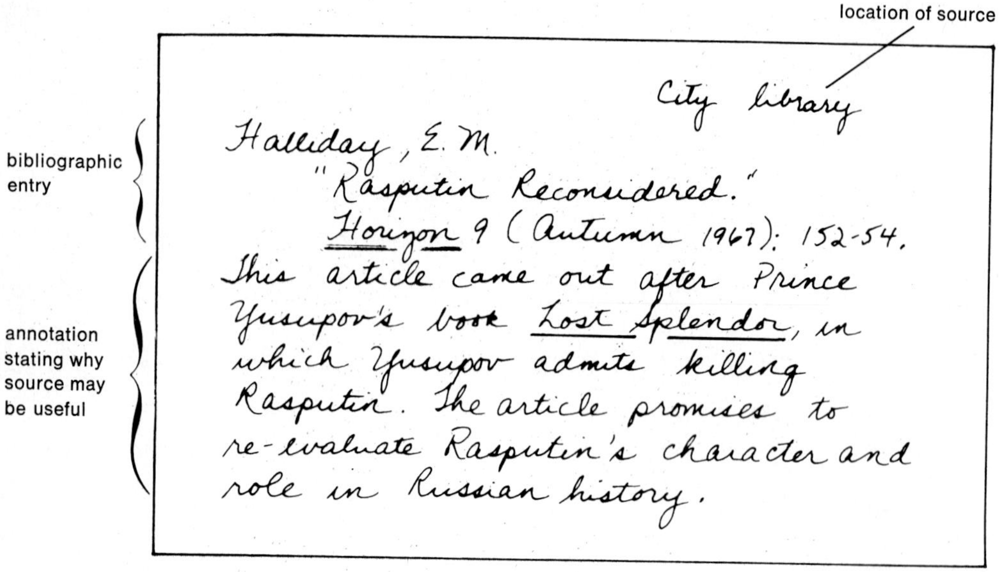

location of source

bibliographic
entry

Halliday, E. M.
   "Rasputin Reconsidered."
      Horizon 9 (Autumn 1967): 152-54.

annotation
stating why
source may
be useful

This article came out after Prince Yusupov's book _Lost Splendor_, in which Yusupov admits killing Rasputin. The article promises to re-evaluate Rasputin's character and role in Russian history.

**Figure 4-3**   Bibliography card for a periodical

**Figure 4-4**   Bibliography card for a newspaper article

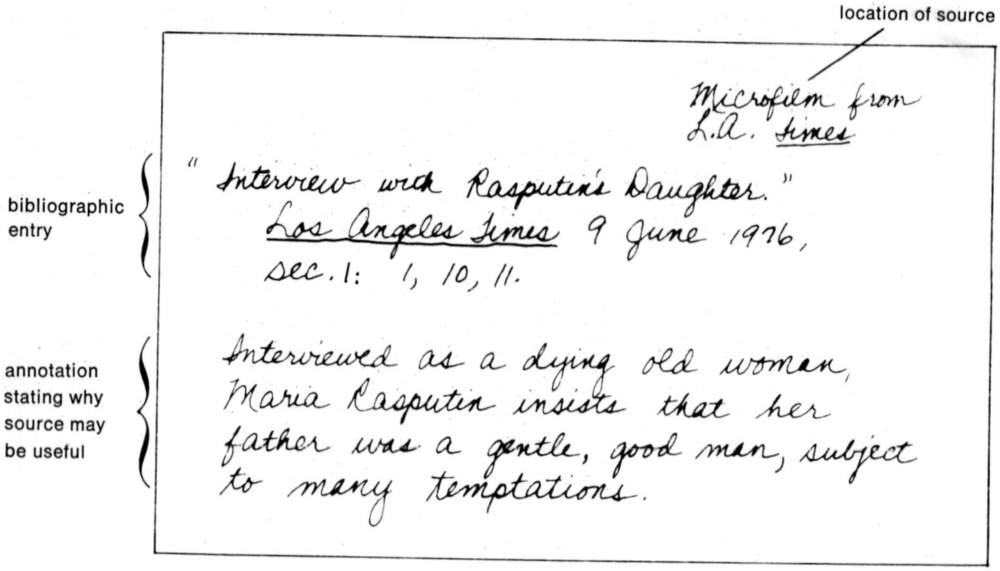

location of source

Microfilm from L.A. _Times_

bibliographic
entry

" Interview with Rasputin's Daughter."
   _Los Angeles Times_ 9 June 1976,
      sec. 1:   1, 10, 11.

annotation
stating why
source may
be useful

Interviewed as a dying old woman, Maria Rasputin insists that her father was a gentle, good man, subject to many temptations.

- In the upper right-hand corner of the card, name the library or place where the source was found, as for example, "Main City Library."
- In the upper left-hand corner of the card, cite the library call number of the source, so that it can be easily found even if reshelved.

Generally you will end up with many more sources in the working bibliography than are listed in the final bibliography. This is as it should be. Many sources will be consulted, but few chosen. False starts and dead-end trails are to be expected. Books will lure one on with a promising table of contents and title, but once skimmed, will prove to be excessively technical, dated, or simply beside the point. The researcher must good-naturedly ignore the irrelevant and worthless sources, while studiously tracking down those articles, essays, and books that promise to be worthwhile and useful.

# 4b

## Selecting your sources

Researchers seldom have time to faithfully read every book or article written about their subject. Instead, the experienced researcher will initially skim a source to determine its usefulness. In skimming, one searches for major ideas in a piece of writing merely to confirm its appropriateness as a research source. If an initial skimming indicates that source is helpful and to the point, it can be read carefully later. However, if the source appears to be farfetched, ponderous, dated, irrelevant, or otherwise useless, then it should be set aside and more promising leads pursued. Do not, however, destroy the bibliography card of the discarded source, since you may wish to return to it later.

Skimming, like most skills, improves with practice. Here are some hints on how to skim a piece of writing for major ideas:

- Glance at the preface of a book. Often an author will state there what the book is about. Likewise, an afterword will often recount the major ideas of a book.
- Look up the subject in the index of the book. Frequently one can tell from the number of pages devoted to the subject whether or not the book is likely to be useful. For instance, if you are looking in a Russian history book for information on Rasputin, and see from its index that it contains only two pages about him, you should probably move on to some other source.
- Read the chapter headings. Often these will reveal what the chapter is about. Similarly, the major ideas in a chapter are sometimes summarized in headnotes to its various sections.

- Read the first and last two sentences in a paragraph to find out what information it contains. Generally, the main idea of a paragraph is stated in its initial sentences, and summed up in its final sentences.
- Glance at the opening paragraph of an article, essay, or book chapter. Often the author's thesis will be stated in the first paragraph or two of an article or essay. Similarly, the thesis of a chapter may be given in its initial paragraph.
- Glance at concluding paragraphs in an article, essay, or book chapter. Often these final paragraphs will sum up the discussion and restate major ideas.
- Run your eye down the page, reading randomly every fourth or fifth sentence. Most readers who do this can get a fair inkling of what the material is about.

### 4b-1  Primary and secondary sources of evidence

The judgments or conclusions in your paper must be based on evidence. *Primary sources of evidence* are original writings by an author, documents, artifacts, laboratory experiments, or other data providing firsthand information. A literary paper about an author might quote letters, memoirs, an autobiography, novels, short stories, plays, personal notes by the author and the like as primary sources of evidence.

*Secondary sources of evidence* are writings, speeches, and other documents *about* a primary source. The opinions of critics are important and widely used secondary sources. An experiment may be a primary source; commentary on it by others is a secondary source. Making a legalistic distinction between these two is not necessary. It is merely necessary to know that your papers will consist of both kinds of evidence. You should also know that for some kinds of papers—especially those on literary topics—primary sources are best. But primary sources require that you expend the effort to interpret them.

### 4b-2  Evaluating sources of evidence

All sources are not created equal. They vary in quality of scholarship, force of argument, and acuracy of detail. Some sources are useful, scholarly, and accurate; others are worthless, silly, and misleading. For example, a student writing a paper on human evolution would be grievously mistaken in taking the fossil remains of the Piltdown Man to be the "missing link"—no matter how many library sources said so. In a brief burst of glory the Piltdown Man was hailed as the "missing link" in human evolution. Many articles and books in the library still make this claim, though their authors would now dearly love to retract, since the

Piltdown Man has been exposed as an elaborate hoax. Anthropologists know all about the Piltdown Man's checkered career, though a student researcher might not. All fields are similarly littered with past errors preserved in the collections of libraries. Yet the researcher, who is often a novice in the subject, must nevertheless dicriminate between error and truth in the writings of experts—a tricky thing to do.

Fortunately, there are some common-sense ways of evaluating sources of evidence. We list them below.

- Verify one opinion against another. No one who conscientiously researched the literature on human fossils would be duped by the early claims on behalf of Piltdown Man, for these have been thoroughly discredited in later writings. In any given field authors often comment on the work of their peers. The diligent researcher soon perceives a consensus of opinion among the experts that can be used to judge the reputation of an author or source.
- Note the date of the evidence. In researching any topic you should attach greatest importance to the most recent data. If two sources are identical except in date, cite the later one as your authority.
- Use common sense. Try to evaluate the logic and probable authenticity of any source you intend to use. For example, if you are doing a paper on the possible existence of UFOs, you can and should carefully analyze the testimony of alleged eyewitnesses. Common sense and keen attention to detail are the chief requirements for evaluating this kind, as well as many other kinds, of evidence.
- Check your evaluations against those of professionals. For example, the opinions of critics can give you an inkling of how experienced readers have viewed a certain novel. *The Book Review Digest* is a good source for critical opinions on books. You can also check the credentials of an author or expert in any of the various biographical dictionaries or *Who's Who* volumes to judge how much weight an expert evaluation should be given.
- Beware of statistics. Because we tend to believe that figures are more accurate than words, we can easily be duped by statistics. A student reading, "At present 35% of children 12 to 18 use alcohol, compared with only 1% in 1940" needs to note carefully that the statistic does not apply to *all* children. The accuracy and inclusiveness of the study that produced the statistics should also be determined. You should question the credibility of a source that uses general and exaggerated numbers such as, "Millions of black youths walk the streets of Atlanta, unemployed." The attentive reader will recognize this assertion as figurative language and strive for impartiality. Admittedly this is hard to do, especially if your position is already biased. Nevertheless, you should try to evaluate all data and statistics with an open mind.

# 4c

## Note-taking

The information uncovered on your topic through research should be transcribed onto $4 \times 6$ note cards and eventually incorporated into the body of the paper. Bear in mind, as you read and take notes, that a research paper should contain a variety of material taken from different sources. It is not enough to simply write down your own ideas and speculations, while ignoring everyone else's opinion on the subject. Your own ideas should be derived from evidence and information uncovered on the subject through research, and the reader should be made aware not only of your conclusions, but also of the substance and reasoning that led you to them.

Students are often puzzled about how much of the paper should consist of their original writing, and how much of material drawn from researched sources. No exact rule exists. You should not write a paper consisting of a string of quotations and paraphrases but containing nothing of your own. Nor should you glut the paper entirely with your own notions, with only a token quotation or paraphrase added here and there to give the illusion of research. Ideally, the paper should consist of information from sources blended judiciously with your own commentary and interpretation. Certainly you should say what you think, but you should also say why you think it—what evidence exists to support your opinions; which authorities on the subject agree with you; and why those of a different opinion are probably in error. In sum, the paper demands not merely opinionated conclusions, but conclusions supported by other opinions.

### 4c-1 Format of the note cards

- Use $4 \times 6$ cards for note-taking. Large enough to accommodate fairly long notes, $4 \times 6$ cards are also unlikely to be confused with the smaller $3 \times 5$ bibliography cards.
- Write in ink rather than pencil so that the cards can be shuffled without blurring the notes.
- Write down only one idea or quotation on each card. Cards with only a single note can be put in any sequence simply by shuffling. If the note is so long that two cards have to be used, staple them together.
- Identify the source of the note in the upper left-hand corner of the card. Since the bibliography card already lists complete information on the source, use only the author's last name or key words from the title followed by a page number. For example, use "Fülöp-Miller 10,"

or "Holy Devil 10," to identify a note taken from page 10 of *Rasputin, the Holy Devil*, by René Fülöp-Miller.

■ Jot down in the upper right-hand corner of the card a general heading for the information the card contains. These headings make it easy to organize the notes by shuffling the cards. (Write in pencil so that the heading can be changed.)

### 4c-2  Kinds of note cards

The notes gathered from your research must be blended into the body of the paper to provide documentation, proof, and evidence in support of the thesis. These notes are of four kinds: the *summary*, the *paraphrase*, the *quotation*, and the *personal comment*.

### a.  The summary

A summary is a condensation of significant facts from an original piece of writing. A chapter is condensed into a page, a page into a paragraph, or a paragraph into a sentence, with the condensation in each case retaining the essential facts of the original. Consider the following summary of an eight-page description of Rasputin:

Fülöp-Miller 3-10.                    Rasputin's appearance

Rasputin's appearance was a combination of coarse, unkempt peasant burliness and mystical, poetic religiosity. He was at once repulsive and attractive. Strangers who met him were first disgusted by such details as his pock-marked skin and his dirty fingernails, but inevitably they came under the spell of his urgent, probing blue eyes.

**Figure 4-5**  Sample note card containing a summary

Common sense should govern your use of the summary. Some facts need to be quoted in detail, but others do not, and can be just as effectively summarized. For instance, the note card shown was for a paper on Rasputin that dealt mainly with the historical truth about the man, not with his physical appearance. It was therefore enough for the student to summarize certain features of Rasputin that made him simultaneously repulsive and attractive. In another context, say in a paper on the physical disfigurement of famous people, it might have been necessary for the student to quote generously from the eight-page description which, in this instance, she needed only to summarize.

### b.  The paraphrase

To paraphrase means to say in one's own words what someone else has said. The paraphrase—unlike the summary—does not condense, but restates a passage in approximately the same number of words as the original, using the syntax and vocabulary of the paraphraser. Ordinarily, the paraphrase is the most frequently used note in the preparation of a research paper.

Paraphrasing achieves two purposes: first, it shows that the student has mastered and assimilated the material to the extent of being able to state, it in his or her own words. Second, it gives the paper an even, consistent style, since both original and source material are cast in the words of the student writer. Below is a short passage from *The Fall of the Russian Monarchy* by Bernard Pares. An appropriate student paraphrase is given in Figure 4-6.

> Meanwhile Rasputin, as he appears to have done earlier, disappeared into the wilds of Russia. Here too he was true to an historical type. Always, throughout Russian history, there had been *stranniki* or wanderers who, without any ecclesiastical commission, lived in asceticism, depriving themselves of the most elementary of human needs, but gladly entertained by the poor wherever they passed. Some of them went barefoot even throughout the winter and wore chains on their legs. This self-denial gave them a freedom to address as peasant equals even the Tsars themselves, and there are many instances of their bold rebuke scattered over Russian history.

### c.  The quotation

The quotation reproduces an author's words exactly as they were spoken or written, preserving even peculiarities of spelling, grammar, or punctuation. Use of an occasional quotation is justified only where the authority of the writer is being evoked, or where the original material is so splendidly expressed as to be altogether ruined by any attempt at either summary or paraphrase.

Student papers are commonly flawed by the overuse of quoted mate-

Pares 134-35.             Rasputin as nomad, ca. 1902

For some time Rasputin became like the well-known strannidi, those wandering ascetics who, without official priestly license, wandered all over Russia depending, wherever they passed, on the poor for food and shelter. Some of the nomads even walked barefoot in the freezing Russian winter with chains clinking around their legs. This kind of self-denial bestowed on them the peculiar right to address even a Tsar as their peasant equal. In this role of half priest half beggar, Rasputin roamed the wilds of Russia.

**Figure 4-6**   Sample note card containing a paraphrase

**Figure 4-7**   Sample note card containing a quotation

Fülöp-Miller 366.          The murder of Rasputin

Farewell letter from Empress Alexandra to the murdered Rasputin:

" My dear martyr, grant me your blessing to accompany me on the sorrowful road I have still to tread here below. Remember us in Heaven in your holy prayers. Alexandra."

rial. Moreover, many teachers regard the excessive inclusion of quotations as a sign of padding. A good rule of thumb is therefore to limit quoted material to no more than ten percent of the total paper. Another good rule is to quote only when the authority of the writer is needed, or when the material simply cannot be either paraphrased or summarized.

The rules for placing quotations on note cards are:

- Place quotation marks around the quotation.
- Introduce the quotation or place it in proper context.
- Copy quotations exactly as they are written. (See pp. 65–73 for how to introduce quotations, and pp. 75–77 for how to use ellipses.)

Occasionally, a summary or paraphrase is combined with a quotation on a note card, the key phrases or words from the original source being used to add literary flavor or authenticity to the note. Below is an original passage from *The Fall of the Russian Monarchy* by Bernard Pares, followed by a note card that combines a paraphrase with a quotation from this source.

> Nothing is more untrue than the easy explanation that was so often given, that he became the tool of others. He was far too clever to sell himself to anyone. He did not ask for presents and had no need; he had only to accept all that was showered upon him, and that he did briefly and almost casually, in many cases at once passing on the largess to the poor; his position was that of one who plundered the rich for the poor and was glad to do it.

**Figure 4-8**    Sample note card combining paraphrase and quotation

Pares  140, 141.                    Rasputin's generosity to the poor

Some critics have accused Rasputin of becoming "the tool of others" in order to acquire expensive personal gifts or other material advantage. Nothing could be further from the truth. Rasputin was too clever "to sell himself to anyone." He did not need to. All he had to do was sit back and accept all the luxuries offered to him by high society. And, in fact, one of his favorite roles was that of a Russian Robin Hood who "plundered the rich for the poor" by taking gifts offered and immediately passing them on to people in need.

*d. The personal comment*

Personal-comment notes can be used to record any ideas, conjectures, or conclusions that occur to you during the research. These notes are generally used to explicate a fuzzy statement, stress a particular point, draw a conclusion, clarify an issue, identify an inconsistency, or introduce a new idea. Jot down these ideas as they dawn on you. If the personal-comment note deals with material contained on another card, staple the two cards together. An example of a personal-comment note card is given below.

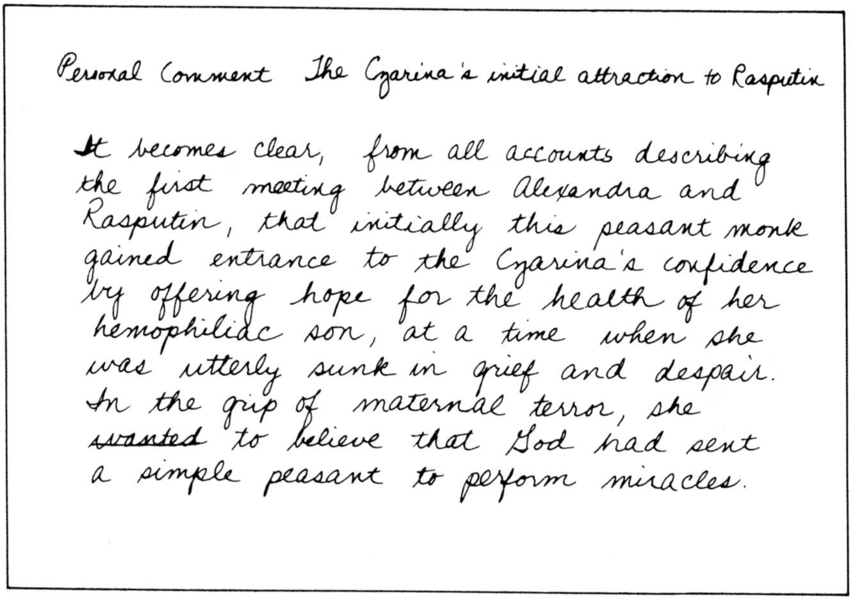

Personal Comment The Czarina's initial attraction to Rasputin

It becomes clear, from all accounts describing the first meeting between Alexandra and Rasputin, that initially this peasant monk gained entrance to the Czarina's confidence by offering hope for the health of her hemophiliac son, at a time when she was utterly sunk in grief and despair. In the grip of maternal terror, she wanted to believe that God had sent a simple peasant to perform miracles.

**Figure 4-9** Sample note card containing a personal comment

# 4d

## Plagiarism: what it is and how to avoid it

Plagiarism is the act of passing off another's words and ideas as one's own. The question of when one has plagiarized and when one has simply asserted a general truth from an unknown source, can be sometimes puzzling. In a cosmic sense, the process of learning is made up of countless tiny crimes of plagiarism, since we all borrow freely from one another. No generation speaks a language of its own invention; few people are creators of the proverbs and sayings that they utter daily. The mother who tells her child, "A thing of beauty is a joy forever," is plagiarizing from the poet John Keats; the father who warns his son, "Hell hath no fury like a woman scorned," has plagiarized from the playwright William Congreve. Innumerable other examples can be given to show how we freely and wantonly borrow ideas and expressions from one another.

Blatant plagiarism, however, involves the conscious and deliberate stealing of another's words and ideas, generally with the motive of earning undeserved rewards. The student who copies the paper of a friend is guilty of blatant plagiarism. Likewise, the student who steals an idea from a book, expresses it in his or her own words, and then passes it off as original, has committed an act of plagiarism.

The conventions of writing research papers dictate that students must acknowledge the source of any idea or statement not truly their own. This acknowledgment is made in a note specifying the source and author of the borrowed material. All summaries, paraphrases, or quotations must be documented; only personal comments may remain un-documented. In sum, to avoid plagiarism students must:

- Provide a note for any idea borrowed from another.
- Place quoted material within quotation marks.
- Provide a bibliography entry at the end of the book for every source used in the text or in a note.

Not every assertion is documentable, nor is it necessary for students to document matters of general and common knowledge. For instance, it is commonly known that the early settlers of America fought wars with the Indians—an assertion a student could safely make without documenta-tion. Similarly, a student could write, "Russia was in turmoil during the years preceding the Bolshevik Revolution," without documenting this statement, since the turmoil of prerevolutionary Russia is common knowledge. As a rule of thumb, a piece of information that occurs in five or more sources may be considered general knowledge. Proverbs, and sayings of unknown origins, are also considered general knowledge and do not have to be documented.

The following, however, must be accompanied by a citation specifying author and source:

- Any idea derived from any known source.
- Any fact or data borrowed from the work of another.
- Any especially clever or apt expression, whether or not it says some-thing new, that is taken from someone else.
- Any material lifted verbatim from the work of another.
- Any information that is paraphrased or summarized and used in the paper.

In writing research papers, students are expected to borrow heavily from the works of experts and authorities—indeed, this is partly the purpose of the research; but they are also expected to acknowledge the sources of this borrowed material.

To illustrate plagiarism in different degrees, we have reproduced a passage from a book, followed by three student samples, two of which are plagiarisms.

*Original passage*

Alexander III died on 20 October, 1894, and was succeeded by his son Nicholas. The new emperor was more intelligent and more sensitive than his father. Both those who knew him well, and those who had brief and superficial contact with him, testify to his exceptional personal charm. The charm was, however, apparently associated with weakness and irresolution. Nicholas appeared to agree with the last person he had talked to, and no one could tell what he would do next.

*Student Version A (plagiarized)*

When Alexander III died on October 20, 1894, he was followed by his son Nicholas, who was more intelligent and more sensitive than his father. People who knew him well and also some who knew him only superficially testify that he was exceptionally charming as a person. This charm, however, was associated with weakness and an inability to make decisions. Nicholas always seemed to agree with the last person he had talked to, and no one could predict what he would do next.

This is an example of outright plagiarism. No documentation of any sort is given. The student simply repeats the passage almost verbatim, as though he or she had written it.

*Student Version B (plagiarized)*

When Alexander III died on October 20, 1894, he was followed by his son Nicholas, who was more intelligent and more sensitive than his father. People who knew him well, and also some who knew him only superficially, testify that he was exceptionally charming as a person. This charm, however, was associated

with weakness and an inability to make decisions.
Nicholas always seemed to agree with the last person
he had talked to, and no one could predict what he
would do next.[3]

    [3] Hugh Seton—Watson, The Russian Empire, 1801–
1917, vol. 3 of The Oxford History of Modern Europe
(Oxford: Oxford UP, 1967) 547.

    Though documented with a footnote, the passage is still a plagiarism because the student has merely changed a word or two of the original, without doing a proper paraphrase.

*Student
Version C
(acceptable)*

Emperor Nicholas II, who came to the throne of Russia
following the death of his father, Alexander III, was
apparently a man of exceptional personal charm and
deep sensitivity.  Ample testimony has come to us
from both intimate as well as casual acquaintances,
indicating that indeed he possessed a magnetic
personality.  However, the general consensus is also
that he was a man who lacked the ability to make hard
decisions, preferring to agree with the last person
he had seen, and thus making it impossible to predict
what he would do next.[3]

    [3] Hugh Seton—Watson, The Russian Empire, 1801–
1917, vol. 3 of The Oxford History of Modern Europe
(Oxford: Oxford UP, 1967) 547.

    This is an acceptable use of the material. The original is properly paraphrased and its source documented with a footnote.

Thesis: After six decades of being judged a demoniacal libertine, Rasputin now deserves to be viewed from another point of view—as a man who was intensely religious, who passionately desired peace, and who was deeply devoted to his family and friends.

Notice that the thesis, as worded, specifies exactly what the writer has to do, and what information she will need to do it. To begin with, she will have to document Rasputin's reputation as a demoniacal libertine. Having done that, she will have to support her three contrary assertions: that Rasputin was intensely religious, that he passionately desired peace, and that he was deeply devoted to his family and friends. The thesis, moreover, suggests exactly the kind of information that the student will need to write the paper. First, she must cite historical opinion that portrays Rasputin as a demoniacal libertine. Second, she will need to produce anecdotal material, eyewitness accounts, biographical opinions, and similar evidence that support her contrary assertions about Rasputin.

### 5a-2 Rules for wording the thesis

To be useful, the thesis must be properly worded. A vague, confused, or lopsided thesis will either inflict similar miseries on the paper, or cause the writer to flounder helplessly among a disarray of note cards. Properly worded, the thesis should: (1) be clear, comprehensible, and direct; (2) predict major divisions in the structure of the paper; (3) commit the writer to an unmistakable course, argument, or point of view. The thesis on Rasputin is clear, implies a four-part division in the structure of the paper, and obligates the writer to argue a single proposition: that Rasputin was harshly judged by history. Likewise, the thesis on the *Titanic* disaster is clear and direct, divides the paper into two principal parts, and commits the writer to a single argument: that the ocean liner sank because of defects in her steering and bulkheads. Listed below is a series of rules to guide you in properly wording your thesis.

- *The thesis should commit the writer to a single line of argument*. Consider for instance this example:

    Poor    The Roman theater was inspired by the Greek theater, which it imitated, and eventually the Romans produced great plays in their <u>theatrons</u>, such as those by Plautus, who was the best Roman comic writer because of his robustness and inventiveness.

# Five
# The Thesis and the Outline

## 5a The thesis: definition and function

## 5b The outline

# 5a

## The thesis: definition and function

The thesis is a statement that summarizes the central idea of the paper. By convenience and custom, this statement is usually the final sentence of the opening paragraph, as in the following example.

```
                    The Bilingually Handicapped Child


        There are approximately five million children in the United

    States who attend public schools and speak a language other than

    English in their homes and neighborhoods.  Many of these children

    are handicapped in communication and thought processes, and have

    to repeat the first grades in school several times.  The bilingual

    child is usually unable to conceptualize in the English language

    taught at school, since he is from a different cultural and lan-

    guage background.  Early compensatory educational programs would

    give the bilingual child a head start and he would be better pre-

    pared for handling school work.
```

The underlined sentence is the thesis—the central idea for which the writer intends to argue. Once readers have gotten through this first paragraph, the aim of the paper is abundantly clear to them; they know what to anticipate.

The thesis serves at least three functions. First, it establishes a boundary around the subject that discourages the writer from wandering aimlessly. Most of us are often tempted to stray from the point when we write. We begin by intending to write a paper about Rasputin's place in history, then stumble onto some fascinating fact about Russian monasteries and become eager to somehow work it in. With a clear thesis before us, however, we are less likely to be seduced by a digression. Formulated before the actual writing of the paper begins, the thesis commits us to argue one point, discuss one subject, clarify one issue. Writers so committed will not leapfrog from topic to topic, nor free-associate erratically from one minor point to another.

Second, the thesis—if worded properly—can chart an o[...] for the paper, making it easier to write. Consider for instan[...]

```
        Two defects in the design of the Titanic contribu[...]

    sinking: her steering was sluggish and unresponsive, e[...]

    ship of her immense size; her traverse bulkheads, whic[...]

    have made her virtually unsinkable, did not extend all

    to her deck.
```

The course before the writer is as plain as day: first, the slug[...] of the *Titanic* must be discussed and clarified with appropri[...] details; second, the design of her traverse bulkheads must b[...] and the defect thoroughly explained. The writer's job is ea[...] the thesis has conveniently divided the paper into two parts, [...] not only the topics to be discussed, but also their sequence. [...] and easier by far to write about such a thesis than to writ[...] about the sinking of the *Titanic*.

Third, the thesis gives the reader an idea of what to expect, [...] paper consequently easier to read. Textbooks have elabor[...] headings and section headnotes just for this purpose. Newspa[...] are captioned and headlined for a similar reason. It is eas[...] virtually anything if we have an idea of what to anticipate[...] anticipation narrows and focuses our attention. A paper with[...] creates no such anticipation in a reader and is therefore more[...] follow.

### 5a-1  Choosing the thesis

There is no chicken-and-egg mystery about which comes first—[...] or the thesis. One cannot formulate a thesis about a subject [...] first knows a great deal about it. Ordinarily, students will the[...] well into the research and notes before they can formulate the[...]

Basically, you are looking for a central idea that summa[...] information you have gathered on the subject. Consider for ins[...] paper on Rasputin, which we have been using as our prime [...] The student, after much reading and note-taking, discovered [...] spite his diabolic reputation, Rasputin did do some good. Specif[...] discovered that: (1) Rasputin had intense religious feelings; (2)[...] passionate desire for peace in Russia; (3) he was deeply devot[...] family and friends. She therefore summarized her findings abou[...] tin in the following thesis:

A single topic is difficult enough to research and write about; with two topics in a single paper, the writer's task becomes almost impossible. The thesis just given threatens to wrench the paper in two contrary directions: it commits the student to cover both the origins of Roman theater and the theatrical career of Plautus, one of Rome's greatest comic playwrights. This dual thesis came about because the student had laboriously accumulated two sets of notes—one on the origins of Roman theater and another on the career of Plautus—and was determined to devise a thesis that would allow him to use both. The result is this curiously dual thesis that skews the paper in two contrary directions. Persuaded to relinquish the notes on the origins of the Roman theater and to focus the paper entirely on the career of Plautus, the student drafted the following improved thesis:

> *Better*   Because of his robust language and novel comic plots,
>
> Titus Maccicus Plautus can be considered the best Ro-
>
> man comic playwright; his plays are still success-
>
> fully staged today.

The paper is now committed to a single line of argument, and its focus is therefore vastly improved.

■ *The thesis should not be worded in figurative language*. The reasoning behind this rule is obvious: figurative language is too indefinite and oblique to constitute the central idea of a paper. Consider this thesis:

> *Poor*   Henry James is the Frank Lloyd Wright of the American
>
> novel.

No doubt the writer knew exactly what she meant by this allusion, but its significance is murky to a reader. If one cannot understand the central idea of a paper, what hope does one have of understanding the paper? The following plainly expressed thesis is vastly better:

> *Better*   The novels of Henry James have internal consistency
>
> because of the way he unifies his themes, patterns his
>
> episodes, and orders his images.

- *The thesis should not be vaguely worded.* Vagueness may tantalize, but it does not inform. Moreover, a paper with a vague thesis is a paper without direction, and all the more difficult to write. Consider this example of a vague thesis:

      *Poor*    Cigarette smoking wreaks havoc on the body.

Doing a paper on such a thesis will truly put a writer to the test. The thesis suggests no direction, provides no structure, proposes no arguments. Contrast it with this improved version:

      *Better*    Cigarette smoking harms the body by constricting the

      blood vessels, accelerating the heartbeat, paralyz-

      ing the cilia in the bronchial tubes, and activating

      excessive gastric secretions in the stomach.

The writer knows exactly what points to argue and in what order.

- *The thesis should not be worded as a question.* The thesis worded as a question does not provide the writer with the kind of obligatory direction given by the one phrased as a statement. Here is an example:

      *Poor*    Who makes the key decisions in U.S. cities?

This is the sort of question that makes a good starting point for research. Indeed, most research will begin with an unanswered question in the mind of the researcher. But the eventual thesis should not be your original question; it should be the answer uncovered in your research.

      *Better*    Key decisions in large U.S. cities are made by a hand-

      ful of individuals, drawn largely from business, in-

      dustrial, and municipal circles, who occupy the top

      of the power hierarchy.

- *The thesis should be as concise as possible.* If ever a writer should try for conciseness, it is in the drafting of the thesis. A long, cumbersome thesis is likely to muddle the writer and send the paper flying off in

different directions. The reader who cannot fathom the thesis of a paper is even less likely to make sense of its contents. Here is a muddled thesis:

> *Poor*  Despite the fact that extensive time consumed by television detracts from homework, competes with schooling more generally, and has contributed to the decline in the Scholastic Aptitude Test score averages, television and related forms of communication give the future of learning its largest promise, the most constructive approach being less dependent on limiting the uses of these processes than on the willingness of the community and the family to exercise the same responsibility for what is taught and learned this way as they have exercised with respect to older forms of education.

This is of course garbled nonsense. Pity the student who has written a paper based on this tortured thesis. Here is an improved version:

> *Better*  While numerous studies acknowledge that the extensive time spent by students watching television has contributed to the decline in the Scholastic Aptitude Test scores, leading educators are convinced that television holds immense promise for the future of learning, provided that the family and the community will prudently monitor its use.

To paraphrase an old saying, "Like thesis, like paper." A muddled, incoherent thesis will generate an equally muddled and incoherent paper.

### 5a-3   Placing the thesis

The thesis is usually introduced in the final sentence of the first paragraph—a position that gives the writer a chance to establish an opening context yet is still emphatic enough to draw attention to the thesis. Some variation in placement of the thesis does exist, but most teachers distinctly prefer it to be stated as the final sentence of the initial paragraph. Here are three examples of theses introduced in this customary place:

He is a vagabond in aristocratic clothing——shabby but grand.  As he scurries along in his cutaway and derby hat, aided by a cane, he is obviously a tramp, but a tramp with the impeccable manners of a dandy.  He is willing to tackle any job, but seldom does it properly.  He often falls in love, but usually the affair sours in the end.  His only enemies are pompous people in places of authority.  The general public adores

*Thesis*   him because he is everyman of all times.  <u>Charlie Chaplin's ''Tramp'' has remained a favorite international character because he is a character with whom the average person can empathize.</u>

A quarter of a million babies are born each year with birth defects.  Of these defects, only 20 percent are hereditary.  Most of them could have been prevented because they are the tragic results of poor prenatal

*Thesis*   care.  <u>An unfavorable fetal environment, such as can be caused by malnutrition in the mother or her use of drugs, is a primary cause of many kinds of birth defects.</u>

> Theodor Seuss Geisel writes and illustrates zany
>
> children's books, usually in verse, under the
>
> pseudonym of ''Dr. Seuss.'' He has written twenty-six
>
> best sellers over a period of thirty years, and they
>
> are all still in print. In story after story, this
>
> author creates a topsy-turvy world where the normal
>
> becomes aberrant and the aberrant becomes normal.

*Thesis*  The simple vocabulary and rhyming lines of Dr.

Seuss's books make them easy for children to read, but

the author's illustrations are primarily responsible

for the imaginative flair in his work.

# 5b
## The outline

The outline is an ordered listing of the topics covered in the paper. Varying in complexity and style, outlines are nevertheless useful to both the writer and the reader. The writer who writes from an outline is less likely to stray from the point, or to commit a structural error such as overdeveloping one topic while skimping on another. The reader, on the other hand, benefits from the outline as a complete and detailed table of contents.

### 5b-1   Visual conventions of the outline

The conventions of formal outlining require that main ideas be designated by Roman numerals such as I, II, III, IV, V. Subideas branching off from the main ideas are designated by capital letters A, B, C, D, and so on. Subdivisions of these subideas are designated by Arabic numerals 1, 2, 3, 4, and so forth. Minor ideas are designated by lower-case letters a, b, c, d, etc. Here is an example of the proper form of an outline:

```
I.  Main idea

   A.  Subidea
```

```
     B.  Subidea

          1.  Division of a subidea

          2.  Division of a subidea

               a.  Minor idea

               b.  Minor idea

  II.  Main idea
```

The presumption behind this sort of arrangement is obvious: namely, that students will not merely generalize, but will support their contentions and propositions with examples and details. Indeed, that is exactly what the writer of a research paper is expected to do—to make assertions that are supported by concrete examples and specific details. If you have done your research badly and have not been diligent in gathering specific facts about the topic, this deficiency will now become painfully obvious.

Notice that every category must be subdivided at least once, since it is impossible to divide anything into fewer than two parts. An outline dividing the subject into three or four levels—that is, down to examples or details—is generally adequate for most college-level research papers. If further subdivisions are necessary, the format is as follows:

```
  I.
     A.
          1.
               a.
                    (1)
                         (a)
```

The basic principle remains the same: larger ideas or elements are stacked to the left, with smaller ideas and elements to the right.

### 5b-2   Equal ranking in outline entries

The logic of an outline requires that each entry be based on the same organizing principle as another entry of equal rank. All capital-letter entries must consequently be equivalent in importance and derived from the same organizing principle. Notice the lack of equal ranking in the following example:

```
  I.  Rousseau gave the people a new government to work toward.

     A.  It would be a government based on the general will.
```

B.   The new government would serve the people instead of the
     people serving the government.

C.   The people tore down the Bastille.

The C entry is out of place because it is not of equal rank with entries A
and B. A and B are subideas that characterize the new government
proposed by Rousseau; C is a statement that describes the revolt of the
French people against the old government.

### 5b-3   Parallelism in outline entries

The clarity and readability of an outline are immeasurably improved if
its entries are worded in similar grammatical form. Notice the lack of
parallelism in the following outline:

I.   The uses of the laser in the military

A.   For range-finding

*wrong*   B.   For surveillance

C.   To illuminate the enemy's position

Entries A and B consist of a preposition followed by a noun, while entry
C is worded as an infinitive phrase. C should therefore be reworded to
make it grammatically similar to entries A and B:

I.   The uses of the laser in the military

A.   For range-finding

*correct*   B.   For surveillance

C.   For illuminating an enemy's position

The outline is now easier to read because its entries are grammatically
parallel.

### 5b-4   Types of outlines

The three main types of outlines are the topic outline, the sentence
outline, and the paragraph outline. The formats of these different outlines cannot be mixed or combined; one type of outline must be used
exclusively.

## a. *The topic outline*

The topic outline words each entry as a phrase, breaking down the subject into major subheadings. Topic outlines are particularly useful for outlining relatively simple subjects. Here is a topic outline of the paper on Rasputin:

Rasputin's Other Side

Thesis: After six decades of being judged a demoniacal libertine, Rasputin how deserves to be viewed from another point of view——as a man who was intensely religious, who passionately desired peace, and who was deeply devoted to his family and friends.

I.   The ambiguity of the real Rasputin

   A.  His birth

   B.  Popular historical view

      1.  His supporters

      2.  His detractors

II.  Rasputin's religious feelings

   A.  His rich nature and exuberant vitality

   B.  His simple peasant faith

III.  Rasputin's desire for peace in Russia

   A.  His concern for the Russian underdog

      1.  His loyalty to the peasantry

      2.  His opposition to anti-Semitism

   B.  His opposition to all wars

IV.  Rasputin's gentle, compassionate side

   A.  His kindness to the Romanovs

   B.  His love for family

Notice that the thesis of the paper is placed as a separate entry immediately after the title. It is also customary to omit "introduction" and "conclusion" entries.

### b. The sentence outline

The sentence outline uses a complete grammatical sentence for each entry. (Some instructors allow the entries to be worded as questions, but most prefer declarative sentences.) Sentence outlines are especially well suited for complex subjects, the detailed entries giving the writer an excellent overview of the paper. Here is a sentence outline of the paper on Rasputin:

```
                    Rasputin's Other Side


Thesis: After six decades of being judged a demoniacal libertine,

        Rasputin now deserves to be viewed from another point of

        view——as a man who was intensely religious, who passion-

        ately desired peace, and who was deeply devoted to his

        family and friends.

   I.  The real Rasputin is difficult to discover.

       A.  The birth of Rasputin coincided with a ''shooting

           star.''

       B.  The popular historical view of Rasputin portrays him as

           primarily evil.

           1.  Supporters called him a spiritual leader.

           2.  Detractors called him a satyr and charged that his

               depraved faithful were merely in awe of his sexual

               endowments.

  II.  Rasputin had intense religious feelings.

       A.  He had a rich nature and exuberant vitality.

       B.  He had a simple peasant faith in God.
```

III.  Rasputin's passionate desire for peace in Russia revealed

itself in several ways.

A.  He was concerned for the Russian underdog.

1.  He wanted a Tsar who would stand mainly for the

peasantry.

2.  He spoke out boldly against anti—Semitism.

B.  Because of his humanitarian spirit, he was opposed to

all wars.

IV.  Rasputin had a gentle, compassionate side.

A.  He showed great kindness to the Romanovs.

B.  Maria Rasputin tells of her father's love for his

family.

## c. The paragraph outline

The paragraph outline records each entry as a complete paragraph, thus providing a condensed version of the paper. This form is useful mainly for long papers whose individual sections can be summarized in whole paragraphs, but is seldom recommended by instructors for ordinary college papers. Here is the Rasputin paper in the form of a paragraph outline:

Rasputin's Other Side

Thesis: After six decades of being judged a demoniacal libertine,

Rasputin now deserves to be viewed from another point of

view——as a man who was intensely religious, who passion—

ately desired peace, and who was deeply devoted to his

family and friends.

I.  Rasputin himself always attached great significance to the

fact that at the time of his birth, a shooting star was seen streaking across the horizon. He saw this phenomenon as an omen that he was fated to have influence and special powers. The popular historical view of Rasputin paints him primarily as evil. In his day, however, he attracted numerous supporters who viewed him as their spiritual leader. But he also had many detractors who called him a satyr and accused his followers of sexual depravity.

II. Rasputin had intense religious feelings. He was so filled with exuberance and vitality that he could stay awake until the early hours of the morning, dancing and drinking in frenzied religious fervor. He did not have the theology of a sophisticated church cleric, but rather he expressed his religion in the simple terms of a Russian peasant.

III. Rasputin's passionate desire for peace in Russia revealed itself in several ways. For instance, he was concerned for such Russian underdogs as the peasants and the Jews, always encouraging the Tsar to protect these unfortunate groups. Also, his humanitarian and pacifist nature made him a determined opponent of all wars.

IV. Rasputin had a gentle, compassionate side. He was completely devoted to the Tsar's family and was known to have had a calming influence on the hemophiliac son of the Tsar. Maria Rasputin gives a glowing report of her father's kindness and love.

## 5b-5   The decimal notation of an outline

Other outline forms exist that use various methods of indenting, labeling, and spacing. One form that has been gaining favor in business and science is the decimal outline. Based on the decimal accounting system, this outline form permits an infinite number of possible subdivisions through the simple addition of another decimal place. Here is the body of the Rasputin paper notated in the decimal outline form:

```
                      Rasputin's Other Side


  1.  The ambiguity of the real Rasputin
      1.1.  His birth
      1.2.  Popular historical view
            1.2.1.  His supporters
            1.2.2.  His detractors

  2.  Rasputin's religious feelings
      2.1.  His rich nature and exuberant vitality
      2.2.  His simple peasant faith

  3.  Rasputin's desire for peace in Russia
      3.1.  His concern for the Russian underdog
            3.1.1.  His loyalty to the peasantry
            3.1.2.  His opposition to anti-Semitism
      3.2.  His opposition to all wars

  4.  Rasputin's gentle, compassionate side
      4.1.  His kindness to the Romanovs
      4.2.  His love for family
```

Notice that though a decimal notation is used, this outline arranges its entries on the same indentation principle used in other outlines, with larger ideas stacked to the left, and smaller ideas to the right.

### 5b-6   Which kind of outline should you use?

If you have a choice, if you are a beginning writer, and if your research has uncovered much detail on your subject, don't hesitate a minute: use a detailed sentence outline. Develop it at least down to the third level— the level of Arabic numerals. In doing so you actually erect a kind of scaffolding for the essay. To write the rough draft, you merely transcribe from the outline, fill in the blanks, insert transitions and connectives, and you have an essay.

The main entries of this outline should be the topic sentences of various paragraphs. Its details should be exactly the kind you intend to use to support the topic sentence. Here, as an example, is an outlined paragraph from a sentence outline of a paper on Agatha Christie's fictional sleuth, Hercule Poirot:

```
I.  Hercule's unique personality and character set him apart from
    other fictional detectives.
    A.  His physical appearance was unique.
        1.  He was 5'4", had a black handlebar mustache, an egg-
            shaped head, and catlike eyes that grew greener as the
            solution to a crime drew near.
        2.  He wore a black coat, pin-striped pants, a bow tie,
            shiny black boots, and, usually, a coat and muffler.
```

Here is the paragraph as it appeared in the essay:

```
    Hercule's unique personality and character set him apart from
other fictional detectives.  One of the memorable features of his
personality and character was his physical appearance.  He was "a
diminutive five foot four inches tall and slender."⁷  His hair was
an "unrepentant" black, neatly groomed with hair tonic.  His up-
per lip displayed his pride and joy and his more distinctive fea-
ture, a small black handlebar mustache.⁸  He had catlike eyes that
grew greener as the solution to a crime drew near and a head the
shape of an egg.  Thus Poirot has been referred to as a "mus-
tachioed Humpty Dumpty."⁹  This "extraordinary looking little
man, who carried himself with immense dignity," almost always
wore the same outfit, consisting of a black jacket, striped pants,
a bow tie, and, in all but the hottest weather, an overcoat and
muffler.  He also wore patent leather boots that almost always
displayed a dazzling shine.¹⁰
```

Notice the close correspondence between the outline and the final paragraph. First, the main entry of the outline is exactly the same as the topic sentence of the paragraph. Second, subidea A is fleshed out and used in the paragraph to introduce the details that follow. Third, the details in the outline are used nearly word-for-word in the paragraph. Naturally, there is more material in the paragraph than in the outline, which is not surprising, since the second is a short-hand version of the first.

If you are going to be following an outline as you write, this is the kind that is especially useful. Once drafted, it becomes a condensed version of the essay. Any paragraph is easy to write when you know exactly what its main point must be and what details it should contain. That and more is provided by the detailed sentence outline.

# Six
## Transforming the Notes into a Rough Draft

**6a** Preparing to write the rough draft: a checklist

**6b** Incorporating note-taking into the flow of the paper

**6c** Writing the paper with unity, coherence, and emphasis

**6d** Using the proper tense

# 6a

## Preparing to write the rough draft: a checklist

The following is a practical checklist of things you should do before beginning to write the rough draft:

- You should formulate a thesis. The research paper is the sort of writing that requires considerable premeditation from a writer. Information sifted from the sources and assembled on the note cards has to be carefully grafted into the main body of the paper. Arguments have to be thought out in advance and checked against the opinions of experts. In sum, no matter how spontaneous a writer you may be, you should nevertheless have a definite thesis in mind before you begin to write the rough draft.

- You should go over the note cards, picking out those cards relevant to the thesis, and setting aside all others. Bear in mind, moreover, that you are very likely to have more notes than you can use. To attempt to cram every single note into the paper is to be misled by an impulse that has ruined thousands of papers. You must exercise selectivity over the note cards, based upon the wording of the thesis, or the paper will end up an incoherent muddle of unrelated notes.

- You should arrange and rearrange the cards until they are organized in the order in which they will be used. This order in turn will be dictated by the wording of the thesis, and the nature of the information entered on the individual cards.

- You should sketch an outline of the paper, breaking down the thesis into an ordered listing of topics. This is the stage at which you should experiment with different approaches to your research subject. Juggle the topics until they are arranged in the most logical and emphatic order. If necessary, rephrase the thesis until it generates a more definite structure for the paper.

Once you have formulated the thesis, sorted the cards in their proper sequence, and drafted the outline, you are ready to begin writing the rough draft. Work from the outline and note cards. Triple space the rough draft to allow room for penciling in afterthoughts or corrections. Use a separate sheet for each paragraph so that additional ideas, words, or phrases that occur to you can be tacked on to the paragraphs without creating an unreadable jumble. Keep a dictionary and thesaurus handy, using the first to avoid misspelled or incorrect words, and the second to insure word precision and variety.

# 6b

## Incorporating note-taking into the flow of the paper

The notes you have taken must be blended smoothly into the natural flow of the paper—this is the prime rule for writing the rough draft. Documentation should add clarity, not clutter. Paraphrases, summaries, indirect quotations, and allusions must be edited for smoothness. Quotations, of course, have to be used verbatim, and must not be tampered with. Transitions between ideas should be made logically and smoothly. The paper should not seem a cut-and-paste hodgepodge bristling with numerous unrelated quotations. In sum, you must observe the rhetorical principles of unity, coherence, and emphasis (see 6c).

### 6b-1   Voice, tone, and audience

Strive for an objective voice and a formal tone, assuming your audience to be critical and well-educated. A research paper is not the proper vehicle for flippant language, meaningless jargon, or self-indulgent outbursts. Furthermore, your paper should not be written from the "I" point of view, since you must avoid any impression of bias or personal prejudice. If you wish to include a relevant personal observation or experience, refer to yourself as "the author" or "the writer." While you certainly should avoid pomposity or excessive artificiality, a serious, judicial style is expected.

### 6b-2   Using summaries and paraphrases

The sources of summaries and paraphrases must be given within the text or in parentheses. Below is an example of a paraphrase used without mention of its source in the text:

> When the court life of Russia died out at the imperial palace
> of Tsarskoe Selo, all kinds of political salons suddenly made
> their appearance in various sections of St. Petersburg.  While
> these new salons became the breeding ground for the same kinds of
> intrigues, plots, counterplots, and rivalries that had taken place
> at the imperial palace, somehow their activities seemed dwarfed
> and their politics lacked the grandeur and dazzle that had accom-
> panied the political style at the palace (Fülöp-Miller 101).

In this case, parenthetical documentation of the paraphrase is sufficient. However, the writer who wishes to state a paraphrase more emphatically, or to throw the weight of an expert or authority behind the summary, should mention the source in the text, as in the following example:

```
As Hugh Seton-Watson points out in the preface to his book on the

Russian empire, most people tend to forget that the Russian empire

was multinational and therefore peopled with many non-Russian

citizens, most important of which were the Polish (ix).
```

The summary here is more emphatic because it is coupled with the name of the authority whose work is being summarized.

Sometimes students are so dazzled by the writing style of a source that they unwittingly adopt its flavor and language in their summaries; the result is a discordant mixture of styles within a single paragraph. Here is an example:

```
The hull of the Titanic was traversed by watertight bulkheads,

capable of withstanding enormous pressure.  The engineering no-

tion was that if the ship sprang a leak, water would seep into in-

dividual compartments and be harmlessly trapped. At worse, the

liner would list, and her passengers be slightly uncomfortable as

she limped her way back to port.  Metallurgical fabrication tech-

niques employed in the construction and deployment of each bulk-

head were consonant with the best engineering and metallurgical

knowledge extant at the time of the Titanic's construction.  In

short, the Titanic, though considered ''unsinkable,'' was neither

better nor worse built than any of her other sisters then at sea.
```

The underscored sentence is a summary of information found in a book on marine engineering. Notice how stylistically different the summary seems from the rest of the paragraph. Having pored over the book, the student then unconsciously mimicked its wooden flavor when writing the summary. Before using it, she should have edited the summary to blend it in with the style of the paragraph. Here is an improved version.

```
The hull of the Titanic was traversed by watertight bulkheads,

capable of withstanding enormous pressure.  The engineering no-

tion was that if the ship sprang a leak, water would seep into in-

dividual compartments and be harmlessly trapped.  At worse, the

liner would list, and her passengers be slightly uncomfortable as

she limped her way back to port.  These bulkheads were built ac-

cording to the best metallurgical techniques known at the time of

the Titanic's construction.  In short, the Titanic, though con-

sidered ''unsinkable,'' was neither better nor worse built than

any of her other sisters then at sea.
```

### 6b-3   Using direct quotations

Quotations must be reproduced in the exact phrasing, spelling, capitalization, and punctuation of the original. Staple or paste the quotation note card to the rough draft rather than copying the quotation. Later, when you write the final draft, you will have to transcribe the quotation from the note card onto the paper. By stapling the note card to the rough draft, you avoid having to transcribe quotations twice, thus reducing the chance of error.

Any modification made in a quotation—no matter how minor—must be indicated either in a note placed in square brackets within the quotation, or in parentheses at the end of the quotation.

```
Milton was advocating freedom of speech when he said, ''Give me

the liberty to know, to think, to believe, and to utter freely

[emphasis added] according to conscience, above all other

liberties'' (120).
```

Quotations must fit logically into the syntax of surrounding sentences, so as not to produce an illogical or mixed construction. The following quotation is poorly integrated:

```
Chung—Tzu describes a sage as ''suppose there is one who insists on

morality in all things, and who places love of truth above all

other values'' (58).
```

Here is the same quotation properly integrated into the sentence:

```
Chung—Tzu describes a sage as ''one who insists on morality in all

things, and who places love of truth above all other values'' (58).
```

Here is another example of a badly integrated quotation:

```
The poet showed his belief in self—criticism by writing that ''I am

a man driven to scold myself over every trivial error'' (15).
```

Here is the quotation properly handled:

```
The poet showed his belief in self—criticism when he wrote this

about himself: ''I am a man driven to scold myself over every triv—

ial error'' (15).
```

### a.  Overuse of quotations

No passage in the paper should consist of an interminable string of quotations. A mixture of summaries, paraphrases, and quotations is smoother and easier to read; moreover, such a mixture gives the impression that students have done more than patch together bits and pieces from books and articles they have read. Here is an example of a paragraph littered with too many quotations:

```
According to McCullough, ''the groundswell of public opinion

against the Japanese started in the early 1900s'' (191).  This is

when the United States Industrial Commission issued a report stat—
```

ing that the Japanese ''are more servile than the Chinese, but less obedient and far less desirable'' (Conrat 18). At about the same time, the slogan of politician and labor leader Dennis Kearney was ''the Japs must go!'' (10). The mayor of San Francisco wrote that ''the Japanese cannot be taken into the American culture because they are not the stuff of which American citizens are made'' (Daniels 9–10). In 1905, writes McCullough, ''the Japanese and Korean Expulsion League held its first meeting and spawned many other such similar organizations'' (102).

Here is an improved version, which deftly turns many of the quotations into summaries and paraphrases, resulting in a cleaner, less cluttered paragraph:

The anti–Japanese movement in America goes back to the turn of the century, when the United States Industrial Commission claimed that the Japanese ''are more servile than the Chinese, but less obedient and far less desirable'' (Conrat 18). At about the same time, the slogan of politician and labor leader Dennis Kearney was ''The Japs must go!'' while the mayor of San Francisco insisted that it was impossible for the Japanese to assimilate into American culture and that they were ''not the stuff of which American citizens are made'' (Daniels 9–10). In this xenophobic atmosphere, the Japanese and Korean Expulsion League was formed in 1905 and a number of other anti–Japanese societies followed (McCullough 102).

Notice, by the way, that the improved version contains fewer references than the original. In the first version, the student was forced to document every quotation, even though successive quotations some-times came from the same source. The blend of summaries, paraphrases, and quotations not only reduced clutter, but also cut down on the number of notes by combining references from the same source into a single sentence and under a single note.

### b. Using brief quotations

Brief quotations (four lines or less) may be introduced with a simple phrase:

Betty Friedan <u>admits</u> that it will be quite a while before women know ''how much of the difference between women and men is cultur-ally determined and how much of it is real.''

''God is the perfect poet,'' <u>said</u> Browning in ''Paracelsus.''

Hardin Craig <u>suggests</u> that ''in order fully to understand and appreciate Shakespeare, it is necessary to see him as a whole.''

In Shakespeare's <u>Antony and Cleopatra</u>, Cleopatra <u>prefers</u> ''a ditch in Egypt'' as her grave to being hoisted up and shown to the ''shouting varletry of censuring Rome'' (<u>Ant</u>. 4.1.55-60).

<u>According to</u> David Halberstam, when McNamara began to take over the Vietnam problem, ''there was a growing split between the civilians and the military over the assessment of Vietnam.''

In contrast to Eichmann's concept of justice, Thoreau <u>believed</u> that ''a true patriot would resist a tyrannical majority.''

Note that if the quotation is grammatically part of the sentence in which it occurs, the first word of the quotation does not need to be capitalized, even if it is capitalized in the original.

*Original*      "Some infinitives deserve to be split."
*quotation*                                          Bruce Thompson

*Quotation used*  Bruce Thompson affirms what writers have always sus-
*as part of a*
*sentence*    pected, namely that ''some infinitives deserve to be

         split.''

Moreover, if the quotation is used at the end of a declarative sentence, it will be followed by a period whether or not a period is used in the original.

*Original*      "Love is a smoke rais'd with the fume of sighs; . . ."
*quotation*                                          Shakespeare

*Quotation used*  In Act I Romeo describes love as ''a smoke rais'd with
*in a declarative*
*sentence*    the fume of sighs.''

Finally, you should strive for variety in the introduction of quotations, rather than ploddingly serving them up with the same words and phrases. If you introduce one quotation with, "So-and-so says," try something different for the next, such as, "In the opinion of at least one critic," or "A view widely shared by many in the field affirms that," and so on.

### c.  Using long quotations

Unlike quotations of four lines or less, longer quotations need to be introduced by a formal sentence, placed in context, and properly explained. Moreover, long quotations must be set off from the text by triple spacing, indented ten spaces from the left margin, and typed with double spacing but without quotation marks (unless the quotation itself contains quotation marks). If two or more paragraphs are quoted, then the sentence beginning each paragraph should be indented three spaces. Each long quotation should be preceded by a colon:

**Figure 6-1**    A long quotation of two paragraphs

The final paragraphs of "A Rose for Emily" bring to a

horrifying climax all elements of Gothic horror

that have pervaded the story:

quotation set apart
from the text by
double spacing

opening sentence of
paragraph indented 5
spaces

      For a long while we just stood there,

looking down at the profound and fleshless

grin. The body had apparently once lain in

the attitude of an embrace, but now the long

sleep that outlasts love, had cuckolded him.

body of quotation
indented 10 spaces
from left margin

What was left of him, rotted beneath what was

left of the nightshirt, had become inextric-

able from the bed in which he lay; and upon

him and upon the pillow beside him lay that

even coating of the patient and biding dust.

opening sentence
of second paragraph
indented 5 spaces

      Then we noticed that in the second pillow

was the indentation of a head. One of us

lifted something from it, and leaning for-

ward, that faint and invisible dust dry and

acrid in the nostrils, we saw a long strand

of iron-gray hair.

If the quotation consists of only a single paragraph, or if the opening
sentence of the quotation is not the start of a paragraph, then the first
line of the quotation need not be indented three spaces:

In his novel Lady Chatterley's Lover, D. H. Lawrence creates a

mesmeric and ritualistic effect as he describes the love scene be-

tween Mellors and Connie:

> But he drew away at last, and kissed her and covered her
>
> over, and began to cover himself. She lay looking up to
>
> the boughs of the tree, unable as yet to move. He stood
>
> and fastened up his breeches, looking round. All was
>
> dense and silent, save for the awed dog that lay with
>
> its paws against its nose. He sat down again on the
>
> brushwood and took Connie's hand in silence. (150)

Lawrence has created a trancelike mood that conveys the symbolic

importance of this scene.

Notice how the author has provided a context for the quotation by alluding to it as "mesmeric and ritualistic"; how she has provided a formal introduction; and how, following the quotation, she has provided an explanation of why the quotation was presented.

### d.  Using quotations from poetry

Unless the stanzaic line needs to be preserved for stylistic emphasis, short passages of verse should be enclosed by quotation marks and incorporated into the text. Quotations of two or three lines may also be part of the text, but with the lines separated by a slash (/) with a space on each side of the slash:

> The line "I have been half in love with easeful Death" expresses
>
> a recurrent theme in Keats's poetry––the desire for permanent res-
>
> idence in a world free from pain and anguish.

> "The raven's croak, the low wind choked and drear, / The baffled
>
> stream, the gray wolf's doleful cry" are typical Romantic images
>
> used by William Morris to create a mood of idle despair.

Verse quotations that exceed three lines should be separated from the text by triple spacing, indented ten spaces from the left margin (or less, if the line is so long that it would cause the page to look unbalanced), double-spaced without quotation marks (unless the poem itself contains quotation marks), and introduced with a colon. The spatial arrangement of the original poem (indentation and spacing within and between lines) should be reproduced with accuracy:

```
In the following lines from ''You Ask Me Why, Tho' Ill at Ease,''

Tennyson expresses the poet's desire for freedom to speak out:


        It is the land that freemen till,

            That sober-suited Freedom chose,

            The land, where girt with friends or foes

        A man may speak the thing he will.
```

The quotation beginning in the middle of a line of verse should be reproduced exactly that way and not shifted to the left margin:

```
As Cordelia leaves her home, exiled by Lear's folly, she reveals

full insight into her sisters' evil characters:


            I know you what you are;

        And like a sister am most loath to call

        Your faults as they are nam'd.  Love well our father:

        To your professed bosoms I commit him:

        But yet, alas, stood I within his grace,

        I would prefer him to a better place. (Lr. 1.1.272-77)
```

### e. Using a quotation within another quotation

Use single quotation marks to enclose a quotation within another brief quotation:

```
Rollo May is further exploring the daimonic personality when he

states that ''in his essays, Yeats goes so far as to specifically

define the daimonic as the 'Other Will.'''
```

For quotations within long, indented quotations, use double quotation marks:

In his essay ''Disease As a Way of Life,''  Eric J. Cassell makes

the following observation:

> As the term ''diarrhea—pneumonia complex'' suggests, in-
>
> fants in the Navajo environment commonly suffered or
>
> died from a combination of respiratory and intestinal
>
> complaints that are not caused by any single bacterium
>
> or virus.

## f. Punctuating quotations

The rules for punctuating quotations are few and simple:

- Place commas and periods inside the quotation marks:

''Three times today,'' Lord Hastings declares in Act 3, ''my foot-

cloth horse did stumble, and started, when he look'd upon the

Tower, as loath to bear me to the slaughter—house.''

- Place colons and semicolons outside the quotation marks:

Brutus reassures Portia, ''You are my true and honourable wife, as

dear to me as are the ruddy drops that visit my sad heart''; conse-

quently, she insists that he reveal his secrets to her.

- Place question marks and exclamation marks inside the quotation marks if they are part of the quotation, but outside if they are not:

King Henry asks, ''What rein can hold licentious wickedness when

down the hill he holds his fierce career?''

But:

Which Shakespearean character said, ''Fortune is painted blind,

with a muffler afore her eyes''?

## g.  Interpolations in quoted material

Personal comments or explanations within a quotation must be placed in square brackets (not parentheses), which may be handwritten if no such key exists on your typewriter. The word "sic" within square brackets means that the quotation—including any errors—has been exactly copied.

```
The critical review was entitled ''A Cassual [sic] Analysis of

Incest and Other Passions.''
```

The "sic" indicates that "cassual" is reproduced exactly as it is spelled in the quotation.

Here is an explanatory interpolation, also set off in square brackets:

```
Desdemona answers Emilia with childlike innocence: ''Beshrew me if

I would do such a wrong [cuckold her husband] for all the whole

world.''
```

## h.  The ellipsis

The ellipsis—three dots ( . . . ) with a space before and after each dot—is used to indicate the omission of material from a quotation. Such omissions are necessary when only a part of the quotation is relevant to the point you are making. Use of the ellipsis, however, does not free a researcher from an obligation of remaining faithful to the intent of the author's original text. The following example illustrates the misuse of the ellipsis to distort an author's meaning:

*Original*   Faulkner's novels have the quality of being lived, absorbed, remembered rather than merely observed.

Malcolm Cowley

*Quotation*
```
Malcolm Cowley further suggests that ''Faulkner's

novels have the quality of being . . . merely

observed.''
```

If you are quoting no more than a fragment and it is clear that something has been left out, no ellipsis is necessary:

```
Malcolm Cowley refers to Faulkner's ''mythical kingdom.''
```

But when it is not clear that an omission has been made, the ellipsis must be used.

■ *Omissions within a sentence* are indicated by three spaced dots:

*Original*   Mammals were in existence as early as the latest Triassic, 190 million years ago, yet for the first one hundred and twenty million years of their history, from the end of the Triassic to the late Cretaceous, they were a suppressed race, unable throughout that span of time to produce any carnivore larger than cat-size or herbivore larger than rat-size.

Adrian Desmond

*Quotation*   Adrian Desmond, arguing that the dinosaurs were once dominant over mammals, points out that ''mammals were in existence as early as the latest Triassic . . . yet for the first one hundred and twenty million years of their history . . . they were a suppressed race, unable to produce any carnivore larger than cat–size or herbivore larger than rat–size.''

Two omissions are made in the quotation, and both indicated by an ellipsis of three spaced dots.

■ *Omissions at the end of a sentence* use a period followed by three spaced dots:

Adrian Desmond, arguing that the dinosaurs were once dominant over mammals, points out that the mammals were, for millions of years, ''a suppressed race, unable throughout that span of time to pro–duce any carnivore larger than cat–size. . . .''

Notice that the first dot is a period, and is placed immediately after the last word without an intervening space.

If the ellipsis is followed by parenthetical material at the end of a sentence, use three spaced dots and place the sentence period after the final parenthesis:

Another justice made the following, more restrictive, statement: ''You have the right to disagree with those in authority . . . but you have no right to break the law . . .'' (Martin 42).

■ *Omissions of a sentence or more* are also indicated by four dots, but with this proviso: that a complete sentence must both precede and follow the four dots. Here is an example:

*Original*    *Manuscript Troana* and other documents of the Mayas describe a cosmic catastrophe during which the ocean fell on the continent, and a terrible hurricane swept the earth. The hurricane broke up and carried away all towns and forests. Exploding volcanoes, tides sweeping over mountains, and impetuous winds threatened to annihilate humankind, and actually did annihilate many species of animals. The face of the earth changed, mountains collapsed, other mountains grew and rose over the onrushing cataract of water driven from oceanic spaces, numberless rivers lost their beds, and a wild tornado moved through the debris descending from the sky.

                                                              Immanuel Velikovsky

*Unacceptable*     That species of animals may have been made extinct by
*use of four*
*dots to mark*     some worldwide catastrophe is not unthinkable. Im—
*an omission*
                   manuel Velikovsky states that according to ''<u>Manu-</u>

                   <u>script Troana</u> and other documents. . . . The face of

                   the earth changed, mountains collapsed, other moun-

                   tains grew and rose over the onrushing cataract of wa-

                   ter driven from oceanic spaces, numberless rivers

                   lost their beds, and a wild tornado moved through the

                   debris. . . .''

The quotation is unacceptably reproduced because the fragment "*Manuscript Troana* and other documents," rather than an entire sentence, is placed before the four dots. Here is an acceptable use of this material:

That species of animals may have been made extinct by some world—

wide catastrophe is not unthinkable.  Immanuel Velikovsky states

that ''<u>Manuscript Troana</u> and other documents of the Mayas describe

a cosmic catastrophe. . . . The face of the earth changed, moun-

tains collapsed, other mountains grew and rose over the onrush-

ing cataract of water driven from oceanic spaces, numberless

```
rivers lost their beds, and a wild tornado moved through the

debris. . . .''
```

Complete sentences are reproduced before and after the four periods, which satisfies the convention.

- *Omissions of long passages*, such as several stanzas, paragraphs, or pages, are marked by a single typed line of spaced dots.

```
Speaking through the prophet Amos, the God of the Israelites warns

sternly:
```

```
            For you alone have I cared

            among all the nations of the world;

            therefore will I punish you

            for all your iniquities.

            . . . . . . . . .

            An enemy shall surround the land;

            your stronghold shall be thrown down

            and your palaces sacked.
```

- *Omissions that immediately follow an introductory statement* require no ellipsis.

```
Acceptable   In Booth's fantastic mind, his act was to be ''the

             perfect crime of the ages and he the most heroic

             assassin of all times.''
```

```
Unacceptable  In Booth's fantasic mind, his act was to be ''. . .

              the perfect crime of the ages and he the most heroic

              assassin of all times.''
```

Although an omission has been made in the beginning of the quotation, the use of an ellipsis following the introductory remark is unnecessary.

## 6b-4   Using indirect quotations

There are times when you will want to quote an author indirectly. An indirect quotation reports what someone said or wrote but not in the exact words of the original passage. Indirect quotations should not appear in quotation marks. Study the following examples:

*Direct quotation*   J. K. Galbraith makes the following statement: ''In the Affluent Society no useful distinction can be made between luxuries and necessaries.''

*Indirect quotation*   J. K. Galbraith suggests that in an affluent society rich people don't make any useful distinction between luxuries and necessities.

*Direct quotation*   After defining the qasida as a ''pre-Islamic ode,'' Katharine Slater Gittes comments: ''These wholly secular odes glorify the Bedouin life, the life of the wanderer.''

*Indirect quotation*   According to Katharine Slater Gittes, the main purpose of the qasida, a pre-Islamic ode, is to glorify the life of the Bedouin wanderer.

The purpose of using indirect quotations is to avoid a choppy style that evolves when one uses a string of direct quotations. Indirect quotations maintain the continuity of the writer's own style, giving the text a smoother flow.

**NOTE:** Whether using a short, long, or indirect quotation, be sure to avoid vague pronoun references in your introductory phrasing:

*Poor*   In one article it stated, ''Numerous victims. . . .''

*Better*   In his article ''Anorexia Nervosa,'' Petersen states, ''Numerous victims. . . .''

78

*Poor*   In the introduction <u>they</u> point out that the vote was

59 to 38 against the bill.

*Better*   The Introduction points out that the vote was 59 to 38

against the bill.

### 6b-5   How to place and punctuate the page reference parentheses

This section applies only if your paper is documented in the parenthetical style used by the Modern Language Association (MLA) and the American Psychological Association (APA) (see 7d and 7e).

### a.  Short quotations

When using a quotation of one sentence or less in your running text, place the page reference parentheses *after* the closing quotation mark but *before* the end punctuation, thus including the parentheses within your own sentence:

Noyes, for example, insisted that ''there is a language in the

Canticles which I could not apply to the Supreme Being . . . with-

out feeling guilty of blasphemy'' (125).

### b.  Long quotations

When using a *long, indented quotation*, omit quotation marks and place the page reference parentheses *after* the final period with no period following the parentheses:

Gail Sheehy characterizes certain successful males as <u>wunder-</u>

<u>kinder</u>:

> The <u>wunderkind</u> often seems to possess a boundless capac-
>
> ity to bounce back from career failures.  Business
>
> losses, power struggles, lost elections, even criminal
>
> charges are viewed as temporary setbacks; they merely
>
> stiffen his resolve to come out a winner. (191)

### c. Quotations ending in an ellipsis

If the quotation (long or short) ends in an ellipsis, place the final period after the parentheses. (See 6b-3*h*, p. 75.)

### 6b-6   Using personal comments

Students are expected to do more in a research paper than simply preside over the opinions of their sources. Naturally, the bulk of the paper will consist of material accumulated in research. But without the interpretation of the student, none of this material is likely to make any sense to a reader. A prime function of the personal comment, therefore, is to supply the reader with information otherwise unobtainable from the stark research data. Personal comments serve to interpret material, mark transitions from one idea to another, and draw conclusions. In a manner of speaking, the thesis statement can also be regarded as an elaborate personal comment in which the student enunciates a general design and focus for the entire paper.

The example below illustrates the use of the personal comment to interpret material. The student's paper is on the career of Pope Innocent III; the discussion in the preceding paragraph centered on a crusade that Innocent III had just called for. Interjecting a personal comment, the student interprets the motive of Innocent III in launching this crusade:

```
Innocent III's call for this crusade shows that he was trying to

establish that the Papacy was the temporal authority on earth.  As

the head of Christendom, he couldn't tolerate any philosophy that

would divert attention away from the teaching of the Catholic

church.
```

Personal comments are also used to establish smooth transitions as the discussion moves from one idea to another. Here is an example, taken from this same student paper. The preceding paragraph has just summarized the reaction of Innocent III to the heresy of the Cathars.

```
The heresy of the Cathars was not the only anti-Catholic philoso-

phy that Innocent III endeavored to crush.  He desired to crush

the heresy of the Moslems as well.
```

The paper then moves on to a discussion of the efforts of Pope Innocent III to crush the Moslems.

Finally, the personal comment is widely used to make summations and draw conclusions. The paper on Innocent III ends with this summation of the Pontiff's career:

```
Innocent III's pontificate was the zenith of the medieval papacy.

He involved himself in world affairs by endeavoring to stop heresy

and by exerting his authority over kings.  He crushed the Cathar

heresy and brought the Greek church under his control.  He used

the kings of Europe like pawns on a chessboard.  Therefore one can

conclude that Innocent III made the theory of papal theocracy into

a reality.
```

# 6c

## Writing the paper with unity, coherence, and emphasis

### 6c-1   Unity

The rhetorical principle of unity dictates that a paper should stick to its chosen thesis without rambling or digressing. If the thesis states that Japanese art influenced French Impressionism, the paper should cover exactly that subject and nothing more. If the thesis proposes to contrast the life styles of inner city residents and suburban dwellers, the paper should concisely pursue such a contrast, ignoring all side issues, no matter how personally fascinating to the writer.

To observe the principle of unity, a writer has merely to follow the lead of the thesis. Properly drafted, the thesis will predict the content of a paper, control its direction, and obligate the writer to a single purpose. The writer introduces only material relevant to the thesis, suppressing the urge to dabble in side issues or to stray from the point. Such admirable single-mindedness will produce a paper written according to the principle of unity, and consequently easier for a reader to follow.

The principle of unity should govern the progression of ideas within an individual paragraph as well as throughout the entire structure of an essay. Paragraphs should be written to scrupulously deliver exactly what the topic sentence promises, for the content of a paragraph is controlled by its topic sentence much as the structure and direction of an essay are determined by its thesis.

## 6c-2 Coherence

Coherence is said to exist in a paragraph whose sentences are arranged in a clear, logical, and intelligible order. If the sentences of a paragraph are illogically or unintelligibly arranged, the paragraph is said to be incoherent, as for instance this one:

In the past year it's been through times of extreme highs and lows in my emotional outlook on life. The trend of any life seems to follow this general pattern. Some of the high moments were meeting new people that turned out to be much more than mere acquaintances, having the newly met person turn into a friend a person could know for the rest of their life. Also competing in sports and in the area of track and field and baseball. Meeting and going out with a few girls, which in our relationship between each other bloomed into a special kind of affection for ourselves.

The paragraph is so muddled and incoherent that it is nearly impossible to read.

Incoherent writing is primarily caused by a writer's inability to perceive the paragraph as a whole. Instead, the writer becomes preoccupied with individual sentences, and fashions them as though they existed in isolation on the page. The result is the splintered writing seen in the paragraph above. To avoid incoherence, a writer must conceptualize the paragraph as a unit of expression to which individual sentences contribute an increment of meaning. Sentences must be written down in such a way as to coexist harmoniously with their neighbors. If you have trouble writing coherently, consult a good handbook or your instructor.

## 6c-3 Emphasis

The rhetorical principle of emphasis requires the expression of more important ideas in main or independent clauses, and of less important ideas in dependent or subordinate clauses. In sum, properly emphatic writing will attempt to rank ideas through grammatical structure. Here is an example of an unemphatic piece of writing:

*Poor emphasis*   The gifted child is a high achiever on a specific
                  test, either the Otis or Binet I.Q. test. These tests

```
            are usually administered at the end of the second

            grade.  They determine the placement of the child in

            third grade.  These tests are characterized by writ-

            ten as well as verbal questions, so that the child has

            the opportunity to express himself creatively.
```

The grammatical treatment of ideas is altogether too egalitarian. A reader simply cannot distinguish between the important and the unimportant ideas, because they are all expressed in a similar grammatical structure. Here is the same passage made emphatic:

```
Improved     A child is considered gifted if he has achieved a high
emphasis
             score on a specific test such as the Otis or Binet

             I.Q. test.  Characterized by written as well as ver-

             bal questions so that the child has the opportunity to

             express himself creatively, these tests are adminis-

             tered at the end of the second grade in order to de-

             termine the proper placement of the child in

             third grade.
```

By placing subordinate ideas in subordinate clauses, the writer achieves a purposeful focus missing from the unemphatic version.

# 6d
## Using the proper tense

### 6d-1 Maintain the present tense except when reporting an event that happened in the past.

In the following passage, note the appropriate shift from past to present.

```
    In the 1950s there was among the medical profession a sudden en-

    thusiasm for the surgical removal of infected lung tissue, and ex-
```

pensive plans <u>were</u> made to build new surgical wards in many hos-
pitals. But when streptomycin <u>came</u> along, much of this surgery
<u>became</u> unnecessary. Thus huge amounts of money <u>had been</u> wasted.
The truth <u>is</u> that a much higher priority needs to be given to
basic research in biologic science. This <u>is</u> the best way of sav-
ing health care expenses in the long run.

Beginning with the sentence "The truth is . . . ," the shift from past to
present is smoothly accomplished.

### 6d-2  Keep your tense or mood consistent.

*Wrong*  The wildlife of the beaches <u>would be</u> contaminated in

the event of an oil spill. The sand and water <u>becomes</u>

covered with oil sludge and residue.

*Right*  The wildlife of the beaches <u>would be</u> contaminated in

the event of an oil spill. The sand and water <u>would</u>

<u>become</u> covered with oil sludge and residue.

The writer began the idea in the conditional and must complete it in that
mood.

### 6d-3  Use the present tense for most comments by authorities because they usually continue to be true and in print.

Thomas Jefferson <u>supports</u> the idea of . . .

Gilbert Highet <u>criticizes</u> . . .

Milton and Shakespeare, like Homer, <u>acknowledge</u> the desire . . .

''Art rediscovers . . . what is necessary to humanness,'' <u>declares</u>

John Gardner.

But use the past tense for actions or events completed in the past.

When Horace <u>wrote</u> the <u>Ars Poetica</u>, . . .

The nationwide founding of the Brewers Association <u>was</u> a factor

contributing . . .

In the 17th century, Seventh—day Baptists <u>were</u> among the followers

of Oliver Cromwell.

# Seven
# Systems of Documentation

**7a** When to provide documentation

**7b** Types of documentation

**7c** Guide to systems of documentation

**7d** Parenthetical documentation: Author and work (MLA style)

**7e** Parenthetical documentation: Author and date (APA style)

**7f** Parenthetical documentation: Numbers

**7g** Traditional documentation: Footnotes/endnotes

**7h** Content notes

**7i** Consolidation of references

# 7a

## When to provide documentation

Neither general knowledge, common sayings, nor self-evident opinions or conclusions need to be documented. The rule of thumb is simply this: if the idea, opinion, or conclusion is of the kind that any well-read person is likely to know, then no documentation is necessary. For instance, the assertion that the Nazi regime under Hitler committed atrocities against the Jews is common knowledge and therefore requires no documentation. However, if you quote from eyewitness accounts of these atrocities, acknowledgment must be given in either a footnote, an endnote, or in parentheses. In sum, any idea, conclusion, information, or data specifically derived from the work of someone else must be acknowledged. (See also 4d, pp. 39–42—Plagiarism: what it is and how to avoid it.)

# 7b

## Types of documentation

Documentation is the process by which you give credit to the appropriate sources for every borrowed idea used in your paper. Borrowed ideas may be incorporated into the paper either as direct quotations, summaries, or paraphrases. But no matter what form you use to incorporate the idea of another into your paper, you must give appropriate credit in a specific and conventional style that allows a reader to trace your sources and, if necessary, to investigate their accuracy or applicability. (See also 4c-2, pp. 35–39.)

Two basic styles of documentation are now used in research: (1) note citations and (2) parenthetical citations. The older style, note citations, calls for footnotes or endnotes. This style is preferred by two major fields, the humanities (but *not* language and literature) and the fine arts (music, art, and dance). Footnotes and endnotes both require superscript numbers within the text and corresponding documentary notes either at the bottom of the page (footnotes) or at the end of the paper (endnotes). For example, a paper on Salvador Dali's religious paintings might include the following passage:

```
One of Dali's most popular paintings, Christ of Saint John of the

Cross, pictures the crucified Christ suspended over Iligat Bay, a

port on the east coast of Spain.   Christ is symbolized as the nu-

cleus of the atom, that is, the unity of the universe.[3]
```

In the footnote style, the superscript *3* would have the following corresponding footnote at the bottom of the same page on which the superscript *3* appeared:

> [3] Salvador Dali, <u>Dali</u>, trans. Eleanor R. Morse (New
> York: Abrams, 1968) 33.

The endnote style requires the same reference note (only double spaced within and between notes) in numerical order according to the superscripts, in a separate section entitled "Notes" at the end of the paper. (See p. 106.)

The note citation style also requires a separate bibliography at the end of the paper in which all sources used are listed alphabetically by the surnames of the authors or, in cases where there is no author, by the first significant word of the title of the work. An example follows:

> Dali, Salvador. <u>Dali</u>. Trans. Eleanor R. Morse. New York:
>
> Abrams, 1970.

Each source will therefore be documented at least twice: in a footnote or endnote, and in a bibliography entry. Slight differences exist in the format of each kind of documentation—differences which must be observed. Footnotes or endnotes cannot simply be transferred to the bibliography page of the paper; nor can a bibliography entry serve as a note.

A second style of documentation, which uses parenthetical citations, now dominates in the sciences as well as in language and literature. Here references are placed not in endnotes or footnotes but in parentheses within the text itself. The parenthetical note refers the reader to a bibliography entry, which includes complete publication details on the source. Let us assume, for instance, that a paper on the history of passive resistance alludes to a work by Ralph Templin. In the new parenthetical documentation style, all of the important documenting information would appear in the text, with only a short reference in parentheses:

> As Ralph Templin notes (253), nonviolence does not simply ignore
>
> evil so that peace can be maintained.

or

> Nonviolence does not simply ignore evil so that peace can be main-
>
> tained (Templin 253).

For the full Templin reference, the reader then consults the bibliography section at the end of the paper—labelled "Works Cited" or "Reference List." Simplicity is the main virtue of this new style. In the past, beleaguered students had to perform double labor in documenting their papers. First, they had to laboriously type out footnotes on the bottoms of their pages, often ruining otherwise good pages because they had miscounted the number of lines a note required. Next, they had to repeat the nearly identical information in a bibliography citation. The use of endnotes required the same double labor. But the new style calls for only one complete citation—the bibliography entry. Within the text itself the parenthetical reference consists of author and page (or, in the case of scientific papers, author and date). This text favors parenthetical documentation, and that is the style it explains in detail. However, for those students whose teachers still prefer the traditional note style, summary guidelines to it, with examples, are provided as well.

# 7c

## Guide to systems of documentation

The following list can help you decide which type of documentation your paper requires. Disciplines are listed alphabetically within each group.

GUIDE TO SYSTEMS OF DOCUMENTATION

| | | |
|---|---|---|
| **Author/Work (MLA)** (See 7d.) | Language Literature | |
| **Author/Year (APA)** (See 7e.) | Agriculture Anthropology Archaeology Astronomy Biology Botany Business Education | Geology Home Economics Linguistics Physical Education Political Science Psychology Sociology |
| **Traditional** **(Footnote/Endnote)** (See 7g.) | Art Dance History Music | Philosophy Religion Theater |
| **Numbers** (See 7f.) | Chemistry Computer Science Health | Mathematics Medicine Nursing |

# 7d

## Parenthetical documentation: Author and work (MLA style)

College research papers in the field of language and literature have long followed the style laid down by the Modern Language Association (MLA). In 1983 the MLA announced its decision to change to the parenthetical style of documentation. Other changes in style proposed by the MLA are as follows:

- Use of Arabic numerals for everything except titles (*Henry IV*) or preliminary pages of a text traditionally numbered with Roman numerals (i, ii, iv, x, etc.).
- Omission of "p." or "pp." for page numbers.
- Omission of "l." or "ll." in favor or "line" or "lines" until lineation is established in the paper.
- A new form for journal entries, as follows:

```
Sherry, James J. ''Tennyson and the Paradox of the Sign.''  Victo-

    rian Poetry 17 (1979): 204-16.
```

Note the omission of the comma after the journal title, the changed order of entries, and the colon following the year to separate the volume and page.

- Changing the heading of the bibliography section to "Works Cited."

### 7d-1   Reference citations in the text

The new MLA style simplifies the reader's job by suggesting the following rules for in-text citations.

### a.  *Introducing the authority*

Introduce paraphrases or quotations by giving the authority's name. Use both the first name and the surname the first time the authority is used:

```
Robert M. Jordan suggests that Chaucer's tales are held together

by seams that are similar to the exposed beams supporting a Gothic

cathedral (237-38).
```

Subsequent citations will refer simply to the authority's surname:

```
Jordan further suggests:
```

## b. Identifying the source

Whenever possible, identify what makes the source important:

```
Noam Flinker, Lecturer in English at the Ben-Gurion University of
the Negev in Israel, an authority on Biblical literature, repeat-
edly suggests . . .
```

## c. Documenting without mention of authority

When the authority is not mentioned in the introduction to a paraphrase or quotation, place in parentheses the authority's name, followed by a page reference:

```
Democracy is deemed preferable to monarchy because it protects the
individual's rights rather than his property (Emerson 372).
```

## d. Material by two authors

When referrring to material written by two authors, mention the names of both authors:

```
Christine E. Wharton and James S. Leonard take the position that
the mythical figure of Amphion represents a triumph of the spir-
itual over the physical (163).
```

Subsequent references would refer simply to Wharton and Leonard.

## e. Material by more than two authors

For a work with more than three authors or editors, use the first name followed by "et al." or "and others" (without a comma following the name):

```
G. B. Harrison et al. (Major British Writers) provide an
excellent overview of the best in English literature.
```

## f. *Mentioning both author and work*

When it can be accomplished smoothly, mention both the author and the work in your introduction:

> In his essay ''Criticism and Sociology,'' David Daiches insists
>
> that ''sociological criticism can help to increase literary
>
> perception as well as to explain origins'' (17).

## g. *Anonymous author*

When a work is listed as anonymous, mention the fact that it is anonymous in the text and place the title of the work from which the piece was taken, or an abbreviated version if the title is very long, in parentheses:

> Another anonymous poem, ''Driftwood'' (<u>Driftwood</u>), also damns the
>
> city for its thoughtless pollution of the environment.

## h. *No author*

When a work has no author, cite the first two or three significant words from the title:

> Spokane's <u>The Spokesman Review</u> (''Faulkner Dies'') gets at the
>
> heart of America's greatest fiction writer when it states
>
> that . . . .

## i. *More than one work by the same author*

When more than one work by the same author is referred to in the paper, provide a shortened version of the title in each citation. Citing only author and page may confuse the reader since "Works Cited" will contain two references to the same author. The following passage is an example of how to handle two works by the same author:

> Feodor Dostoevsky declares that the ''underground'' rebel is rep-
>
> resentative of our society (<u>Underground</u> 3). He seems to confirm
>
> this view in Raskolnikov's superman speech (<u>Crime</u> 383-84), where
>
> he identifies . . .

### j. Multivolume works

When referring to a specific passage in a multivolume work, give the author, the volume number followed by a colon and a space, and the page reference:

```
Other historians disagree (Durant 2: 25) . . . .
```

When referring to an entire volume, give the name of the author, followed by a comma, and the abbreviation "vol.," followed by the volume number: (Durant, vol. 2).

### k. Double reference—a quotation within a cited work

```
As Bernard Baruch pointed out, ''Mankind has always thought to
substitute energy for reason'' (as qtd. in Ringer 274).
```

"Works Cited" would then contain the following entry:

```
Ringer, Robert J.   Restoring the American Dream.   New York: Harp-
er, 1979.
```

### l. Short passages of poetry

When short passages of poetry are incorporated into your text, observe these rules:

- Set off the quotation with quotation marks.
- Use a slash (with a space before and after the slash) to indicate separate lines of poetry.
- Place the proper documentation in parentheses immediately following the quotation and inside the period, because the reference is part of your basic sentence. The reference will be to the lines of the poem.

Study the following example:

```
Byron's profound sense of alienation is echoed in Canto 3 of
Childe Harold's Pilgrimage: ''I have not loved the World, nor the
World me: / I have not flattered its rank breath, nor bowed / To
its idolatries a patient knee'' (190-91).
```

### m. Using Arabic numerals

Use Arabic numerals for books, parts, volumes, and chapters of works; for acts, scenes, and lines of plays; for cantos, stanzas, and lines of poetry.

IN-TEXT CITATIONS

Volume 2 of *Civilization Past and Present*
Book 3 of *Paradise Lost*
Part 2 of *Crime and Punishment*
Act 3 of *Hamlet*
Chapter 1 of *The Great Gatsby*

PARENTHETICAL DOCUMENTATION

| | |
|---|---|
| (*Tmp.* 2.2.45-50) | for act 2, scene 2, lines 45-50 of Shakespeare's *Tempest* (See 10g-2c for abbreviating titles of Shakespeare's plays.) |
| (*GT* 2.1.3) | for part 2, chapter 1, page 3 of *Gulliver's Travels* by Swift |
| (*Jude* 15) | for page 15 of the novel *Jude the Obscure* by Hardy |
| (*PL* 7.5-10) | for book 7, lines 5-10 of *Paradise Lost* by Milton |
| (*FQ* 1.2.28.1-4) | for book 1, canto 2, stanza 28, lines 1-4 of *The Faerie Queene* by Spenser |

### 7d-2   Varying your introductions

Use variety in your introductions to in-text citations. As you achieve fluency and sophistication in writing, you will find ways to introduce authors and their works smoothly and without boring repetitions. Some possibilities are listed here, but you can create many more:

```
Lionel Trilling, the noted critic and editor, has championed this

idea (108).
```

```
In The Coming of Age, Simone de Beauvoir contends that the de-

crepitude accompanying old age is ''in complete conflict with

the manly or womanly ideal cherished by the young and fully

grown'' (25).
```

```
William York Tindall describes this segment as ''the densest part

of the Wake'' (171).
```

```
This attitude is central to the archetypal approach of interpret-

ing poetry (Fiedler 519).


Richard Chase argues that Billy Budd is a sort of Adam ''as yet un-

tainted by the 'urbane serpent''' (745).


In his eloquent guidebook Style, F. L. Lucas points out that re-

vision in writing is ''a means not only of polishing, but also of

compressing'' (261).


Others, like Booth (51) and Warren (33), take the opposite point

of view.
```

# 7e

## Parenthetical documentation: Author and date (APA style)

Established by the American Psychological Association (APA), this style is used by the social sciences, business, anthropology, and some of the life sciences (see 7c for a list of the disciplines using it). The APA style favors a system of parenthetical citations within the text much like the style now recommended by MLA. But there is a significant difference between the two. An in-text citation done in the APA style mentions only the author and date of the cited publication, not the author and work.

### 7e-1 Reference citations in the text

On the whole, scientific papers favor a parenthetical style of documentation that briefly identifies the source of a quotation or a piece of information so that the reader can find it in the alphabetical list of references at the end of the paper. Because in scientific research the date of publication is often crucial, APA emphasizes the date by placing it in parentheses following the name of the author. All notes are so treated except for content notes (see 7h). This system, like the new MLA system, simplifies the job of documentation by eliminating all reference notes at the bottom of the paper or at the end of the paper, requiring instead only a final "Reference List."

APA distinguishes between a *reference list*, which is a list of works specifically used in the research and preparation of your paper, and a *bibliography,* a list of works used for background reading or for further reading on the subject. A paper in the sciences, therefore, will end with a reference list, not with a bibliography.

### a. One work by a single author

The APA style sheet requires an author-date method of citation; that is, the surname of the author and the year of publication are inserted in the text of the paper at the appropriate point:

```
Johnson (1983) discovered that children were more suscep-

tible. . . .
```

or

```
In a more recent study (Johnson, 1983), children were found to be

more susceptible. . . .
```

or

```
In 1983 Johnson did another study that indicated children were

more susceptible. . . .
```

If the name of the author appears as an integral part of your sentence, then cite only the year of publication in parentheses, as in the first example. Otherwise, show both the author and the date of publication in parentheses, as in the second example. If, however, both the year and the author are cited in the textual discussion, then nothing need appear within parentheses, as in the third example.

### b. Subsequent references

If you continue to refer to the same study within a paragraph, subsequent references do not need to include the year as long as the study cannot be confused with other studies in your paper:

```
In a more recent study, Johnson (1983) found that children were

more susceptible. . . .  Johnson also found that. . . .
```

### c. One work by two or more authors

Scientific papers commonly reflect multiple authorship because so much of scientific research involves team work or cooperative studies.

When a work has two authors, always mention both names each time the reference occurs in your text:

```
In a previous study of caged rats (Grant & Change, 1958) the sur-

prising element was . . .
```

or

```
Much earlier, Grant and Change (1958) had discovered . . .
```

Notice that each time you refer to a work by two authors, you must name both authors.

### d.  One work by up to six authors

For works with up to six authors, mention all authors the first time the reference occurs; however, in subsequent citations, include only the surname of the first author followed by "et al." (not underlined and without a period after "et") and the year of publication:

■ First citation:

```
Holland, Holt, Levi, and Beckett (1983) indicate that . . .
```

■ Subsequent citation:

```
Holland et al. (1983) also found . . .
```

An exception occurs when two separate references have the same first author and same date and would thus shorten to the same reference. For example, Drake, Brighouse, and High (1983) and Drake, High, and Guilmette (1983) would both shorten to Drake et al. (1983). In such a case always cite both references in full to avoid confusion. Also, all multiple-author citations in footnotes, tables, and figures should include the surnames of all authors every time the citations occur.

### e.  Work of six or more authors

When a work has six or more authors, name only the surname of the first author followed by "et al." (not underlined and without a period after "et") and the year, in the first as well as in subsequent citations. In the final reference list, the names of all authors will appear in full. An exception occurs when two separate references would shorten to the same form. In such a case, list as many authors as are necessary to distinguish the two references, followed by "et al." For instance,

```
Cotton, Maloney, Brauer, Martin, Rodiles, and Tscharner (1970)
```

and

```
Cotton, Maloney, Jenkins, Martin, Rodiles, and Tscharner (1970)
```

would be cited as follows in the text:

```
Cotton, Maloney, Brauer, et al. (1970)
```

and

```
Cotton, Maloney, Jenkins, et al. (1970)
```

NOTE: In your running text, join the names of multiple-author citations by the word *and*; however, in parenthetical material, in tables, and in the final reference list, join the names by an ampersand (&), as follows:

```
Anderson and Raoul (1984) demonstrated clearly that . . .
```

but

```
As was clearly demonstrated earlier (Anderson & Raoul, 1984), cer-

tain factors remain . . .
```

### f. Corporate authors

Sometimes a scientific work is authored by a committee, an institution, a corporation, or a governmental agency. The names of most such corporate authors should be spelled out each time they appear as a reference source in your text. Occasionally, however, the name is spelled out in the first citation only and is abbreviated in subsequent citations. The rule of thumb for abbreviating is that you must supply enough information in the text for the reader to track down this source in your final reference list. In the case of long and cumbersome corporate names, abbreviations are acceptable in subsequent citations as long as the name is recognized and understood.

■ First citation in the text:

```
(National Institutes of Mental Health [NIMH], 1984)
```

■ Subsequent citations:

```
(NIMH, 1984)
```

■ First citation in the text:

```
(Santa Barbara Museum of Natural History [SBMNH], 1984)
```

■ Subsequent citations:

(SBMNH, 1984)

If the name is short or its abbreviation would not be understood easily, spell out the name each time the reference occurs.

(Harvard University, 1984)

(Russell Sage Foundation, 1984)

(Bendix Corporation, 1984)

The point is that the names of all of these corporate authors are simple enough to be written out each time they are cited.

*g. Works with an anonymous author or without an author*

When the author of a work is listed as "Anonymous," show the word "Anonymous" in parentheses in the text, followed by a comma and the date:

(Anonymous, 1984)

In your final reference list, the work will be alphabetized under "A" for "Anonymous."

When a work has no author, simply show, in parentheses, the first two or three words from the title of the book or article, followed by a comma and the year:

. . . as seen in most cases ("Time graphs," 1983)

The study shows that 55% of seniors (College bound seniors, 1979)

have serious difficulty with . . .

In the final reference list, works without authors are alphabetized according to the first significant word in the title. Articles (*the, a, an*), prepositions (*from, between, behind,* etc.), and pronouns (*this, those, that,* etc.) do not count. References to statutes and other legal materials are treated like references to works without authors; that is, you will cite the first few words of the reference and the year. Note that court cases cited in the text must be underlined.

```
(Baker v. Carr, 1962)

(National Environmental Protection Act, 1970)

(Civil Rights Act, 1964)
```

### h. Authors with the same surname

If your paper includes two or more authors with the same surname, include the authors' initials in all text citations even if the date differs. In this way you will be sure to avoid confusion:

```
D. L. Spencer (1965) and F. G. Spencer (1983) studied both as-

pects of . . .
```

### i. Two or more works within the same parentheses

Sometimes your paper may require that you cite within parentheses two or more works supporting the same point. In such a case, you will list the citations in the same order in which they appear in the reference list and according to reference list guidelines (see 8a-1). The following rules will be helpful:

■ *Two or more works by the same author(s)* are arranged in the same order by year of publication. If a work is in press (in the process of being published) cite it last:

```
Research of the past two years (Jessup & Quincy, 1983, 1984) has

revealed many potential . . .
```

or

```
Past studies (Eberhard, 1980, 1981, in press) reveal . . .
```

Different works by the same author that have the same publication date must be identified by "a," "b," "c," etc.:

```
According to these studies (Rodney & Campbell, 1980a, 1980b, in

press) the prevalent attitude is . . .
```

102

■ *Two or more works by different authors* cited within the same parentheses should be listed alphabetically according to the first authors' surnames. Use semicolons to separate the studies:

```
Three separate studies (Delaney & Rice, 1980; Rodney & Hollander,

1980; Zunz, 1981) tried to build on the same theory, but . . .
```

### j. References to specific parts of a source

Anytime you refer to a specific quotation, figure, or table, you must supply the appropriate page, figure number, or table number:

```
(Spetch & Wilkie, 1983, pp. 15–25)

(Halpern, 1982, Fig. 2)
```

Note that the words *page* and *Figure* are abbreviated.

### k. Personal communications

Personal communications include such items as letters, memos, and telephone conversations. Since they do not represent recoverable data, such items will not be reflected in your reference list. You will cite them in your text only. Give the initials and the surname of the communicator, and the date on which the communication took place:

```
(R. J. Melrose, personal communication, November 19, 1984)
```

or

```
R. J. Reiss (personal communication, November 19, 1984) provided

considerable insight on . . .
```

### l. Citation as part of a parenthetical comment

When a citation appears as part of a parenthetical comment, use commas rather than brackets to set off the date:

```
(See also Appendix A of Jenkins, 1983, for additional proof)
```

### 7e-2  Minimizing awkward placement of references

Many scholars favor the APA system of documentation because it helps the reader identify authority and date immediately without looking to the bottom of the page or flipping to the end of the article. However, you should guard against having so many references on one page that they become intrusive and hamper readability. The following passage, for example, is cluttered with parenthetical information:

```
The protocol itself was faulty (Jacobson, 1950); thus the result-

ing research was also seriously flawed (Zimmerman, 1955; Masters,

1956; Lester, 1956), and millions of dollars in time and equipment

were wasted (Smith, 1957).
```

To avoid this kind of congestion, some references can be given in the text:

```
In 1950, Jacobson acknowledged that the original protocol was

faulty, so that when Zimmerman (1955), Masters (1956), and Lester

(1956) performed their experiments, these too were flawed. The

consequent loss of thousands of dollars in time and equipment has

been well documented (Smith, 1957).
```

A prudent mixture of parenthetical and in-text references is best when a page threatens to become gorged with research citations.

# 7f

## Parenthetical documentation: Numbers

We shall make only brief mention of the numbers system, used mainly in the applied sciences (chemistry, computer science, mathematics, and physics) and in the medical sciences (medicine, nursing, and general health). Simply stated, this system requires an in-text number in place of an author, work, or page reference. That number will be used each time the source is cited within the text and will also appear in front of the work listed in "Works Cited." Observe the following rules, when using number citations in your text:

- Place the citation enclosed within parentheses, immediately after the authority's name:

```
Caffrey's (1) first description of child abuse included . . .
```

An alternate style is to place the citation as an elevated numeral:

```
Zimmerman et al.⁴ found cerebral infarctions in 50% of the cases.
```

- If your running text does not use the authority's name, insert both the name and number within parentheses:

```
Table 3 (Kaplan 4) displays the response distribution . . .
```

Alternate style:

```
Table 3 (Kaplan⁴) displays the response distribution . . .
```

- If necessary, add specific data to the entry:

```
The self-reported symptoms as analyzed by Wynder (3 Table 6) indi-
cate a significant increase . . .
```

(The reference is to Table 6 on page 3).

Alternate style:

```
The self-reported symptoms³˙ ᵀᵃᵇˡᵉ ⁶
```

- If you are citing more than one authority in your text, use the following format:

```
Other authors have confirmed Caffrey's observations concerning
the pathogenesis of the injuries (4-6).
```

Alternate style:

```
Other authors have confirmed Caffrey's observations concerning
the pathogenesis of the injuries.⁴⁻⁶
```

The reference is to three sources in "Works Cited": 4, 5, and 6.

# 7g
## Traditional documentation: Footnotes/endnotes

Notes serve two purposes in a research paper: (1) They acknowledge the source of a summary, paraphrase, or quotation; (2) they add explanatory comments that would otherwise interrupt the flow of the paper. Explanatory notes are often called "content notes" (See 7h).

Some teachers require that notes be typed at the bottom of the page on which the source is cited; others prefer that all notes appear in a separate listing at the end of the paper, before the bibliography. A *foot*note appears at the *foot* of the page whereas an *end*note appears at the *end* of the paper.

The examples in this section follow the new MLA guidelines for documentation, insofar as those guidelines are applicable to traditional footnotes and endnotes. Note that your instructor may want you to use a documentation style that differs in some ways from these examples. To avoid extra work, consult your instructor before your paper is typed in final form.

### 7g-1   Format for endnotes

Endnotes occur in the following format, and are typed together on a separate sheet at the end of the paper:

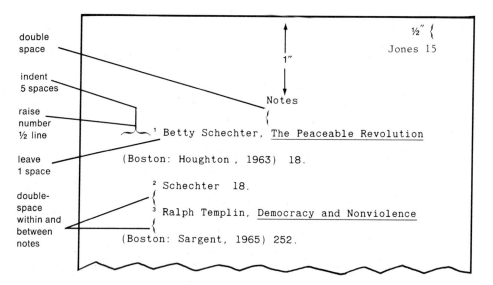

**Figure 7-1**   Format for endnotes

### 7g-2   Format for footnotes

Footnotes are placed at the bottom of the page on which the cited source occurs, and in the following format:

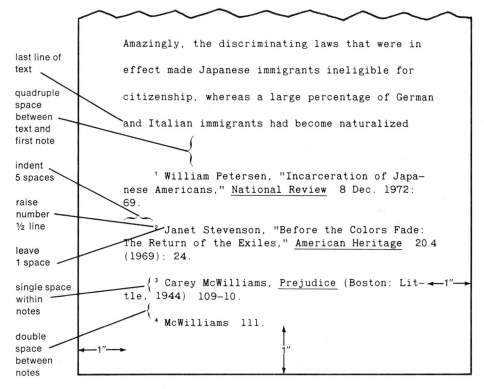

**Figure 7-2**  Format for footnotes

### 7g-3  Numbering of notes

Notes are numbered by Arabic numerals elevated one half space above the line and placed as close as possible to the end of the material cited. All notes should be numbered consecutively throughout the paper (1, 2, 3, etc.). Note numbers are not followed by periods or enclosed in parentheses. Moreover, they follow without space all punctuation marks except the dash.

### 7g-4  Proper placement of note numbers

The prime rule is that a note number should be placed as near as possible to the *end* of cited material.

> *Wrong*    In A Matter of Life Bertrand Russell emphasizes that
>
> law ''substitutes a neutral authority for private

> bias,''[13] and he believes this to be the main advan-
>
> tage of the law.

*Better*    In <u>A Matter of Life</u> Bertrand Russell emphasizes that

        law ''substitutes a neutral authority for private

        bias,'' and he believes this to be the main advantage

        of the law.[13]

However, if cited material is followed by material quoted or paraphrased from another source, then each note should be placed immediately after the material to which it refers.

> Whereas Herbert Read suggests passive resistance as ''the weapon
>
> of those who despair of justice,''[14] Ralph Templin warns that non-
>
> violence must never overlook evil for the sake of peace.[15]

(In the preceding example, note 14 cites quoted material from one source, while note 15 cites paraphrased material from another source.)

Finally notes should not be placed immediately after an author's name, or immediately after the verb or colon that introduces a documented passage:

*Wrong*    Justice Abe Fortas[1] states, for example, that civil

        disobedience should be directed only against ''laws

        or practices that are the subject of dissent.''

*Wrong*    Justice Abe Fortas states,[1] for example, that civil

        disobedience should be directed only against ''laws

        or practices that are the subject of dissent.''

*Right*    Justice Abe Fortas states, for example, that civil

        disobedience should be directed only against ''laws

        or practices that are the subject of dissent.''[1]

### 7g-5 Sample footnotes for books

Below you will find examples of most of the kinds of notes you will be using in your research paper if you do not use an in-text parenthetical style for citations. These samples, however, cannot anticipate every conceivable kind of citation. If you need to cite a source for which this book provides no model, use your common sense. Bear in mind, moreover, that the purpose of documentation is to allow a reader to reconstruct your research and thinking. You should therefore provide enough information to enable a reader to easily locate any cited source.

All samples are given in the footnote format, with single spacing. They can easily be converted to endnotes by double spacing within each note and between notes. Study each entry carefully to determine the proper punctuation, spacing, and underlining.

*a. Book with a single author*

[1] Fawn M. Brodie, Thomas Jefferson: An Intimate History (New York: Norton, 1974) 181.

*b. Book with two or more authors*

Cite all authors (up to three) in order of appearance on the title page. For a book written by more than three authors, use in full the first name listed, followed by "et al." with no comma in between:

[2] John C. Bollens and Grant B. Geyer, Yorty: Politics of a Constant Candidate (Pacific Palisades: Palisades Pub., 1973) 73.

[3] Gordon W. Allport, Philip E. Vernon, and Gardner Lindzey, Study of Values (New York: Houghton, 1951) 12.

[4] Ruth Brown et al., Agricultural Education in a Technical Society: An Annotated Bibliography of Resources (Chicago: American Library Assn., 1973) 220.

*c. Book with a corporate author*

Organizations that author books are treated like authors:

[5] American Institute of Physics, Handbook, 3rd ed. (New York: McGraw, 1972) 10.

### d. Book with an anonymous or pseudonymous author

When the author of a book is anonymous, merely list the title. Neither "anonymous" nor "anon." needs to be added:

> [6] Current Biography (New York: Wilson, 1976) 20–22.

The name of an author who writes under a pseudonym (or *nom de plume*) may be given in brackets:

> [7] George Eliot [Mary Ann Evans], Daniel Deronda (London, 1876) 58.

**NOTE:** Since the book was published before 1900, no publisher has to be named.

### e. Work in several volumes or parts

In a reference to a multivolume work in its entirety, state the number of volumes after the title:

> [8] T. Walter Wallbank and Alastair M. Taylor, Civilization Past and Present, 2 vols. (New York: Scott, 1949).

Since the reference is to the entire work, no page is cited.

If the reference is to a specific page in a specific volume, the number of volumes is still given after the title. Then the volume number must be listed again in Arabic numerals after the facts of publication and separated from the page number(s) by a colon and a space:

> [9] T. Walter Wallbank and Alastair M. Taylor, Civilization Past and Present, 2 vols. (New York: Scott, 1949) 2: 217.

For multivolume works published over a number of years, show the total number of volumes and the range of years as well as information on specific volumes used:

> [10] LeRoy Edwin Froom, The Prophetic Faith of Our Fathers. 4 vols. (Washington: Review and Herald, 1950–54) 1: 16–17.

For individual volumes of a multivolume work with separate titles, use the following form:

> [11] Paul Jacobs, Saul Landen, and Eve Pell, Colonials and So-
> journers, vol. 2 of To Serve the Devil (New York: Random, 1971)
> 37–39.

## f. Collections: anthologies, casebooks, and readers

For a work included in a casebook, anthology, essay collection, or the like—that is, a collection of different pieces by different authors—use the following form:

> [12] Eudora Welty, ''The Wide Net,'' Story: An Introduction to
> Prose Fiction, ed. Arthur Foff and Daniel Knaff (Belmont: Wads-
> worth, 1966) 166.

## g. Double reference—a quotation within a cited work

Use the following form for referring to a quotation within a cited work:

> [13] Lin Piao as quoted in Jean Daubier, A History of the
> Chinese Cultural Revolution, trans. Richard Seaver (New York:
> Random, 1974) 83.

## h. Reference work

For signed articles in well-known encyclopedias, supply name of author, title of entry, name of encyclopedia, and year of edition:

> [14] Albert George Ballert, ''Saint Lawrence River,'' Encyclo-
> paedia Britannica, 1963 ed.

The authors of articles in reference works are usually identified by initials that are decoded in a special index volume. If the article is unsigned, begin with the title entry:

> [15] ''House of David,'' Encyclopedia Americana, 1974 ed.

> [16] ''Telegony,'' Dictionary of Philosophy and Psychology,
> 1902 ed.

## i. Work in a series

> [17] Louis Auchincloss, Edith Wharton, University of Minnesota
> Pamphlets on American Writers 12 (Minneapolis: U of Minnesota P,
> 1961) 17.

## j. Edition

The word *edition* can be understood in three different ways: it can mean (1) a revised printing of a work; (2) a collection of items edited by one or several authors; (3) the edited version of one or more works by an editor or editors. The proper forms to use in each of these cases are as follows:

*(i) FOR A REVISED EDITION:*

   [18] Porter G. Perrin and Jim W. Corder, Handbook of Current English, 4th ed. (Glenview: Scott, 1975) 304-05.

*(ii) FOR AN EDITED COLLECTION:*

   [19] Charles Clerc, ''Goodbye to All That: Theme, Character and Symbol in Goodbye, Columbus,'' Seven Contemporary Short Novels, ed. Charles Clerc and Louis Leiter (Glenview: Scott, 1969) 107.

The reference here is to an editorial critique on one of the novels in the collection.

*(iii) FOR THE WORK OF AN EDITOR:*

   [20] Hardin Craig and David Bevington, eds., The Complete Works of Shakespeare, rev. ed. (Glenview: Scott, 1973) 31-38.

Because the reference is to the editorial work of Craig and Bevington, the names of these editors are listed in place of the author's. But when the paper deals with the work of the original author, rather than with the work of an editor or translator, the author's name must then be listed first:

   [21] Sylvia Plath, Letters Home, ed. Aurelia Schober Plath (New York: Harper, 1975) 153-54.

## k. Translation

   [22] Benvenuto Cellini, Autobiography of Benvenuto Cellini, trans. John Addington Symons (New York: Washington Square, 1963) 75-79.

## l. *Pamphlet*

Citations of pamphlets should conform as nearly as possible to the format used for citations of books. Give as much information about the pamphlet as is necessary to help a reader find it:

> [23] Calplans Agricultural Fund, An Investment in California Agricultural Real Estate (Oakland: Calplans Securities, n.d.) 3.

## m. *Government publication or legal reference*

Because of their complicated origins, government publications can be difficult to document. Generally, the citation of a government publication should list first the author or agency, then the title of the publication (underlined), followed by the publication facts (place, publisher, date) and the page reference. Although no standard format exists for all such publications, we have tried to supply samples for the kinds of government sources most often cited in undergraduate papers.

### (i) THE CONGRESSIONAL RECORD

A citation to the *Congressional Record* requires only title, date, and page(s):

> [24] Cong. Rec., 15 Dec. 1977: 19740.

### (ii) CONGRESSIONAL PUBLICATIONS

The authors are listed either as "U.S. Cong., Senate," "U.S. Cong., House," or "U.S. Cong., Joint":

> [25] U.S. Cong., Senate, Permanent Subcommittee on Investigations of the Committee on Government Operations, Organized Crime—Stolen Securities, 93rd Cong., 1st sess. (Washington: GPO, 1973) 1–4.

"GPO" is the accepted abbreviation for "U.S. Government Printing Office."

> [26] U.S. Cong., House, Committee on Foreign Relations, Hearings on S. 2793, Supplemental Foreign Assistance Fiscal Year 1966—Vietnam, 89th Cong., 2nd sess. (Washington: GPO, 1966) 9.

The titles of government publications, although long and cumbersome, must nevertheless be accurately cited.

*(iii) LEGAL PUBLICATIONS*

> ²⁷ Office of the Federal Register, ''The Supreme Court of the United States,'' United States Government Manual (Washington: GPO, 1976) 67.

Names of laws, acts, and the like are generally neither underlined nor placed within quotation marks: Constitution of the United States, Declaration of Independence, Bill of Rights, Humphrey-Hawkins Bill, Sherman Anti-Trust Act. Citations of legal sources usually refer to sections rather than to pages. Certain conventional abbreviations are also used in such citations:

> ²⁸ U.S. Const., art. I, sec. 2.

> ²⁹ 15 U.S. Code, sec. 78j(b) (1964).

> ³⁰ U.C.C., art. IX, pt. 2, par. 9–28.

Names of law cases are abbreviated, and the first important word of each party is spelled out: Brown v. Board of Ed. stands for Oliver Brown versus the Board of Education of Topeka, Kansas. Cases, unlike laws, are italicized in the text but not in the notes. Text: *Miranda v. Arizona.* Note: Miranda v. Arizona. The following information must be supplied in a citation of a law case: (1) the name of the first plaintiff and the first defendant; (2) the volume, name, and page (in that order) of the law report cited; (3) the name of the court that decided the case; (4) the year in which the case was decided:

> ³¹ Richardson v. J. C. Flood Co., 190 A. 2d 259 (D.C. App. 1963).

Interpreted, this footnote means that the Richardson v. J. C. Flood Co. case can be found on page 259 of volume 190 of the Second Series of the *Atlantic Reporter.* The case was settled in the District of Columbia Court of Appeals during the year 1963. For further information on the form for legal references, consult *A Uniform System of Citation*, 12th ed. (Cambridge: Harvard Law Review Association, 1976).

*n. Classical works*

In citing a classical work that is subdivided into books, parts, cantos, verses, and lines, specify the appropriate subdivisions so that a reader using a different edition of the work can easily locate the reference:

[32] Homer, The Iliad, trans. Richmond Lattimore (Chicago: U of Chicago P, 1937) 101 (3.15–20).

[33] Dante Alighieri, The Inferno, trans. John Ciardi (New York: NAL, 1954) 37 (2.75–90).

Books or parts have traditionally been indicated by large Roman numerals, cantos or verses by small Roman numerals, and lines by Arabic numerals. However, the modern trend is toward Arabic numerals for everything (see 7d-1k).

### o.  The Bible

Because the King James Bible is such a familiar document, only the appropriate book and verse need be cited. Translations other than the King James must be indicated within parentheses.

■ King James Bible

> [34] Isaiah 12:15.    or    [34] Isaiah 12.15.

■ Other translation

> [35] 2 Corinthians 2:10 (Revised Standard Version).

or

> [35] 2 Corinthians 2.10 (Revised Standard Version).

### 7g-6   Sample footnotes for periodicals

### a.  Anonymous author

> [1] ''Elegance Is Out,'' Fortune 13 Mar. 1978: 18.

Most periodical articles are written by unidentified correspondents.

### b.  Single author

> [2] Hugh Sidey, ''In Defense of the Martini,'' Time 24 Oct. 1977: 38.

### c.  More than one author

> [3] Clyde Ferguson and William R. Cotter, ''South Africa—What Is to Be Done?'' Foreign Affairs 56 (1978): 254.

The format of a citation to a multiple authored magazine article is the same as for a multiple authored book. For three authors, list the names of the authors exactly as they appear in the article. Separate the first and second name by a comma, and the second and third by a comma followed by the word "and." For more than three authors, list the name of the first author followed by "et al." with no comma in between.

*d. Journal with continuous pagination throughout the annual volume*

⁴ Anne Paolucci, ''Comedy and Paradox in Pirandello's Plays,'' <u>Modern Drama</u> 20 (1977): 322.

Since there is only one page 322 throughout volume 20 of 1977, it is unnecessary to add the month.

*e. Journal with separate pagination for each issue*

⁵ Claude T. Mangrum, ''Toward More Effective Justice,'' <u>Crime Prevention Review</u> 5 (Jan. 1978): 7.

⁶ Janet Stevenson, ''Before the Colors Fade: The Return of the Exiles,'' <u>American Heritage</u> 20.4 (1969): 24.

Since each issue of these journals is paged anew, page 7, for example, will occur in all issues of volume 5; therefore, the addition of the month is necessary. Some journals use numbers to distinguish different issues. Footnote 6, for example, refers the reader to issue 4 of volume 20. Follow the style of the individual journal.

⁷ Robert Brown, ''Physical Illness and Mental Health,'' <u>Philosophy and Public Affairs</u> 7 (Fall 1977): 18–19.

Since this journal is published quarterly and in volumes that do not coincide with the year, adding the season of publication makes the source easier to locate.

*f. Monthly magazine*

⁸ Flora Davis and Julia Orange, ''The Strange Case of the Children Who Invented Their Own Language,'' <u>Redbook</u> Mar. 1978: 113, 165.

Note the split page reference to the article, which began on one page and was continued at the back of the magazine.

## g. *Weekly magazine*

[9] Suzy Eban, ''Our Far-Flung Correspondents,'' The New Yorker 6 Mar. 1978: 70–72.

## h. *Newspaper*

[10] James Tanner, ''Disenchantment Grows in OPEC Group with Use of U.S. Dollar for Oil Pricing,'' Wall Street Journal 9 Mar. 1978: 3, cols. 3–4.

See also footnote 13 below.

Listing the columns as well as the page makes the article easier to locate; however, listing the column(s) is optional.

**NOTE:** If the first word of a newspaper's title is an article, the article is deleted. For example, above, *The Wall Street Journal* becomes *Wall Street Journal*.

[11] Daniel Southerland, ''Carter Plans Firm Stand with Begin,'' Christian Science Monitor 9 Mar. 1978, western ed.: 1, 9.

Supply the edition or section when available.

## i. *Editorial*

Signed:

[12] William Futrell, ''The Inner City Frontier,'' editorial, Sierra 63.2 (1978): 5.

Unsigned:

[13] ''Criminals in Uniform,'' editorial, Los Angeles Times 7 Apr. 1978, pt. 2: 6.

Listing the part as well as the page makes this newspaper article easier to locate.

## j. *Letter to the editor*

[14] Donna Korcyzk, letter, Time 20 Mar. 1978: 4.

## k. *Critical review*

[15] Peter Andrews, rev. of The Strange Ride of Rudyard Kipling: His Life and Works, by Angus Wilson, Saturday Review 4 Mar. 1978: 24.

### 7g-7 Sample footnotes for special items

Citation samples of other sources commonly used in research papers are given below. For citation forms on sources not covered here, consult your instructor. Bear in mind that the prime rule of documentation is to provide the information necessary for a reader to trace any cited source.

### a. Lecture

As minimum information cite the speaker's name, the title of the lecture in quotation marks, the sponsoring organization, the location, and the date. If the presentation has no title, use an appropriate label, such as lecture, speech, or address.

[1] Gene L. Schwilck, ''The Core and the Community,'' Danforth Foundation, St. Louis, 16 Mar. 1978.

[2] Jesse Jackson, address, Democratic National Convention, San Francisco, 17 July 1984.

### b. Film

Film citations should include the title of the film (underlined), the director's name, the distributor, and the year of release. Information on the producer, writer, performers, and size or length of the film may also be supplied, if necessary to your study:

[3] The Turning Point, dir. Herbert Ross, with Anne Bancroft, Shirley MacLaine, Mikhail Baryshnikov, and Leslie Brown, Twentieth Century—Fox, 1978.

### c. Radio or television program

Citations should include the title of the program (underlined), the network or local station, and the city and date of broadcast. If appropriate, the title of the episode is listed in quotation marks before the title of the program, while the title of the series, neither underlined nor in quotation marks, comes after the title of the program. The name of the writer, director, narrator, or producer may also be supplied, if significant to your paper:

[4] ''Diving for Roman Plunder,'' narr. and dir. Jacques Cousteau, The Cousteau Odyssey, KCET, Los Angeles, 14 Mar. 1978.

[5] World of Survival, narr. John Forsythe, CBS Special, Los Angeles, 29 Oct. 1972.

*d. Recording (disc or tape)*

For commercially available recordings, cite the following: composer or performer, title of recording or of work(s) on the recording, artist(s), manufacturer, catalog number, and date of issue (if not known, state "n.d."):

> [6] The Beatles, ''I Should Have Known Better,'' The Beatles Again, Apple Records, SO–385, n.d.

(This is a reference to one of several songs on a disc.) A citation of a recording of classical music may omit the title of the recording and instead list the works recorded. Musical compositions identified by form, key, and number are neither underlined nor placed within quotation marks:

> [7] Johann Sebastian Bach, Toccata and Fugue in D minor, Toccata, Adagio, and Fugue in C major, Passacaglia and Fugue in C minor; Johann Christian Bach, Sinfonia for Double Orchestra, Op. 18, No. 1, cond. Eugene Ormandy, The Philadelphia Orchestra, Columbia, MS 6180, n.d.

(When two or more composers and their works are involved, a semicolon separates each grouping.) Citations of recordings of the spoken word list the speaker first:

> [8] Swift Eagle, The Pueblo Indians, Caedmon TC 1327, n.d.

For a recording of a play, use the following form (the participating actors are listed):

> [9] Shakespeare's Othello, with Paul Robeson, Jose Ferrer, Uta Hagen, and Edith King, Columbia, SL–153, n.d.

In addition to the speaker and title, a citation to a noncommercial recording should state when the recording was made, for whom, and where. The title of the recording is not underlined:

> [10] Michael Dwyer, Readings from Mark Twain, rec. 15 Apr. 1968, Humorist Society, San Bernardino, CA.

*e. Personal letter*

Published letters are treated as titles within a book. Add the date of the letter, if available:

> [11] Oscar Wilde, ''To Mrs. Alfred Hunt,'' 25 Aug. 1880, <u>The Letters of Oscar Wilde</u>, ed. Rupert Hart—Davis (New York: Harcourt, 1962) 67—68.

For letters personally received, use the following form:

> [12] Gilbert Highet, letter to the author, 15 Mar. 1972.

*f. Interview*

Citations of interviews should specify the kind of interview, the name (and, if pertinent, the title) of the interviewed person, and the date of the interview:

> [13] Dr. Charles Witt, personal interview, 23 Mar. 1976.

> [14] Telephone interview with Edward Carpenter, librarian at Huntington Library, 2 Mar. 1978.

### 7g-8  Subsequent references to footnotes/endnotes

Subsequent citations to an already identified source are given in abbreviated form. The rule is to make subsequent citations brief but not cryptic. Ordinarily the author's last name or a key word from the title, followed by a page number, will do. Latin terms such as "op. cit." ("in the work cited"), "loc. cit." ("in the place cited"), and "ibid." ("in the same place") are no longer used.

First reference:

> [1] John W. Gardner, <u>Excellence</u> (New York: Harper, 1961) 47.

Subsequent reference:

> [2] Gardner 52.

If two or more subsequent references cite the same work, simply repeat the name of the author and supply the appropriate page numbers. Do not use "ibid."

<sup>3</sup> Gardner 83.

<sup>4</sup> Gardner 198.

If, however, your paper also contains references to Gardner's other book, *Self-Renewal*, the two books should be distinguished by title in subsequent references:

<sup>5</sup> Gardner, Excellence 61.

<sup>6</sup> Gardner, Self—Renewal 62.

If two of the cited authors share the same last name, subsequent references should supply the full name of each author:

<sup>7</sup> Henry James 10.

<sup>8</sup> William James 23—24.

For a subsequent reference to an anonymous article in a periodical, use a shortened version of the title.

First reference:

<sup>9</sup> ''The Wooing of Senator Zorinsky,'' Time 27 Mar. 1978: 12.

Subsequent reference:

<sup>10</sup> ''Zorinsky'' 13.

For subsequent references to unconventional or special sources, you may need to improvise.

# 7h

## Content notes

Content notes consist of material that is relevant to your research but that does not need to interrupt the flow of your text. Such notes may consist of an explanation, additional information, reference to other sources, information about procedures used to gain information, or acknowledgment of special assistance. The format of content notes is the same no matter which style of documentation is used in the paper. Some instructors insist that all content notes be gathered together on a page entitled "Notes," placed after the text of the paper but before the "Works Cited" page. Other instructors prefer to have them placed at the foot of the appropriate page so that the reader can look down and read them as they occur. The following rules should be observed when typing content notes:

- Indent the first line of each note 5 spaces.
- Double space content notes gathered at the end of the paper (see sample student paper, p. 222), but single space those shown at the foot of a page. In the latter case be sure to allow for enough space for the entire note. Begin the note four lines below the text. Do *not* type a solid line between the text and the note since this would indicate a note continued from the previous page when space ran out. Single space the note but double space between notes if there is more than one note.
- In your text, roll up a half space at the relevant place and strike your note number, as in the following example:

```
The centaur, being half horse and half man, symbolized both the

wild and benign aspect of nature. Thus the coexistence of nature

and culture was expressed. 12
```

The note at the foot of the page then adds the following comment without interrupting the flow of the text:

```
    12 It should be noted that the horse part is the lower and
more animalistic area whereas the human portion is the upper, in-
cluding the heart and head.
```

- Provide complete documentation to content footnote sources in "Works Cited," but do *not* provide complete documentation in the note itself. For instance, the following content footnote might appear in a biology paper:

```
    10 Harvey (1980) disagrees with this aspect of Johnson's in-
terpretation of handwriting.
```

The following full reference would then appear in "Works Cited":

```
Harvey, O. L. (1980). The measurement of handwriting considered as

    a form of expressive movement. Quarterly Review of Biology,

    55, 231-249.
```

**NOTE:** An exception is the traditional footnote or endnote style, which provides full documentation in the note as well as in "Works Cited."

Study the following sample content notes:

**7h-1   Content footnote explaining a term**

[1] The ''Rebellion of 1837'' refers to December of 1837, when William Lyon Mackenzie, a newspaper editor and former mayor of Toronto, led a rebellion intended to establish government by elected officials rather than appointees of the British Crown.

**7h-2   Content footnote expanding on an idea**

[2] This pattern of development was also reflected in their system of allocation: only a small percentage of tax money was used for agriculture, whereas great chunks were apportioned to industry.

**7h-3   Content footnote referring the reader to another source**

[3] For further information on this point, see King and Chang (124–35).

**NOTE:** The "Works Cited" list must provide full documentation for this source:

King, Gilbert W., and Hsien Wu Chang. ''Machine Translation of

Chinese,'' Scientific America 208.6 (1963): 124–35.

**7h-4   Content footnote explaining procedures**

[4] Subjects were classed according to their smoking history as never smokers, cigar and/or pipe smokers exclusively, ex-cigarette smokers (smoked cigarettes regularly in the past but not within the year prior to the time of interview), and current cigarette smokers (smoked cigarettes regularly at the time of the interview for at least one year).

### 7h-5   Content footnote acknowledging assistance

[5] The authors wish to acknowledge the assistance of the Montreal Children's Hospital in providing access to their Hewlett Packard 3000 computer.

# 7i

## Consolidation of references

If a substantial part of your paper is based on several sources that deal with the same idea, consolidating the references into a single note may save space and prevent repetition. The format for handling consolidation of references differs according to the documentation style being used.

### 7i-1   Footnote using author-work style (MLA)

[1] For this idea I am indebted to Holland (32), Folsom (136–144), and Edgar (15–17).

**NOTE:** A "Works Cited" list at the end of the paper must provide full documentation for these sources.

### 7i-2   Footnote using author-date style (APA)

[2] On this point see Hirsbrunner (1981), Florin (1981), and Frey (1981).

**NOTE:** A "Reference List" at the end of the paper must provide full documentation for these sources.

### 7i-3   Footnote using numbers style

[3] This section reflects the conclusions reached by Kuller (3), Thompson (4), Copley (7), Eisenberg (8), and Weaver (17).

**NOTE:** A "Works Cited" list at the end of the paper must provide full documentation for these sources.

## 7i-4 Footnote using traditional style

> ⁴ For this idea I am indebted to Laurence Bedwell Holland, The
> Expense of Wisdom (Princeton: Princeton UP, 1964) 32; James K.
> Folsom, ''Archimago's Well: An Interpretation of The Sacred
> Fount,'' Modern Fiction Studies 7 (1961): 136–44; and Pelham
> Edgar, Henry James: Man and Author (1927; New York: Russell, 1964)
> 15–17.

**NOTE:** Separate the individual citations with a semicolon. The "Works Cited" list must repeat the documentation for these sources.

# Eight
# Bibliography

**8a** The bibliography

**8b** Works Cited (MLA and traditional styles)

**8c** Reference List (APA style)

**8d** Works Cited (numbers system)

# 8a

## The bibliography

The last part of the research paper is a bibliography—a list in alphabetical order of the sources actually used in the paper. The purpose of this list is to allow the reader to identify and retrieve any source used. Every reference cited in the text must therefore appear in the bibliography; conversely, every work appearing in the bibliography must have been used in the text.

Differences in the format of the bibliography are minor among the various documentation styles. Under the MLA and traditional footnote/endnote styles, the bibliography is titled "Works Cited." The APA style labels it a "Reference List." This chapter concentrates on explaining the formats required in these bibliographies; it also gives examples of the format used in the numbers system.

### 8a-1  Alphabetizing bibliography entries

Arrange the entries in your "Works Cited" or "Reference List" in alphabetical order according to the surname of the first author, keeping in mind the following rules:

- Alphabetize letter by letter. Notice, however, that nothing always precedes something. For instance, Rich, Herman B. precedes Richmond, D. L.

- The prefixes *M', Mc,* and *Mac* must be alphabetized literally, not as if they were all spelled *Mac.* Disregard the apostrophe: MacKinsey precedes McCuen, and MacIntosh precedes M'Naughton. If the name of an author includes an article or preposition such as *de, la, du, von, van,* the rule is that when the prefix is part of the surname, then alphabetize according to the prefix (Von Bismarck precedes Vonnegut). If the prefix is not part of the name, treat it as part of the first and middle names (Bruy, Cornelis J. de). When in doubt, consult the biographical section of *Webster's New Collegiate Dictionary* (1981).

- Single-author entries precede multiple-author entries beginning with the same surname:

```
Hirsch, E. D.

Hirsch, E. D., and O. B. Wright.
```

Entries by the same author or authors in the same order are arranged alphabetically by the title, excluding *A* or *The*.

■ A row of three hyphens followed by a period replaces the name of the repeated author(s):

```
Kissinger, Henry Alfred. The Necessity for Choice.

---. Nuclear Weapons and Foreign Policy.
```

■ Works by authors with the same surname are alphabetized according to the first letter of the Christian name:

```
Butler, Alban

Butler, Samuel
```

■ Corporate authors—associations, government agencies, institutions— are alphabetized according to the first significant word of the name. Use the full name, not an abbreviation:

```
Brandeis University (not B.U.)

Southern Asian Institute (not SAI)
```

■ A parent body precedes a subdivision:

```
Glendale Community College, Fine Arts Department
```

■ When a work is anonymous, its title moves into the author's place and is alphabetized according to the first significant word in the title.

■ Alphabetize legal references by the first significant word:

```
Marbury v. Madison

National Labor Relations Act
```

### 8a-2 Sample bibliography page

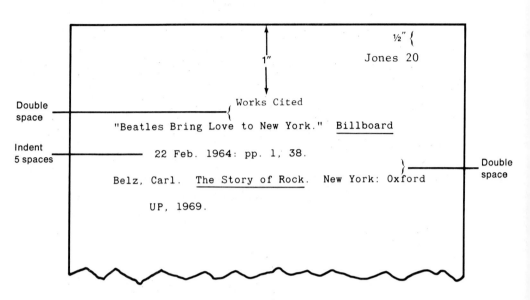

**Figure 8-1**   Sample bibliography page (MLA style)

(See also the sample student papers, pp. 200, 225, and 230.) For details on the form for various bibliographic entries, see 8b and 8c. For rules on alphabetizing the entries, see 8a-1.

# 8b

## Works Cited (MLA and traditional styles)

If you were careful in copying your sources accurately on the bibliography cards, preparing the bibliography will be mainly a matter of transcribing information. But you must still observe the following:

- The bibliography must occupy a separate page.
- Center the title, "Works Cited," one inch from the top of the page. Leave two spaces between the title and the first entry (see 8a-2, Fig. 8-1).
- List all entries in alphabetical order by first author (see 8a-1). Anonymous works are listed alphabetically according to the first word of the title, disregarding *a, an,* or *the* if such a word begins the title.
- Place the author's last name first. In case of two or more authors, all authors' names except the first retain their normal order.

■ Second and subsequent entries by the same author(s) are listed with a line of three hyphens followed by a period:

```
Lewis, Sinclair.  Babbitt.  New York: Harcourt, 1922.

---. Main Street.  New York: Harcourt, 1920.
```

■ Indent the second line of each entry five spaces.
■ Double space throughout the "Works Cited" list.

Study "Works Cited" at the end of two sample student papers (pp. 223 and 236). Note, however, that for a paper for a course in a field other than the modern languages or literature, your instructor may want you to use a documentation style that differs in some ways from the examples shown in this chapter and in the sample student papers in Chapter 11. To avoid extra work, consult your instructor before the final draft of your paper is typed.

### 8b-1   General order for bibliographic references to books in "Works Cited"

Bibliographic references to books list items in the following order:

*a. Author*

The name of the author comes first, alphabetized by surname. If more than one author is involved, invert the name of only the first and follow it by a comma:

```
Brown, Jim, and John Smith
```

For more than three authors, use the name of the first followed by "et al.":

```
Foreman, Charles, et al.
```

In some cases the name of an editor, translator, or compiler will be cited before the name of an author, especially if the actual editing, translating, or compiling is the subject of discussion (see 8b-1c).

*b. Title*

Cite the title in its entirety, including any subtitle, exactly as it appears on the title page. A period follows the title unless the title ends in some other mark, such as a question mark or an exclamation mark. Book titles are underlined; titles of chapters are set off in quotation marks. The initial word and all subsequent words (except for articles and short prepositions) in the title are capitalized. Ignore any unusual typographical style, such as all capital letters, or any peculiar arrangement of capitals and lower-case letters, unless the author is specifically known to insist on such a typography. Separate a subtitle from the title by a colon:

D. H. Lawrence: His Life and Work.

### c. Name of editor, compiler, or translator

The name(s) of the editor(s), compiler(s), or translator(s) is given in normal order, preceded by "Ed(s).," "Comp(s).," or Trans.":

Homer.  The Iliad.  Trans. Richard Lattimore.

However, if the editor, translator, or compiler was listed in your textual citation, then his name should appear first, followed by "ed.," "trans.," or "comp." and a period:

TEXTUAL CITATION:

Gordon's Literature in Critical Perspective offers some . . .

"WORKS CITED" ENTRY:

Gordon, Walter K., ed.  Literature in Critical Perspective.  New

York: Appleton, 1968.

If you are drawing attention to the translator, use the following format:

TEXTUAL CITATION:

The colloquial English of certain passages is due to Ciardi's

translation.

"WORKS CITED" ENTRY:

Ciardi, John, trans.  The Inferno.  By Dante Alighieri.  New York:

NAL, 1961.

### d. Edition (if other than first)

The edition being used is cited if it is other than the first. Cite the edition in Arabic numerals (3rd ed.) without further punctuation. Always use the latest edition of a work, unless you have some specific reason of scholarship for using another.

```
Holman, C. Hugh.  A Handbook to Literature.  3rd ed.  Indianapo-

    lis: Odyssey, 1972.
```

### e. Series name and number

Give the name of the series, without quotation marks and not under-lined, followed by a comma, followed by the number of the work in the series in Arabic numerals, followed by a period:

```
Unger, Leonard.  T. S. Eliot.  University of Minnesota Pamphlets

    on American Writers 8.  Minneapolis: U of Minnesota P, 1961.
```

### f. Volume numbers

An entry referring to all the volumes of a multivolume work cites the number of volumes *before* the publication facts:

```
Durant, Will, and Ariel Durant.  The Story of Civilization.  10

    vols.  New York: Simon, 1968.
```

An entry for only selected volumes still cites the total number of volumes after the title. The volumes actually used are listed *after* the publication facts:

```
Durant, Will, and Ariel Durant.  The Story of Civilization.  10

    vols.  New York: Simon, 1968.  Vols. 2 and 3.
```

For multivolume works published over a number of years, show the total number of volumes, the range of years, and specific volumes if not all of them were actually used.

```
Froom, LeRoy Edwin.  The Prophetic Faith of Our Fathers.  4 vols.

    Washington: Review and Herald, 1950–54.  Vol. 1.
```

## g. *Publication facts*

Indicate the place, publisher, and date of publication for the work you are citing. A colon follows the place, a comma the publisher, and a period the date unless a page is cited.

You may use a shortened form of the publisher's name as long as it is clear: Doubleday (for Doubleday & Company), McGraw (for McGraw-Hill), Little (for Little, Brown), Scott (for Scott, Foresman), Putnam's (for G. Putnam's Sons), Scarecrow (for Scarecrow Press), Simon (for Simon and Schuster), Wiley (for John Wiley & Sons), Holt (for Holt Rinehart & Winston), Penguin (for Penguin Books), Harper (for Harper & Row). For example:

```
Robb, David M., and Jessie J. Garrison.  Art in the Western

     World.  4th ed.  New York: Harper, 1963.
```

But list university presses in full (except for abbreviating "University" and "Press") so as not to confuse the press with the university itself: Oxford UP, Harvard UP, Johns Hopkins UP.

```
Gohdes, Clarence.  Bibliographical Guides to the Study of Litera-

     ture of the U.S.A.  3rd ed.  Durham: Duke UP, 1970.
```

If more than one place of publication appears, give the city shown first on the book's title page.

If more than one copyright date is given, use the latest unless your study is specifically concerned with an earlier edition. (A new printing does not constitute a new edition. For instance, if the title page bears a 1975 copyright date but a 1978 fourth printing, use 1975.) If no place, publisher, date, or page numbering is provided, insert "n.p.," "n.p.," "n.d.," or "n. pag.," respectively. "N. pag." will explain to the reader why no page numbers were provided in the text citation. If the source contains neither author, title, or publication information, supply in brackets whatever information you have been able to obtain:

```
Photographs of Historic Castles.  [St. Albans, England]: N.p.,

     n.d.  N. pag.

Farquart, Genevieve.  They Gave Us Flowers.  N.p.: n.p., 1886.

Dickens, Charles.  Master Humphrey's Clock.  London: Bradbury and

     Evans, n.d.
```

134

### *h. Page numbers*

Bibliographical entries for books rarely include a page number; however, entries for shorter pieces appearing within a longer work—articles, poems, short stories, and so on, in a collection—should include a page reference. In such a case, supply page numbers for the entire piece, not just for the specific page or pages cited in the text:

> Daiches, David.  ''Criticism and Sociology.''  Literature in Crit-
>
>     ical Perspective.  Ed. Walter K. Gordon.  New York: Apple-
>
>     ton, 1968.  7–18.

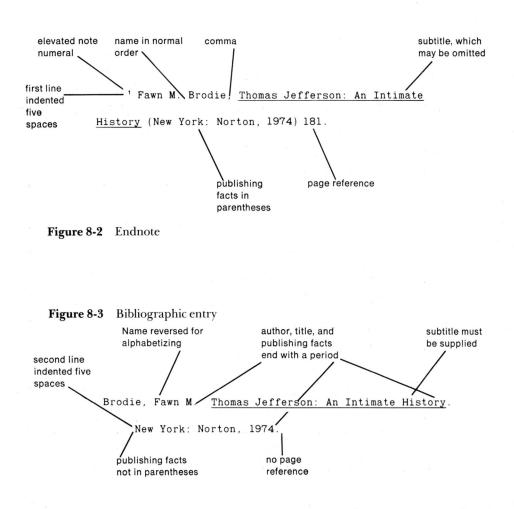

**Figure 8-2**　Endnote

**Figure 8-3**　Bibliographic entry

### i. Differences between endnotes and bibliography entries

Endnotes and bibliography entries contain the same information, with the exception of page numbers, but differ considerably in form, as the following examples make clear:

### 8b-2　Sample bibliographic references to books

### a. Book with a single author

> Brodie, Fawn M.　Thomas Jefferson: An Intimate History.　New York:
>
> 　　Norton, 1974.

### b. Book with two or more authors

> Bollens, John C., and Grand B. Geyer.　Yorty: Politics of a Con-
>
> 　　stant Candidate.　Pacific Palisades: Palisades Pub., 1973.

> Allport, Gordon W., Philip E. Vernon, and Gardner Lindzey.　Study
>
> 　　of Values.　New York: Houghton, 1951.

> Brown, Ruth, et al.　Agricultural Education in a Technical
>
> 　　Society: An Annotated Bibliography of Resources.　Chicago:
>
> 　　American Library Assn., 1973.

### c. Book with a corporate author

> American Institute of Physics.　Handbook.　3rd ed.　New York:
>
> 　　McGraw, 1972.

**NOTE:** If the publisher is the same as the author, repeat the information, as shown here:

> Defense Language Institute.　Academic Policy Standards.　Mon-
>
> 　　terey: Defense Language Institute, 1982.

*d. Book with an anonymous or pseudonymous author*

No author listed:

> Current Biography.  New York: Wilson, 1976.

If you are able to research the author's name, supply it in brackets:

> [Stauffer, Adlai].  Cloudburst.  Knoxville: Review and Courier
>
>     Publishing Assn., 1950.

The name of an author who writes under a pseudonym (or *nom de plume*) may also be given in brackets:

> Eliot, George [Mary Ann Evans].  Daniel Deronda.  London, 1876.

*e. Work in several volumes or parts*

When citing the whole multivolume work:

> Wallbank, T. Walter, and Alastair M. Taylor.  Civilization Past
>
>     and Present.  2 vols.  New York: Scott, 1949.

When citing a specific volume of a multivolume work:

> Wallbank, T. Walter, and Alastair M. Taylor.  Civilization Past
>
>     and Present.  2 vols.  New York: Scott, 1949.  Vol. 2.

When citing a multivolume work whose volumes were published over a range of years:

> Froom, LeRoy Edwin.  The Prophetic Faith of Our Fathers.  4 vols.
>
>     Washington: Review and Herald, 1950-54.

When citing a multivolume work with separate titles:

> Jacobs, Paul, Saul Landen, and Eve Pell. <u>Colonials and Sojourn-</u>
>
> <u>ers</u>. Vol. 2 of <u>To Serve the Devil</u>. 4 vols. New York:
>
> Random, 1971.

*f.  Work within a collection of pieces, all by the same author*

> Johnson, Edgar. ''The Keel of the New Lugger.'' <u>The Great</u>
>
> <u>Unknown</u>. Vol. 2 of <u>Sir Walter Scott</u>. 3 vols. New York:
>
> Macmillan, 1970. 763–76.

> Selzer, Richard. ''Liver.'' <u>Mortal Lessons</u>. New York: Simon,
>
> 1976. 62–77.

**NOTE:** The MLA no longer recommends the use of the word "In" preceding the title of the collection or anthology.

*g.  Chapter or titled section in a book*

> Goodrich, Norma Lorre. ''Gilgamesh the Wrestler.'' <u>Myths of the</u>
>
> <u>Hero</u>. New York: Orion, 1960.

**NOTE:** List the chapter or titled section in a book only when it demands special attention.

*h.  Collections: anthologies, casebooks, and readers*

> Welty, Eudora. ''The Wide Net.'' <u>Story: An Introduction to Prose</u>
>
> <u>Fiction</u>. Ed. Arthur Foff and Daniel Knapp. Belmont: Wads-
>
> worth, 1966. 159–77.

Cowley, Malcolm. ''Sociological Habit Patterns in Linguistic
Transmogrification.'' The Reporter 20 Sept. 1956: 257–61.
Rpt. in Readings for Writers. Ed. Jo Ray McCuen and Anthony
C. Winkler. 2nd ed. New York: Harcourt, 1977. 489–93.

### i. Double reference—a quotation within a cited work

Daubier, Jean. A History of the Chinese Cultural Revolution.
Trans. Richard Seaver. New York: Random, 1974.

Only the secondary source is listed in "Works Cited." See 7d-1k, p. 95,
for an example of how the source of such an entry would appear in text.

### j. Reference works

#### (i) ENCYCLOPEDIAS

Ballert, Albert George. ''Saint Lawrence River.'' Encyclopaedia
Britannica. 1963 ed.

''House of David.'' Encyclopedia Americana. 1974 ed.

Berger, Morroe, and Dorothy Willner. ''Near Eastern Society.''
International Encyclopedia of the Social Sciences. 1968 ed.

#### (ii) DICTIONARIES AND ANNUALS

''Barsabbas, Joseph.'' Who's Who in the New Testament (1971).

''Telegony.'' Dictionary of Philosophy and Psychology (1902).

## *k. Work in a series*

### *(i) A NUMBERED SERIES*

Auchincloss, Louis. <u>Edith Wharton</u>. University of Minnesota Pam—
phlets on American Writers 12. Minneapolis: U of Minnesota
P, 1961.

### *(ii) AN UNNUMBERED SERIES*

Miller, Sally. <u>The Radical Immigrant</u>. The Immigrant Heritage of
America Series. New York: Twayne, 1974.

## *l. Reprint*

Babson, John J. <u>History of the Town of Gloucester, Cape Ann, In—
cluding the Town of Rockport</u>. 1860. New York: Peter Smith,
1972.

Thackeray, William Makepeace. <u>Vanity Fair</u>. London, 1847–48.
New York: Harper, 1968.

## *m. Edition*

Perrin, Porter G., and Jim W. Corder. <u>Handbook of Current En—
glish</u>. 4th ed. Glenview: Scott, 1975.

Rowland, Beryl, ed. <u>Companion to Chaucer: Studies</u>. New York: Ox—
ford UP, 1979.

## *n. Edited work*

If the work of the editor(s) rather than that of the author(s) is being
discussed, place the name of the editor(s) first, followed by a comma,
followed by "ed." or "eds.":

Craig, Hardin, and David Bevington, eds. The Complete Works of

    Shakespeare. Rev. ed. Glenview: Scott, 1973.

If you are stressing the text of the author(s), place the author(s) first:

Clerc, Charles. ''Goodbye to All That: Theme, Character and Sym-

    bol in Goodbye, Columbus.'' Seven Contemporary Short

    Novels. Ed. Charles Clerc and Louis Leiter. Glenview:

    Scott, 1969. 106–33.

### o. Book published in a foreign country

Vialleton, Louis. L'Origine des êtres vivants. Paris: Plon, 1929.

Ransford, Oliver. Livingston's Lake: The Drama of Nyasa. London:

    Camelot, 1966.

### p. Introduction, preface, foreword, or afterword

Davidson, Marshall B. Introduction. The Age of Napoleon. By

    J. Christopher Herold. New York: American Heritage, 1963.

### q. Translation

Symons, John Addington, trans. Autobiography of Benvenuto Cel-

    lini. By Benvenuto Cellini. New York: Washington Square,

    1963.

### r. Book of illustrations

Janson, H. W. History of Art: A Survey of the Major Visual Arts

    from the Dawn of History to the Present. With 928 illustra-

    tions, including 80 color plates. Englewood Cliffs: Pren-

    tice and Abrams, 1962.

## s. *Foreign title*

Use lower case lettering for foreign titles except for the first word and proper names:

```
Vischer, Lukas.  Basilius der Grosse.  Basel: Reinhard, 1953.
```

Supply a translation of the title or city if it seems necessary. Place the English version in brackets immediately following the original, not underlined:

```
Bruckberger, R. L.  Dieu et la politique [God and Politics].

    Paris: Plon, 1971.
```

### 8b-3   General order for bibliographic references to periodicals in "Works Cited"

Bibliographic references to periodicals list items in the following order:

## a. *Author*

List the author's surname first, followed by a comma, followed by the first name or initials. If there is more than one author, follow the same format as for books (See 8b-2b).

## b. *Title of the article*

List the title in quotation marks, followed by a period inside the quotation marks unless the title itself ends in a question mark or exclamation mark.

## c. *Publication information*

List the name of the periodical, underlined, with any introductory article omitted, followed by a space and a volume number, followed by a space and the year of publication within parentheses, followed by a colon, a space, and page numbers for the entire article, not just for the specific pages cited:

```
Smith, Irwin.  ''Ariel and the Masque in The Tempest.''

    Shakespeare Quarterly 21 (1970): 213-22.
```

Journals paginated anew in each issue require the issue number following the volume number, separated by a period:

> Beets, Nicholas.  ''Historical Actuality and Bodily Experience.''
>
>  Humanitas 2.1 (1966): 15–28.

Some journals may use a month or season designation in place of an issue number:

> 2 (Spring 1966): 15–28.

Magazines that are published weekly or monthly require only the date, without a volume number:

> Isaacson, Walter.  ''After Williamsburg.''  Time 13 June 1983:
>
>  12–14.

Newspapers require the section or part number, followed by the page:

> Rumberger, L.  ''Our Work, Not Education, Needs Restructuring.''
>
>  Los Angeles Times, 24 May 1984, pt. 2: 5.

## d. Pages

If the pages of the article are scattered throughout the issue (for example, pages 30, 36, 51, and 52), the following formats can be used:

| | |
|---|---|
| 30, 36, 51, 52 | (This is the most precise method and should be used when only three or four pages are involved.) |
| 30 and passim | (page 30 and here and there throughout the work) |
| 30ff. | (page thirty and the following pages) |
| 30 + | (beginning on page thirty) |

### 8b-4  Sample bibliographic references to periodicals

## a. Anonymous author

> ''Elegance Is Out.''  Fortune 13 Mar. 1978: 18.

*b. Single author*

```
Sidey, Hugh.  ''In Defense of the Martini.''  Time 24 Oct.
     1977: 38.
```

*c. More than one author*

```
Ferguson, Clyde, and William R. Cotter.  ''South Africa——What Is
     to Be Done.''  Foreign Affairs 56 (1978): 254-74.
```

If three authors have written the article, place a comma after the second author, followed by "and" and the name of the third author. If more than three authors have collaborated, list the first author's name, inverted, followed by a comma and "et al."

```
Enright, Frank, et al.
```

*d. Journal with continuous pagination throughout the annual volume*

```
Paolucci, Anne.  ''Comedy and Paradox in Pirandello's Plays.''
     Modern Drama 20 (1977): 321-39.
```

*e. Journal with separate pagination for each issue*

When each issue of a journal is paged separately, include the issue number (or month or season); page numbers alone will not locate the article since every issue begins with page 1.

```
Cappe, Walter H.  ''Humanities at Large.''  The Center Magazine
     11.2 (1978): 2-6.
```

```
Mangrum, Claude T.  ''Toward More Effective Justice.''  Crime Pre-
     vention Review 5 (Jan. 1978): 1-9.
```

```
Brown, Robert.  ''Physical Illness and Mental Health.''  Philoso-
     phy and Public Affairs 7 (Fall 1977): 18-19.
```

## f. Monthly magazine

Miller, Mark Crispin. ''The New Wave in Rock.'' <u>Horizon</u> Mar.

1978: 76–77.

Davis, Flora, and Julia Orange. ''The Strange Case of the Chil-

dren Who Invented Their Own Language.'' <u>Redbook</u> Mar. 1978:

113, 165–67.

## g. Weekly magazine

Eban, Suzy. ''Our Far–Flung Correspondents.'' <u>The New Yorker</u>

6 Mar. 1978: 70–81.

''Philadelphia's Way of Stopping the Shoplifter.'' <u>Business Week</u>

6 Mar. 1972: 57–59.

## h. Newspaper

Tanner, James. ''Disenchantment Grows in OPEC Group with Use of

U.S. Dollar for Oil Pricing.'' <u>Wall Street Journal</u> 9 Mar.

1978: 3.

List the edition and section of the newspaper if specified, as in the examples below:

Southerland, Daniel. ''Carter Plans Firm Stand with Begin.''

<u>Christian Science Monitor</u> 9 Mar. 1978, western ed.: 1, 9.

Malino, Emily. ''A Matter of Placement.'' <u>Washington Post</u>

5 Mar. 1978: L 1.

### i. Editorial

If the section or part is labeled with a numeral rather than a letter, then the abbreviation "sec." or "pt." must appear before the section number. For example, see the unsigned editorial below.

Signed:

Futrell, William. ''The Inner City Frontier.'' Editorial.

Sierra 63.2 (1978): 5.

Unsigned:

''Criminals in Uniform.'' Editorial. Los Angeles Times 7 Apr.

1978, pt. 2: 6.

### j. Letter to the editor

Korczyk, Donna. Letter. Time 20 Mar. 1978: 4.

### k. Critical review

Andrews, Peter. Rev. of The Strange Ride of Rudyard Kipling: His

Life and Works, by Angus Wilson. Saturday Review 4 Mar.

1978: 24–25.

Daniels, Robert V. Rev. of Stalinism: Essays in Historical Inter-

pretations, ed. Robert C. Tucker. The Russian Review

37 (1978): 102–03.

''Soyer Sees Soyer.'' Rev. of Diary of an Artist, by Ralph Soyer.

American Artist Mar. 1978: 18–19.

Rev. of Charmed Life, by Diane Wynne Jones. Booklist 74 (Feb.

1978): 1009.

*l. Published interview*

Leonel J. Castillo, Commissioner, Immigration and Naturalization
Service. Interview. Why the Tide of Illegal Aliens Keeps
Rising. U.S. News and World Report 20 Feb. 1978: 33–35.

*m. Published address or lecture*

Trudeau, Pierre E. ''Reflections on Peace and Security.''
Address to Conference on Strategies for Peace and Security in
the Nuclear Age, Guelph, Ont., Can., 27 Oct. 1983. Rpt. in
Vital Speeches of the Day 1 Dec. 1983: 98–102.

## 8b-5 Nonprint materials

Since nonprint materials come in many forms and with varied information, the rule to follow when dealing with them is to provide as much information as is available for retrieval.

*a. Address or lecture*

O'Banion, Terry. ''The Continuing Quest for Quality.'' Address
to California Assn. of Community Colleges. Sacramento,
30 Aug. 1983.

Schwilck, Gene L. ''The Core and the Community.'' Lecture to Danforth Foundation. St. Louis, 16 Mar. 1978.

For how to handle the reprint of an address or lecture appearing in a periodical, see 8b-4m, above.

*b. Art work*

Angelico, Beato. Madonna dei Linaioli. Museo de San Marco,
Firenze.

For how to handle an illustration in a book of art, see 8b-6a (p. 152).

### c. Computer source

A computer citation will refer to either: (1) a computer program, that is, information received directly from a data bank, or (2) a written publication retrieved by a computer base.

#### (i) COMPUTER PROGRAM

First, list the primary creator of the database as the author. Second, give the title of the program underlined, followed by a period. Third, write "Computer software," followed by a period. Fourth, supply the name of the publisher of the program, followed by a comma and the date the program was issued. Finally, give any additional information necessary for identification and retrieval. This additional information should include, for example, the kind of computer for which the software was created, the number of kilobytes (units of memory), the operating system, and the program's form (cartridge, disk, or cassette):

```
Moshell, J. M., and C. E. Hughes.  Imagination: Picture Program-

     ming.  Computer software.  Wiley, 1983.  Apple II/IIe,

     64KB, disk.
```

#### (ii) SOURCE RETRIEVED FROM A DATABASE

Entire articles and books are now being stored in huge data bases, with companies like ERIC, CompuServe, The Source, Mead Data Control (Nexis, Lexis), and many others providing the access service. These sources should be listed as if they appeared in print, except that you will also list the agency providing the access service. If possible, list any code or file associated with the source:

```
Cohen, Wilbur J.  ''Lifelong Learning and Public Policy.''  Com-

     munity Services Catalyst 9 (Fall 1979): 4-5.  ERIC.  1982.

     Dialog 1, EJ218031.
```

### d. Film

Film citations should include the director's name, the title of the film (underlined), the name of the leading actor(s), the distributor, and the date of showing. Information on the producer, writer, and size or length of the film may also be supplied, if necessary to your study:

```
Ross, Herbert, dir.  The Turning Point.  With Anne Bancroft, Shir-
     ley MacLaine, Mikhail Baryshnikov, and Leslie Brown.  Twen-
     tieth Century-Fox, 1978.
```

### e. Interview

Citations of interviews should specify the kind of interview, the name (and, if pertinent, the title) of the interviewed person, and the date of the interview:

```
Witt, Dr. Charles.  Personal interview.  18 Feb. 1984.
```

```
Carpenter, Edward, librarian at the Huntington Library,
     Pasadena.  Telephone interview.  2 Mar. 1978.
```

### f. Musical composition

Whenever possible, cite the title of the composition in your text, as for instance:

```
Bach's Well-Tempered Clavier is a principal keyboard . . .
```

However, when opus numbers would clutter the text, cite the composition more fully in "Works Cited":

```
Grieg, Edward.  Minuet in E minor, op. 7, no. 3.
```

### g. Radio or television program

Citations should include the title of the program (underlined), the network or local station, and the city and date of broadcast. If appropriate, the title of the episode is listed in quotation marks before the title of the program, while the title of the series, neither underlined nor in quotation marks, comes after the title of the program. The name of the writer, director, narrator, or producer may also be supplied, if significant to your paper:

```
Diving for Roman Plunder.  Narr. and dir. Jacques Cousteau.  KCET,
     Los Angeles.  14 Mar. 1978.
```

''Chapter 2.''  Writ. Wolf Mankowitz.  <u>Dickens of London</u>.  Dir.

and prod. Marc Miller.  Masterpiece Theater.  Introd. Alis-

tair Cooke.  PBS.  28 Aug. 1977.

<u>Dead Wrong</u>.  CBS Special.  24 Jan. 1984.

## h. *Recording (disc or tape)*

For commercially available recordings, cite the following: composer, conductor, or performer, title of recording or of work(s) on the recording, artist(s), manufacturer, catalog number, and year of issue (if not known, state "n.d."):

Beatles, The.  ''I Should Have Known Better.''  <u>The Beatles</u>

<u>Again</u>.  Apple Records, SO–385, n.d.

Bach, Johann Sebastian.  Toccata and Fugue in D minor, Toccata,

Adagio, and Fugue in C major, Passacaglia and Fugue in C

minor; Johann Christian Bach.  Sinfonia for Double Orches-

tra, op. 18, no. 1.  Cond. Eugene Ormandy.  Philadelphia

Orchestra.  Columbia, MS 6180, n.d.

Eagle, Swift.  <u>The Pueblo Indians</u>.  Caedmon, TC 1327, n.d.

<u>Shakespeare's Othello</u>.  With Paul Robeson, Jose Ferrer, Uta Hagen,

and Edith King.  Columbia, SL–153, n.d.

Dwyer, Michael.  Readings from Mark Twain.  Rec. 15 Apr. 1968.

Humorist Society.  San Bernardino.

D. K. Wilgus.  Irish Folksongs.  Rec. 9 Mar. 1969.  U of Califor-

nia, Los Angeles, Archives of Folklore.  T7–69–22.  7½ ips.

Burr, Charles.  Jacket notes.  <u>Grofe: Grand Canyon Suite</u>.  Col-

umbia, MS 6003, n.d.

## *i. Theatrical performance*

Theatrical performances are cited in the form used for films, with added information on the theater, city, and date of performance. For opera, concert, or dance productions you may also wish to cite the conductor (cond.) or choreographer (chor.). If the author, composer, director, or choreographer should be emphasized, supply that information first.

```
Getting Out.  Dir. Gordon Davidson.  By Marsha Norman.  With

     Susan Clark.  Mark Taper Forum, Los Angeles.  2 Apr. 1978.
```

This citation emphasizes the author:

```
Durang, Christopher.  Beyond Therapy.  Dir. John Madden.  With

     John Lithgow and Dianne Wiest.  Brooks Atkinson Theater, New

     York.  26 May 1982.
```

This citation emphasizes the conductor:

```
Conlon, James, cond.  La Bohème.  With Renata Scotto.  Metropoli-

     tan Opera.  Metropolitan Opera House, New York.  30 Oct.

     1977.
```

This citation emphasizes the conductor and the guest performer:

```
Commissiona, Sergiu, cond.  Baltimore Symphony Orchestra.  With

     Albert Markov, violin.  Brooklyn College, New York.  8 Nov.

     1978.
```

This citation emphasizes the choreographer:

```
Baryshnikov, Mikhail, chor.  Swan Lake.  American Ballet Theatre,

     New York.  24 May 1982.
```

### 8b-6  Special items

No standard form exists for every special item you might use in your paper. Again, as a general rule, arrange the information in your bibliographic entry in the following order: author, title, place of publication, publisher, date, and any other information helpful for retrieval. Some examples of common citations follow.

151

## a. *Art work, published*

```
Healy, G. P. A.  The Meeting on the River Queen.  White House,

    Washington, DC.  Illus. in Lincoln: A Picture Story of His

    Life.  By Stefan Lorent.  Rev. and enl. ed.  New York: Harp-

    er, 1957.
```

For how to handle an art work you have actually experienced, see p. 000.

## b. *The Bible*

When referring to the Bible, cite the book and chapter within your text (the verse, too, may be cited when necessary):

```
The city of Babylon (Rev. 18.2) is used to symbolize . . .
```

or

```
In Rev. 18:2 the city of Babylon is used as a symbol of . . .
```

In "Works Cited" the following citation will suffice if you are using the King James version:

```
The Bible
```

If you are using another version, specify which:

```
The Bible, Revised Standard Version
```

## c. *Classical works in general*

When referring to classical works that are subdivided into books, parts, cantos, verses, and lines, specify the appropriate subdivisions within your text:

```
Ovid makes claims to immortality in the last lines of The Meta-

    morphoses (3. Epilogue).
```

```
Francesca's speech (5.118-35) is poignant because . . .
```

In "Works Cited" these references will appear as follows:

```
Ovid.  The Metamorphoses.  Trans. and introd. Horace Gregory.  New

    York: NAL, 1958.


Alighieri, Dante.  The Inferno.  Trans. John Ciardi.  New York:

    NAL, 1954.
```

### d. Dissertation

Unpublished: The title is placed within quotation marks and the work identified by "Diss.":

```
Cotton, Joyce Raymonde.  ''Evan Harrington: An Analysis of George

    Meredith's Revisions.''  Diss.  U of Southern California,

    1968.
```

Published: The dissertation is treated as a book, except that the entry includes the label "Diss." and states where and when the dissertation was originally written:

```
Cortey, Teresa.  Le Rêve dans les contes de Charles Nodier.  Diss.

    U of California, Berkeley, 1975.  Washington, DC: UP of Amer-

    ica, 1977.
```

### e. Footnote or endnote citation

A bibliographical reference to a footnote or endnote in a source takes the following form:

```
Faber, M. D.  The Design Within: Psychoanalytic Approaches to

    Shakespeare.  New York: Science House, 1970.
```

In other words, no mention is made of the note. However, mention of the note should be made within the text itself:

```
In Schlegel's translation, the meaning is changed (Faber

    205, n. 9).
```

The reference is to page 205, note number 9, of Faber's book.

### f. Manuscript or typescript

A bibliographical reference to a manuscript or typescript from a library collection should provide the following information: the author, the title or a description of the material, the material's form (ms. for manuscript, ts. for typescript), and any identifying number. If possible, give the name and location of the library or institution where the material is kept.

```
Chaucer, Geoffrey.  Ellesmere ms., E126C9.  Huntington Library,

    Pasadena.

The Wanderer.  Ms.  Exeter Cathedral, Exeter.

Cotton Vitellius.  Ms., A. SV.  British Museum, London.
```

### g. Pamphlet or brochure

Citations of pamphlets or brochures should conform as nearly as possible to the format used for citations of books. Give as much information about the pamphlet as is necessary to help a reader find it. Underline the title:

```
Calplans Agricultural Fund.  An Investment in California Agri-

    cultural Real Estate.  Oakland: Calplans Securities, n.d.
```

### h. Personal letter

Published:

```
Wilde, Oscar.  ''To Mrs. Alfred Hunt.''  25 Aug. 1880.  The Letters

    of Oscar Wilde.  Ed. Rupert Hart-Davis.  New York: Harcourt,

    1962.  67-68.
```

Unpublished:

```
Thomas, Dylan.  Letter to Trevor Hughes.  12 Jan. 1934.  Dylan

    Thomas Papers.  Lockwood Memorial Library.  Buffalo.
```

Personally received:

Highet, Gilbert. Letter to the author. 15 Mar. 1972.

### i. Plays

#### (i) CLASSICAL PLAY

In your text, provide parenthetical references to act, scene, and line(s) of the play:

Cleopatra's jealousy pierces through her words:

What says the married woman? You may go;

Would she had never given you leave to come:

Let her not say 'tis I that keep you here;

I have no power upon you; hers you are.

(1.3.20–23)

The reference is to Act 1, Scene 3, lines 20–23. In "Works Cited" the play will be cited as follows:

Shakespeare, William. Antony and Cleopatra. The Complete Works

of Shakespeare. Ed. Hardin Craig and David Bevington. Rev.

ed. Glenview: Scott, 1973. 1073–1108.

**NOTE:** When the play is part of a collection, list the pages that cover the entire play.

#### (ii) MODERN PLAY

Many modern plays are published as individual books:

Miller, Arthur. The Crucible. New York: Bantam, 1952.

However, if published as part of a collection, the play is cited as follows:

Chekhov, Anton, The Cherry Orchard. 1903. The Art of Drama. Ed.

R. F. Dietrich, William E. Carpenter, and Kevin Kerrane. 2nd

ed. New York: Holt, 1976. 134–56.

**NOTE:** The page reference is to the entire play.

## *j. Poems*

### *(i) CLASSICAL POEM*

> Lucretius [Titus Lucretius Carus]. Of the Nature of Things.
>
> Trans. William Ellery Leonard. Backgrounds of the Modern
>
> World. Vol. 1 of The World in Literature. Ed. Robert Warnock
>
> and George K. Anderson. New York: Scott, 1950. 343–53.

Or, if published in one book:

> Dante [Dante Alighieri]. The Inferno. Trans. John Ciardi. New
>
> York: NAL, 1954.

### *(ii) MODERN POEM*

Modern poems are usually part of a larger collection:

> Moore, Marianne. ''Poetry.'' Fine Frenzy. Ed. Robert Baylor and
>
> Brenda Stokes. New York: McGraw, 1972. 372–73.

**NOTE:** Cite pages covered by the poem.

Or, if the poem is long enough to be published as a book, use the following format:

> Byron, George Gordon, Lord. Don Juan. Ed. Leslie A. Marchand.
>
> Boston: Houghton, 1958.

## *k. Public documents*

Because of their complicated origins, public documents often seem difficult to cite. As a general rule, follow this order: Government. Body. Subsidiary bodies. Title of document (underlined). Identifying code. Place, publisher, and date of publication. Most publications by the federal government are printed by the Government Printing Office, which is abbreviated as "GPO":

### *(i) THE CONGRESSIONAL RECORD*

A citation to the Congressional Record requires only title, date, and page(s):

> Cong. Rec. 15 Dec. 1977, 19740.

*(ii) CONGRESSIONAL PUBLICATIONS*

United States.  Cong.  Senate.  Permanent Subcommittee on Inves-
tigations of the Committee on Government Operations.  Organized Crime——Stolen Securities.  93rd. Cong., 1st sess.
Washington: GPO, 1973.

United States.  Cong.  House.  Committee on Foreign Relations.
Hearings on S. 2793, Supplemental Foreign Assistance Fiscal
Year 1966——Vietnam.  89th Cong., 2nd sess. Washington:
GPO, 1966.

United States.  Cong.  Joint Economic Committee on Medical Poli-
cies and Costs.  Hearings.  93rd Cong., 1st sess.  Washington:
GPO, 1973.

*(iii) EXECUTIVE BRANCH PUBLICATIONS*

United States.  Office of the President.  Environmental Trends.
Washington: GPO, 1981.

United States  Dept. of Defense.  Annual Report to the Congress
by the Secretary of Defense.  Washington: GPO, 1984.

United States.  Dept. of Education.  National Commission on Ex-
cellence in Education.  A Nation at Risk: The Imperative for
Educational Reform.  Washington: GPO, 1983.

United States.  Dept. of Commerce.  Bureau of the Census.  Statistical Abstracts of the United States.  Washington:
GPO, 1963.

*(iv) LEGAL DOCUMENTS*

When citing a well-known statute or law, a simple format will suffice:

```
US Const.  Art. 1, sec. 2.

15 US Code.  Sec. 78j(b).  1964.

US CC  Art. 9, pt. 2, par. 9–28.

Federal Trade Commission Act.  1914.
```

When citing a little-known statute, law, or other legal agreement, provide all the information needed for retrieval:

```
''Agreement Between the Government of the United States of America

     and the Khmer Republic for Sales of Agricultural Commod-

     ities.''  Treaties and Other International Agreements.  Vol.

     26, pt. 1.  TIAS No. 8008.  Washington: GPO, 1976.
```

Names of court cases are abbreviated and the first important word of each party is spelled out: "Brown v. Board of Ed." stands for "Oliver Brown versus the Board of Education of Topeka, Kansas." Cases, unlike laws, are italicized in the text but not in "Works Cited." Text: *Miranda v. Arizona.* "Works Cited": Miranda v. Arizona. The following information must be supplied in the order listed: (1) name of the first plaintiff and the first defendant, (2) volume, name, and page (in that order) of the law report cited, (3) the place and name of the court that decided the case, (4) the year in which the case was decided:

```
  Richardson v. J. C. Flood Co.  190 A. 2d 259.  D.C. App.  1963.
```

Interpreted, the above means that the Richardson v. J. C. Flood Co. case can be found on page 259 of volume 190 of the Second Series of the *Atlantic Reporter*. The case was settled in the District of Columbia Court of Appeals during the year 1963.

For further information on the proper form for legal citations, consult *A Uniform System of Citation*, 12th ed. Cambridge: Harvard Law Rev. Assn., 1976.

## l. Quotation in a book or article used as a source

### (i) QUOTATION IN A BOOK

> MacDonald, Dwight.  As quoted in John R. Trimble.  Writing With
>
>      Style: Conversations on the Art of Writing.  Englewood
>
>      Cliffs: Prentice, 1975.

### (ii) QUOTATION IN AN ARTICLE

> Grabar, Oleg.  As quoted in Katharine Slater Gittes. ''The Canter-
>
>      bury Tales and the Arabic Frame Tradition.'' PMLA 98 (1983):
>
>      237-51.

## m. Report

Titles of reports in the form of pamphlets or books require underlining. When a report is included within the pages of a larger work, the title is set off in quotation marks. The work must be identified as a report:

> The Churches Survey Their Task.  Report of the Conference on
>
>      Church, Community, and State.  London: Allen & Unwin, 1937.

> Luxenberg, Stan. ''New Life for New York Law.''  Report on New
>
>      York Law School. Change 10 (Nov. 1978): 16-18.

## n. Table, graph, chart, or other illustration

If the table, graph, or chart has no title, identify it as a table, graph, or chart:

> National Geographic Cartographic Division.  Graph on imports
>
>      drive into U.S. market. National Geographic 164 (July
>
>      1983): 13.

**NOTE:** The descriptive label is not underlined or set off in quotation marks.

```
Benson, Charles S.  ''Number of Full-Time Equivalent Employees, by

     Industry, 1929-1959.''  Table.  The Economics of Public Edu-

     cation.  Boston: Houghton, 1961.  208.
```

This time the table has a title, so it is set off in quotation marks.

NOTE: The in-text citation should refer to "Table A.1."

*o. Thesis*

See 8b-6d, "Dissertation."

# 8c

## Reference List (APA style)

Your reference list will contain the following elements listed in the following order: author, year of publication, title, place of publication, and publisher.

The job of preparing your reference list will be easy if you took care to copy your sources accurately onto your bibliography cards. The following rules must be observed:

- Start your reference list on a new page, regardless of how much blank space is left on the last page of your paper.
- Center the title "Reference List" on the page, two inches from the top. Leave four spaces between the title and the first entry (see 8a-2).
- List all entries in alphabetical order (see 8a-1). Anonymous works are listed alphabetically according to the first word of the title, omitting *a*, *an*, or *the* if one of these words begins the title.
- List the names of all initial authors in inverted order.
- Second and subsequent entries by the same author(s) are listed with a line of three hyphens followed by a period: - - -.
- Indent the second line of each entry five spaces.
- Double space throughout the reference list.

Study the reference list at the end of the sample student paper.

### 8c-1   General order for bibliographic references to books in "Reference List" (APA)

Your reference list for books will contain the following elements, listed in the order indicated below:

- Name(s) of author(s) in inverted order, with only the initials of first and middle names.

160

- Year of publication in parentheses, followed by a period.
- Title of the book, underlined, with only the initial letter of the first word capitalized, followed by a period. (In two-part titles separated by a colon, the initial letter of the first word in the second title is also capitalized.)
- Place of publication, followed by a colon.
- Name of publisher, followed by a period. (The name of the publisher is listed in as brief a form as is intelligible. Terms like *Publisher, Co.,* and *Inc.* are omitted. However, names of university presses and associations are spelled out.)

**8c-2   Sample bibliographic references to books**

*a.  Book with a single author*

Jones, E. (1931).  <u>On the nightmare</u>.  London: Hogarth.

A period is placed after the author's name (the period following an initial serves this purpose), after the final parenthesis of the publication date, after the title, and at the end of the entry. A colon separates the city from the publisher.

*b.  Book with two or more authors*

Terman, L. M., & Merrill, M. A.  (1937).  <u>Measuring intelligence</u>.

Cambridge, Mass.: The Riverside Press.

With two names, use an ampersand before the second name and do not use a comma to separate the names. With three or more names, use an ampersand before the last name and use commas to separate the names (Bowen, B. M., Poole, K. J., & Gorky, A.).

*c.  Edited book*

Friedman, R. J., & Katz, M. M. (Eds.).  (1974).  <u>The psychology of</u>

<u>depression: Contemporary theory and research</u>.  New York:

Wiley.

Give the surname and initials of all editors, regardless of how many there are. Show "Ed." or "Eds." in parentheses after the name(s), followed by a period. When referring to an article or chapter in an edited book, use the following form:

```
Waxer, P.  (1979).  Therapist training in nonverbal behavior.  In

    A. Wolfgang (Ed.), Nonverbal behavior: Applications and

    cultural implications (pp. 221–240).  New York: Academic

    Press.
```

When an editor's name is not in the author position, *do not* invert his name. Place "Ed." or "Eds." in parentheses after the name(s), followed by a comma. The title of the article or chapter is *not* placed within quotation marks and only the initial letter in the title is capitalized. Give inclusive page numbers for the article or chapter, in parentheses after the title of the book. Precede the page number(s) by "p." or "pp."

### d. Translated book

The translator of a book (name *not* inverted) is placed within parentheses after the book title and is followed by "Trans." with a period after the end parentheses:

```
Rank, O.  (1932).  Psychology and the soul (William Turner,

    Trans.).  Philadelphia: Univ. of Pennsylvania Press.
```

### e. Book in a foreign language

```
Saint–Exupéry, A. de.  (1939).  Terre des hommes.  Paris: Gal-

    limard.
```

**NOTE:** Titles of foreign books are in lower case except for the initial letter.

### f. Revised edition of a book

Give the edition ("rev. ed.," "4th ed.," etc.) in parentheses following the title. Place a period after the final parenthesis:

```
Boulding, K.  (1955).  Economic analysis (3rd ed.).  New York:

    Harper.
```

### g. Book with a corporate author

When a book is authored by an organization rather than a person, the name of the organization appears in the author's place:

    Committee of Public Finance. (1959). Public finance. New York:

        Pitman.

When the corporate author is also the publisher, place the word *Author* in place of the publisher:

    Commission on Intergovernmental Relations. (1955). Report to

        the President. Washington, DC: Author.

### h. Multivolume book

When citing a multivolume source, place the number(s) of the volume(s) actually used in parentheses immediately following the title. Use Arabic numerals for the volume number(s).

    Ruesch, J. (1980). Communication and psychiatry. In H. I. Kap-

        lan, A. M. Freedman, & B. J. Sadock (Eds.), Comprehensive

        textbook of psychiatry (Vol. 1). Baltimore: Williams &

        Wilkins.

If a multivolume book was published over a number of years, list the years in parentheses following the author's name:

    Brady, V. S. (1978–82).

### i. Unpublished manuscript

Treat an unpublished manuscript the way you would a book except that instead of the place of publication and publishers, you will write "Unpublished manuscript":

    Hardison, R. (1983). On the shoulders of giants. Unpublished

        manuscript.

**NOTE:** For a publication of limited circulation, supply in parentheses, immediately after the title, an address where the publication can be obtained.

### 8c-3   General order for periodicals in "Reference List"

Entries for periodicals in your reference list will contain the following elements, in the order indicated:

- Name(s) of author(s) in inverted order with only the initials of first and middle names.
- Year of publication in parentheses, followed by a period. (For magazines issued on a specific day or month, give the year followed by the month or by the month and day.)
- Title of article not enclosed in quotation marks and with only the initial letter of the first word capitalized, followed by a period.
- Name of the journal or magazine, underlined, with the first word and all other words except articles and prepositions capitalized, followed by a comma.
- Volume number, underlined, followed by a comma. (Do not give volume numbers of periodicals issued on a specific date.)
- Page references, followed by a period.

### 8c-4   Sample bibliographic references to periodicals

*a. Journal article, one author*

> Harvey, O. L. (1980). The measurement of handwriting considered
>
> as a form of expressive movement. Quarterly Review of Biol-
>
> ogy, 55, 231–249.

*b. Journal article, up to six authors*

> Rodney, J., Hollender, B., & Campbell, Perry. (1983). Hypnotiz-
>
> ability and phobic behavior. Journal of Abnormal Psychol-
>
> ogy, 92, 386–389.

Use an ampersand preceded by a comma in front of the last author. Name each author. If the article has more than six authors, use this shortened form for in-text parenthetical references:

> (Frey et al. 1981).

*c. Journal article, paginated anew in each issue*

> Rosenthal, G. A. (1983). A seed-eating beetle's adaptations to
>
> poisonous seed. <u>Scientific American,</u> <u>249</u>(6), 56–67.

If the journal begins each issue with page 1, supply the volume number, underlined, followed immediately by the issue number in parentheses, a comma, and then the page number(s) and a period.

*d. Magazine article, issued monthly*

> Canby, T. Y. (1983, September). Satellites that serve us.
>
> <u>National Geographic,</u> pp. 281–300.

In parentheses after the author, place the year followed by a comma and the month. Place a period after the closing parenthesis. Use "p." or "pp." in front of page number(s).

*e. Magazine article, issued on a specific day*

> Andersen, K. (1983, September 5). Private violence. <u>Time</u>, pp.
>
> 18–19.

In parentheses after the author, place the year followed by a comma and the month and date. Place a period after the closing parenthesis. Use "p." or "pp." in front of page number(s).

*f. Newspaper article*

> Goodman, E. (1983, December 23). Bouvia case crosses the
>
> ''rights'' line. <u>Los Angeles Times</u>, Part 2, p. 5.

Place the exact date in parentheses following the author and indicate the section and page(s) following the newspaper title. Use Arabic numerals throughout the entry. Use "p." or "pp." for page(s). If the newspaper article has no author, begin with the title or headline of the article. Alphabetize works with no author by the first significant word in the title:

> ''Sad plight of anorexics.'' (Full title is ''The sad plight of
>
> anorexics.'')

## g. *Editorial*

Guion, R. M.   (1983).   Comments from the new editor [Editorial].

Journal of Applied Psychology, 68, 547.

When citing an editorial, place the word "Editorial," followed by a period, after the title of the editorial. If the editorial has no title, "Editorial" immediately follows the date. Otherwise treat the entry like any other magazine or journal article.

## h. *Letter to the editor*

Jones, L.   (1983, November).   Bite the bullet [Letter to the edi-

tor].   Psychology Today, p. 5.

**NOTE:** When the month of the magazine is given in parentheses after the author, use "p." or "pp." for page(s). Place "Letter to the editor" in brackets immediately following the title.

## i. *Review*

Boorstein, J. K.   (1983, November/December).   On welfare [Review

of Dilemmas of welfare policy: Why work strategies haven't

worked].   Society, pp. 120–122.

Place "Review of," followed by the title of the work being reviewed, in brackets immediately following the title of the review.

### 8c-5 Sample bibliographic references to nonprint materials

Since nonprint materials come in many forms and with varied information, the rule to follow when dealing with them is to provide as much necessary information as is available.

## a. *Computer sources*

List the primary creator of the database as the author, followed by the date (in parentheses) when the program was produced. Then give the title of the program, and immediately following the title, identify the source [in brackets] as a computer program. Supply the location and

166

name of the publisher of the program. Finally, enclose in parentheses any additional information necessary for identification and retrieval. This additional information should include the kind of computer for which the software was created. Computer citations will refer to material of two kinds: (1) Computer programs—that is, information received directly from data banks—and (2) written publications retrieved by a computer base. Examples of both kinds of citations follow:

*(i) COMPUTER PROGRAM*

Poole, L., & Barchers, M. (1977). <u>Future value of an investment</u>

[Computer program]. Berkeley, CA: Adam Osborne & Associ-

ates. (Basic for a Wang 2200).

Fernandes, F. D. (1972). <u>Theoretical prediction of interference</u>

<u>loading on aircraft stores</u>. [Computer program]. Pomona, CA:

General Dynamics, Electro Dynamics Division. (1650 card im-

ages, Fortran IV, for CDC-6000. Available through the Uni-

versity of Georgia, Athens, Georgia).

**NOTE:** To cite a manual for a computer program, give the same information as you would for a computer program, but in brackets after the title identify the source as a computer manual:

<u>Move-it: Inter-computer communication system</u>. (1982). [Computer

manual]. Canoga Park, CA: Wolfe Software Systems.

*(ii) SOURCE RETRIEVED FROM A DATA BANK*

Ulmer, C. (1981). Competence based instruction. <u>Community Col-</u>

<u>lege Review</u>, <u>8</u>(4), 51-56. Los Angeles: ERIC, Dialog File 1,

EJ27541.

Sources retrieved from a data bank are cited the way you would the original source. Follow the original source citation with a semicolon and

167

"rpt." followed by the city and company providing the computer source service. Add a code, file, or record number when applicable.

### b. Film

```
Cotton, D. H. (Producer), & Correll, J. B. (Director). (1980).

    The Management of hypertension in pregnancies [Film]. Hous-

    ton: University of Texas.
```

When citing a film, name the producer (title in parentheses), followed by the director (title in parentheses), followed by the date of production (in parentheses). Always specify the medium in brackets so that the material cannot be confused with a book or some other source.

### c. Recording (cassette, record, tape)

```
Bronowski, J. (Speaker). (1983). The mind (Cassette Recording BB

    4418.01). Los Angeles: Pacifica Tape Library, 5316 Venice

    Blvd., Los Angeles, CA 90019.
```

When citing a recording, name the primary contributor (Speaker, Narrator, Panel Chair, Forum Director, etc.), followed by the date of production. If the recording has a number, list it in parentheses after specifying the kind of recording. Finally, list the place of publication and the publisher, supplying an exact address if one is available.

### 8c-6  Sample bibliographic references to special items

Sources come in such varied forms that a sample cannot be supplied for every possibility. When listing a source for which there is no exact model, provide enough information to make it possible for your reader to trace the source. In general, follow this order: (1) person or organization responsible for the work, (2) year the work was published, produced, or released, (3) title of the work, (4) identifying code, if applicable, (5) place of origin, (6) publisher. Study the following samples.

### a. Government documents

#### (i) CONGRESS

```
U.S. Cong. House. (1977). U.S. assistance programs in Vietnam.

    92d Cong., 2d sess. Washington, DC: U.S. Government Printing

    Office.
```

U.S. Cong. Senate. (1970). Separation of powers and the indepen-

dent agencies: Cases and selected readings. 91st Cong., 1st

sess. Washington, DC: U.S. Government Printing Office.

U.S. Cong. Joint Committee on Printing. (1983). Congressional

directory. 98th Cong., 1st sess. Washington, DC: U.S. Gov-

ernment Printing Office.

*(ii) EXECUTIVE BRANCH*

Johnson, L. B. (1968). Economic report of the President.

Washington DC: U.S. Government Printing Office.

Executive Office of the President. (1981). Environmental

trends. Washington, DC: U.S. Government Printing Office.

## b. *Legal references*

The only kinds of legal references a student paper is likely to cite are references to court cases or references to statutes. Since legal references can be complex, consult *A Uniform System of Citation*, 12th Edition (Cambridge: Harvard Law Review Association, 1976), if your paper relies heavily on legal references. For common kinds of citations, follow these sample entries:

*(i) COURT CASE*

In general, use the following order when citing court decisions: (1) plaintiff v. defendant, (2) volume, name, and page of law report cited, (3) in parentheses, the name of the court that decided the case.

Clark v. Sumner. 559 S.W.2d. 914 (Tex. civ. app. 1977).

Explanation: The case can be found in the second series, volume 559, beginning on page 914, of the *South Western Reporter*. The case was decided by the Texas Civil Court of Appeals in 1977.

*(ii) STATUTE*

When citing commonly known statutes or laws, a simple format will suffice:

U.S. Const. Art. III, sec. 2.

15 U.S. Code, sec. 78j. (1964).

Sherman Antitrust Act. (1890).

## For lesser-known statutes, supply additional information:

90 U.S. Statutes at Large. 505 (1976).

Nuclear Waste Policy Act, Part I, sec. 112 (a).

Energy Conservation and Production Act, Title I, Part A, sec. 101,
42 U.S.C. 6901, 1976.

### (iii) TREATY

''Technical Cooperation Agreement Between the Government of Royal
Kingdom of Saudi Arabia and the Government of the United
States of America.'' <u>Treaties and Other International Agree-
ments</u>. Vol. 26, Part 1, TAIS No. 8072. Washington, D.C.:
U.S. Government Printing Office, 1976.

### 8c-7  Report

Organization for Economic Cooperation and Development. (1983).
<u>Assessing the impacts of technology on society</u>. (Report).
Washington, D.C.: U.S. Government Printing Office.

## Place "Report" in parentheses after the title. If a code has been assigned to the report, add it also:

(Report No. CSOS-R-292).

170

If the publisher is the same as the author, place "Author" where you would normally give the name of the publisher:

California Postsecondary Education Commission. (1982). Promises

    to keep: Remedial education in California's public colleges

    and universities. (Report). Sacramento, CA: Author.

# 8d
## Works cited: numbers system

Your "Works Cited" list should be arranged in alphabetical order and numbered consecutively. Of course, the numbers will not appear in consecutive order in your text. (Some authorities prefer that you forego an alphabetical arrangement in favor of consecutive numbering according to the order in which the sources appear in the text for the first time.) Study the sample below excerpted from an alphabetical/consecutive number listing. In listing works, follow the APA "Reference List" format as explained in 8c.

Works Cited

1.  Albert, N., & Beck, A. T. (1975). Incidence of depression in

    early adolescence: A preliminary study. Journal of

    Youth and Adolescence, 4, 301-306.

2.  American Heart Association. (1978). Guidelines for a weight

    control component in a smoking cessation program [Pam-

    phlet]. Dallas: Author.

3.  Hankin, J. R., & Locke, B. Z. (1982). The persistence of de-

    pressive symptomatology among prepaid group practice en-

    rolees: An exploratory study. American Journal of Pub-

    lic Health, 72, 1000-1007.

4. Kovacs, M., & Beck, A. T. (1977). An empirical—clinical approach toward a definition of childhood depression. In J. G. Schulterbrandt & A. Raskin (Eds.), Depression in childhood. New York: Raven, 1–25.

5. Nunnaly, J. C. (1967). Psychometric theory. New York: McGraw—Hill.

6. Wahrheit, G. J., Holzer, C. E., & Schwab, J. J. (1973). An analysis of social class and racial differences in de—pressive symptomatology: A community study. Journal of Health and Social Behavior, 14, 291–299.

NOTE: Each of the sources cited by number in the text will correspond to one of the numbered sources listed above.

# Nine
## Finished Form of the Paper

**9a** Finished form of the paper

**9b** Outline

**9c** Title page

**9d** Text

**9e** Tables, charts, graphs, and other illustrative materials

**9f**  **Content notes and endnotes**

**9g**  **Bibliography**

# 9a
## Finished form of the paper

In its finished form the paper consists of the following parts:

> Outline (if required)
> Title page
> Text of the paper
> *N*<sup>c</sup> Content notes (if required)
> *Endnotes or footnotes (if required)
> Works Cited (or Reference List)

The paper should be neatly typed on one side only of each page with a fresh black ribbon. Papers typed in script characters are frequently more difficult to read and therefore unacceptable. Use heavy (20 pound) 8½″ × 11″ white bond paper. Erasable bond smudges too easily for a teacher to pencil in corrections; therefore it should not be used. If you must use erasable bond, have the paper photocopied on plain (uncoated) paper and submit the photocopy. Do not staple the pages or submit the paper inside a folder. Simply clip the pages together with a paper clip and submit the paper as a loose-leaf manuscript. Give the paper a ruthless proofreading before submitting it to the teacher for evaluation.

# 9b
## Outline

The outline that precedes the text of the paper should look uncluttered and balanced. Use small Roman numerals to paginate all pages of the outline. These are not included in the total count of the paper. Place your name, the instructor's name, the name of the course for which the paper was written, and the date in the upper left-hand corner of the paper, just as you are required to do on the title page (See Fig. 9-1).

# 9c
## Title page

A separate title page is not required. Instead, the first page should contain the full title of the paper, your name, the instructor's name, the course for which the paper was written, the date, and the opening text of your paper. The following facsimile of a typical opening page includes marginal measurements and line spacing. (See also the first page of the sample paper on page 203.)

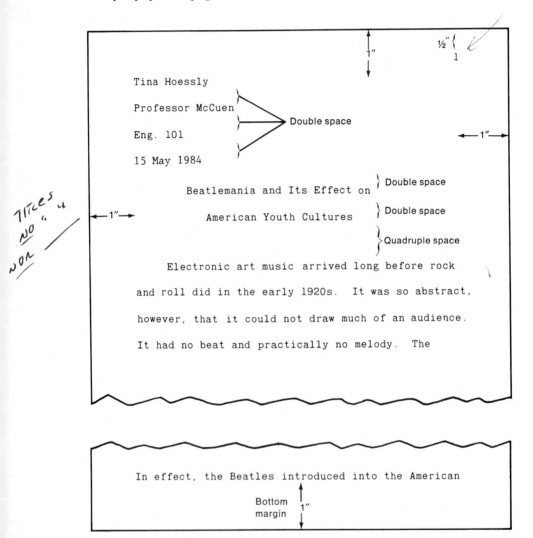

*Titles no " "  nor*

```
                                                    1"      ½" {
                                                     |         1
                                                     ↓
    Tina Hoessly
                        )
    Professor McCuen    )
                        )———> Double space                    ←—1"—→
    Eng. 101            )
                        )
    15 May 1984         )

              Beatlemania and Its Effect on  } Double space
    ←1"→
              American Youth Cultures         } Double space

                                             } Quadruple space

       Electronic art music arrived long before rock

    and roll did in the early 1920s.  It was so abstract,

    however, that it could not draw much of an audience.

    It had no beat and practically no melody.  The
```

```
    In effect, the Beatles introduced into the American
                        Bottom   ↑
                        margin   | 1"
                                 ↓
```

**Figure 9-1**   Sample student title page

This first page, and all subsequent pages, must contain one-inch margins on all sides. All pages, including the first, are numbered. From page 2 on, type your last name before the page number in case a page is misplaced. Except for titles of published works appearing within it, the title of the paper is neither underlined nor entirely placed in capitals. If the title takes up two or more lines, position the extra lines so as to form a double-spaced inverted pyramid, with each line centered on the page:

```
Study of Values: A Scale of Measuring

the Dominant Interests

in Personality
```

Do not use a period at the end of the title.

# 9d

**Text**

- Normal paragraphing must be used throughout the paper. If your paper contains subdivisions (only lengthy papers should), use subtitles either centered on the page or aligned with the left margin. Underline but do not capitalize subtitles. Separate subtitles from the last line of the previous section by quadruple spacing.
- Double-space the text, including quotations. Footnotes are double-spaced between notes but single-spaced within. (See p. 107).
- Number pages, including the first, consecutively in the upper right-hand corner of the paper. Numbers are not followed by hyphens, parentheses, periods, or other characters. "Notes" and "Works Cited" begin on new pages but are numbered as part of the general sequence (see sample student papers, pp. 222, 223).
- Note numerals are placed one half space above the line within the text of the paper. Each superscript numeral should be placed as near as possible to the end of the cited material to which it refers (see 7g-4).
- Unless otherwise indicated by your teacher, a footnote must appear on the bottom of the same page on which its numeral occurs. The first line of each footnote is indented five spaces; second and subsequent lines are aligned with the left margin. For both footnotes and endnotes use elevated numerals (a half space above the line) and follow the numerals with one space. (See pp. 106, 107.)
- For parenthetical citations, see 7d and 7e.
- If possible, use pica type, which is easier to read than elite. Script type and other artistic typefaces are often difficult to read and therefore unacceptable. If in doubt, consult your teacher.
- Avoid multiple corrections. If a correction is unavoidable, type it, or write it in legibly with black ink, *above* the line involved. Do not use the margins. If corrections are extensive, retype the page.

# 9e

## Tables, charts, graphs, and other illustrative materials

Papers in many fields frequently require tables, graphs, charts, maps, drawings, and other illustrations. For example, a paper on the decline of basic skills among high school students may include a graph that plots this decline over the past five years. An economics paper may require charts that explain certain economic changes. An anthropology paper may include drawings of primitive artifacts. A history paper may illustrate some historic battle with a map. A biology paper may include drawings of enlarged cells. The possibilities are nearly endless. The general rule, however, is for all illustrative materials to appear as close as possible to the part of the text that they illustrate.

### 9e-1   Tables

Tables are usually labeled, numbered with Arabic numerals, and captioned. Both labels and captions are capitalized as you would a title (do not use all capital letters). The source of the table and accompanying notes should be placed flush left at the bottom of the table. If no source is listed, a reader will assume that the table is your original work. Indicate notes to tables with lower-case letters, or with asterisks and crosses if you need additional indicators, to avoid confusion with endnotes, footnotes, or other textual notes.

### 9e-2   Other illustrative materials

Other illustrative materials should be labeled "Fig." or "Figure" and numbered with Arabic numerals: Fig. 3. Each figure should be captioned and capitalized with a title:

    Fig. 12.  Chart Tracing the Development of the Alphabet

Again, the source of the illustration and any notes should be placed flush left immediately below the illustration. If no source is cited, a reader will assume that the illustration is your original work. Indicate notes to illustrations with lower-case letters, asterisks, and crosses, so as to avoid confusion with other footnote or endnote numbers in the text. A few sample illustrations follow.

Table 2

Significance of Differences Between Mean Grade Point Averages
of Male Achievers and Underachievers from Grade One Through Eleven

| Grade | Mean grade point average | | F | P | t | P |
|-------|-----------|-----------------|---|---|---|---|
|       | Achievers | Under-achievers |   |   |   |   |
| 1  | 2.81 | 2.56 | 1.97 | n.s.† | 1.44  | n.s. |
| 2  | 2.94 | 2.64 | 1.94 | n.s.  | 1.77  | n.s. |
| 3  | 3.03 | 2.58 | 1.49 | n.s.  | 2.83  | .01* |
| 4  | 3.19 | 2.72 | 1.03 | n.s.  | 2.96  | .01* |
| 5  | 3.28 | 2.75 | 1.02 | n.s.  | 3.71  | .01* |
| 6  | 3.33 | 2.67 | 1.33 | n.s.  | 4.46  | .01* |
| 7  | 3.25 | 2.56 | 1.02 | n.s.  | 5.80  | .01* |
| 8  | 3.36 | 2.50 | 1.59 | n.s.  | 6.23  | .01* |
| 9  | 3.25 | 2.14 | 1.32 | n.s.  | 10.57 | .01* |
| 10 | 3.13 | 1.87 | 1.30 | n.s.  | 10.24 | .01* |
| 11 | 2.81 | 1.85 | 4.05 | .02** | 5.46  | .01* |

\* Yields significance beyond the .01 level.

\*\* Yields significance beyond the .02 level but below the .01 level.

† No significance.

**Figure 9-2**   Sample table

# 9f

## Content notes and endnotes

If you are using the parenthetical style of documentation, content notes, numbered consecutively, would appear at the end of the paper under the heading "Notes." If you are using endnotes, they appear on a separate page at the end of the paper, preceded by the heading "Notes." Any content notes appear either at the bottom of the appropriate page or on a separate page along with the endnotes. (See 7h, pp. 121–124.)

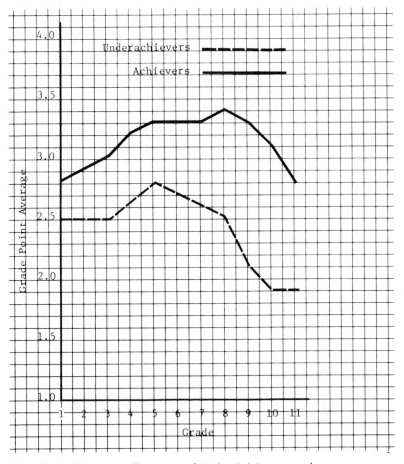

Fig. 1. Achievement Pattern of Male Achievers and
Underachievers from Grades One Through Eleven

**Figure 9-3**   Sample line graph

Fig. 2. African Doll (Akua'ba)
Source: American Museum of
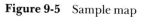
Natural History

**Figure 9-4** Sample illustration

**Figure 9-5** Sample map

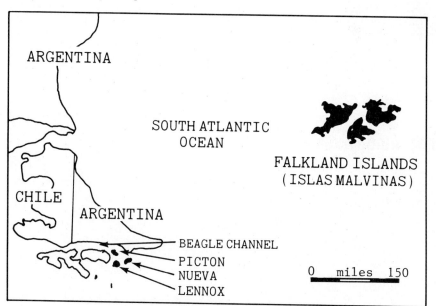

ARGENTINA

SOUTH ATLANTIC
OCEAN

FALKLAND ISLANDS
( ISLAS MALVINAS )

CHILE

ARGENTINA

BEAGLE CHANNEL
PICTON
NUEVA
LENNOX

0   miles   150

Fig. 3. Islands Involved in the Beagle Channel Dispute
Source: U.S. Government Printing Office, 1984

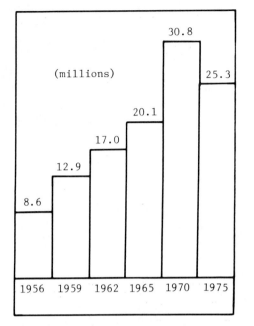

Fig. 4. Number of individuals owning
    shares in public corporations

Source:   New York Stock Exchange

**Figure 9-6**   Sample bar graph

# 9g
## Bibliography

The bibliography appears on a separate page at the end of your paper, marked by the centered heading "Works Cited" or "Reference List." (For sample "Works Cited" pages, see Fig. 8-1, p. 130, and student paper, p. 223; for sample "Reference List," see student paper, p. 229.)

# Ten
# Mechanics

**10a** Using numbers in the paper

**10b** Titles

**10c** Italics

**10d** Names of persons

**10e** Hyphenating words

**10f** Handling foreign-language words

**10g** Abbreviations

# 10a

## Using numbers in the paper

### 10a-1   Numerals

The rule of thumb on the use of numerals is this: use a numeral only if the number cannot be spelled out in two words or less. The MLA prefers that writers spell out numbers from one to nine; use numerals for all numbers 10 and above. For the Roman numeral "one," use a Capital "I"; for the Arabic numeral "one," use either the number "1" on your typewriter keyboard, or the lower case letter "l." Dates and page numbers are usually *not* spelled out: "November 19" or "19 November," and "page 36," are preferred to "the nineteenth of November" and "the thirty-sixth page."

*Wrong*   25,500 voters hailed the passage of the bill.

*Right*   The bill was hailed by 25,500 voters.

### 10a-2   Percentages and amounts of money

Figures of percentages or amounts of money are governed by the rule for numerals. Figures or amounts that can be written out in two words or less may be spelled out; otherwise, they must be expressed as numerals.

| *May be spelled out:* | thirteenth percent | thirteen Deutsche Mark |
|---|---|---|
| | eighty-three percent | fifty British pounds |
| | ten francs | thirty-six dollars |
| *Should be expressed as numerals:* | 133% | 185 DM |
| | 83.5% | £ 550 |
| | 103 fr | $366 |

### 10a-3   Dates

Consistency is the prime rule governing the treatment of dates in the paper. Write either "19 November 1929" or "November 19, 1929," but not a mixture of both. Write either "June 1931" or "June, 1931," but not both. (Note: if a comma is placed between the month and the year, a comma must also follow the year, unless some other kind of punctuation mark is necessary.) The MLA prefers that writers do not use a comma between the month and year. Centuries are expressed in lower-case letters:

```
in the thirteenth century
```

A hyphen must be added when the century is used as an adjective:

```
twelfth-century literature
```

```
seventeenth- and eighteenth-century philosophy
```

Decades can either be written out:

```
during the thirties
```

or expressed in numerals:

```
during the 1930s
```

```
during the '30s
```

The term "B.C." (meaning before Christ's birth) follows the year; "A.D." (meaning after Christ's birth) precedes the year. The MLA recommends omitting the periods in these abbreviations:

```
in 55 BC
```

```
in AD 1066
```

When using both a Western and a non-Western date, place one or the other in parentheses:

```
1912 (Year One of the Republic)
```

Both "in 1929–30" and "from 1929 to 1930" are correct, as is "from 1929–30 to 1939–40." However, do not write "from 1951–72"; confusion may result from the absence of the preposition "to" after 1951. Rather, write "1951 to 1972."

### 10a-4 Numbers connected consecutively

When connecting two numbers, give the second number in full for all numbers from one through ninety-nine. For numbers from one hundred on, give only the last two figures of the second number, if it is within the same hundred or thousand:

```
4–5
```

```
15–18
```

```
        106-07

        486-523

        896-1025

      1,860-1,930

      1,860-75

      1,608-774

    13,456-67

    13,456-14,007
```

The above examples follow the style of the *MLA Handbook*. However, APA and other styles tend to show all digits of the second number, in all cases.

### 10a-5  Roman numerals

The following require capital Roman numerals:

Major divisions of an outline (see 5b-1).

People in a series, such as monarchs, who share a common name:

```
Henry VIII, King of England
```

The following no longer require capital Roman numerals: volumes, books, and parts of major works; acts of plays.

Use lower-case Roman numerals for pages from prefaces, forewords, or introductions to books:

The following no longer require lower-case Roman numerals: chapters of books, scenes of plays, cantos of poems, chapters of books from the Bible.

# 10b

### Titles

The rules that follow apply to titles used in your text. For how to handle titles in notes or bibliography, consult the section on the style you are using in Chapters 7 and 8. The APA, for example, has a special way of handling titles.

### 10b-1 Italicized titles

Certain titles must be italicized and therefore underlined in typewritten work. Underlined titles include the following:

Published books
> <u>A Farewell to Arms</u>

Plays
> <u>The Devil's Disciple</u>

Long poems
> <u>Enoch Arden</u>

Pamphlets
> <u>The Biology of Cancer: A Guide to Twelve College Lectures</u>

Newspapers
> <u>Los Angeles Times</u>, *but* Stoneham <u>Gazette</u>

(Underline only those words that appear on the masthead of the paper.)

Magazines and journals
> <u>U.S. News and World Report</u>; <u>Shakespeare Quarterly</u>

Classical works
> <u>Plutarch's Parallel Lives</u>

Films
> <u>Gone with the Wind</u>

Television and radio programs
> <u>Sixty Minutes</u> (CBS); <u>The Music of Your Life</u> (KNXT)

Ballets
> <u>The Sleeping Beauty</u>

Operas
> <u>Carmen</u>

Instrumental music listed by name
> Brahms's <u>Rinaldo</u>

NOTE: Instrumental music listed by form, number, and key is not underlined:

> Brahms's Piano Concerto no. 1, opus 15 in D minor

Paintings
> Regnault's <u>Three Graces</u>

Sculptures
> Michelangelo's <u>Madonna and Child</u>

Ships
```
U.S.S. Charr
```

Aircraft
```
the presidental aircraft Airforce One
```

**NOTE:** An initial "a," "an," or "the" is italicized and capitalized when it is part of the title:

```
The Grapes of Wrath
```

After the use of the possessive case, delete "The," "A," or "An," in a title:

```
Henry James's Portrait of a Lady
```

(The full title is *The Portrait of a Lady*.)


### 10b-2   Titles within quotation marks

The following items should be placed within quotation marks:

Short stories
```
''The Black Cat''
```

Short poems
```
''The Road Not Taken''
```

Songs
```
''A Mighty Fortress Is Our God''
```

Newspaper articles
```
''It's Drag Racing without Parachutes''
```

Magazine or journal articles
```
''How to Cope with Too Little Time and Too Many Meetings''
```

Encyclopedia articles
```
''Ballet''
```

Subdivisions in books
```
''The Solitude of Nathaniel Hawthorne''
```

Unpublished Dissertations
```
''The Local Communications Media and Their Coverage of Local
     Government in California''
```

Lectures
```
''The Epic of King Tutankhamun: Archeological Superstar''
```

Television episodes
```
''Turnabout,'' from the program The World of Women
```

**NOTE:** Sacred writings, series, editions, societies, conventional titles, and parts of books use neither underlining nor enclosed in quotation marks.

Sacred writings
>      the Bible, the Douay Version, the New Testament, Matthew, the
>          Gospels, the Talmud, the Koran, the Upanishads

Series
>      Masterpiece Theater, the Pacific Union College Lyceum Series

Editions
>      the Variorum Edition of Spenser

Societies
>      L'Alliance française, the Academy of Abdominal Surgeons

Conventional titles
>      Kennedy's first State of the Union Address

Parts of books
>      Preface
>      Introduction
>      Table of Contents
>      Appendix
>      Index

## 10b-3   Titles within titles

If a title enclosed by quotation marks appears within an underlined title, the quotation marks are retained. If an underlined title appears within a title enclosed by quotation marks, the underlining is retained:

>      *Book*      ''The Sting'' and Other Classical Short Stories

>      *Article*      ''Textual Variants in Sinclair Lewis's <u>Babbitt</u>''

Single quotation marks are used with a title requiring quotation marks appearing within another title also requiring quotation marks:

>      *Article*      ''Jonathan's Swift's 'Journal to Stella' ''

A title that would normally be underlined, but that appears as part of another title, is neither underlined nor placed in quotation marks. For example, the title of the book, *The Great Gatsby*, would normally be underlined. But when this title forms part of the title of another book, such as *A Study of* The Great Gatsby, only "A Study of" is underlined:

>      <u>A Study of</u> The Great Gatsby

### 10b-4 Frequent reference to a title

If the research paper refers frequently to the same title, subsequent reference to the title may be abbreviated, once the full title has been initially used. In abbreviating, always use a key word:

Return *for* Return of the Native

Tempest *for* Tempest in a Teapot

''The Bishop'' *for* ''The Bishop Orders His Tomb at Saint Praxis''

UNESCO *for* United Nations Educational, Scientific, and Cultural

      Organization

For citation of titles in subsequent references in notes, see 7g-8.

# 10c

## Italics

In typewritten work, italics are indicated by underlining. Words making up a phrase or title may be continuously, rather than separately, underlined.

- Underline phrases, words, letters, or numerals cited as linguistic examples:

One cannot assume that the Victorian word trump is an amalgamation

of tramp and chump.

- Underline foreign words used in English texts:

It seems clearly a case of noblesse oblige.

He used the post hoc ergo propter hoc fallacy.

**NOTE:** Exceptions to the rule include quotations entirely in another language, titles of articles in another language, and words anglicized through frequent use, such as: détente, laissez faire, gestalt, et al. In papers dealing with the arts, foreign expressions commonly used in the field need not be underlined: hubris, mimesis, leitmotif, pas de deux.

See 10b-1 for italics in titles.

# 10d

## Names of persons

■ In general, omit formal titles (Mr., Mrs., Miss, Ms., Dr., Professor) when referring to persons, living or dead, by their last names. However, convention dictates that certain persons be referred to by title:

Mme de Staël, Mrs. Humphry Ward

■ It is acceptable to use simplified names for famous people:

Dante *for* Dante Alighieri

Vergil *for* Publius Vergilius Maro

Michelangelo *for* Michelangelo Buonarroti

It is also acceptable to use an author's pseudonym rather than the author's real name:

George Sand *for* Amandine–Aurore–Lucie Dupin

Mark Twain *for* Samuel Clemens

Molière *for* Jean–Baptiste Poquelin

■ The *von, van, van der,* and *de* of foreign names are usually not included in references to people:

Goethe (Hans Wolfgang von Goethe)

Frontenac (Louis de Frontenac)

Ruysdael (Salman van Ruysdael)

However, certain names are traditionally not used with the last name alone:

```
Van Dyck not Dyck

De Gaulle not Gaulle

von Braun not Braun

O. Henry not Henry
```

# 10e

## Hyphenating words

- If possible, avoid dividing a word at the end of a typewritten line. But if a word must be divided for the sake of a balanced margin, make the division at the end of a syllable.

```
de-ter-mined      haz-ard-ous

i-vo-ry           grad-u-al

con-clud-ing      dress-er
```

Correct syllabification of words is listed in a dictionary. College dictionaries indicate the syllables of words with dots: bru·tal·i·ty; far·ci·cal.

- Never hyphenate a one-syllable word, such as "twelfth," "screamed," or "brought."
- Do not end or begin a line with a single letter:

```
a-mend, bur-y
```

- Make no division that might cause confusion in either the meaning or pronunciation of a word:

```
sour-ces, re-creation
```

- Divide hyphenated words only at the hyphen:

```
editor-in-chief, semi-retired
```

- Do not divide proper names, such as "Lincoln" or "Italy."
- Do not end several consecutive lines with a hyphen.

# 10f

## Handling foreign-language words

Words or phrases from a foreign language must be reproduced with all their accent marks. If you are doing a lengthy paper on a foreign language or on comparative literature, consider renting a typewriter with an international keyboard. Otherwise, the accent marks of foreign words must be written in by hand. Pay special attention to the following:

- It is not necessary to accent the capital letters of French words.

  énormément, *but* Enormément *or* ENORMEMENT

- For German words with the umlaut, use two dots rather than an "e," even for initial capitals:

  Überhaupt *not* Ueberhaupt

  fröhlich *not* froehlich

- Proper names retain their conventional spelling:

  Boehm *not* Böhm

  Dürrenmatt *not* Duerrenmatt

- Digraphs (two letters that represent only one sound) can be typed without connection (ae, oe), can be written in by hand ( æ , œ ), or can be connected at the top ($\overline{ae}$, $\overline{oe}$). In American English, the digraph "ae" is being abandoned:

  archeology *not* archaeology

  medieval *not* mediaeval

  esthetic *not* aesthetic

# 10g

## Abbreviations

Following is a list of abbreviations commonly encountered in research. The MLA favors dropping periods whenever possible.

### 10g-1   Abbreviations and reference words commonly used

| | |
|---|---|
| AD, A.D. | *anno Domini* 'in the year of the Lord.' No space between; precedes numerals (AD 12). |
| anon. | anonymous |

| | |
|---|---|
| app. | appendix |
| art., arts. | article(s) |
| assn. | association |
| assoc. | associate, associated |
| b. | born |
| BC, B.C. | before Christ. No space between; follows numerals (23 BC). |
| bibliog. | bibliography, bibliographer, bibliographical |
| biog. | biography, biographer, biographical |
| bk., bks. | book(s) |
| © | copyright (© 1975) |
| c., ca. | *circa* 'about.' Used with approximate dates (c. 1851). |
| cf. | *confer* 'compare.' Do not use "cf." if "see" is intended. |
| ch., chs. | chapter(s) |
| chor., chors. | choreographed by, choreographer(s) |
| col., cols. | column(s) |
| comp., comps. | compiled by, compiler(s) |
| cond. | conducted by, conductor |
| Cong. | Congress |
| *Cong. Rec.* | *Congressional Record* |
| d. | died |
| dir., dirs. | directed by, director(s) |
| diss. | dissertation |
| E, Eng. | English |
| ed., eds. | edited by, editor(s), editions(s) |
| e.g. | *exempli gratia* 'for example.' Preceded and followed by a comma. |
| enl. | enlarged (as in "rev. and enl. ed.") |
| esp. | especially (as in "124–29, esp. 125") |
| et al. | *et alii* 'and others' |
| etc. | *et cetera* 'and so forth.' Do not use in text. |
| ex., exs. | example(s) |
| f., ff. | and the following (with no space after a numeral) page(s) or line(s). Exact references are preferable: 89–90 instead of 89f.; 72–79 instead of 72ff. |
| facsim. (or facs.) | facsimile |
| fig., figs. | figure(s) |
| fol., fols. | folio(s) |
| Fr. | French |
| front. | frontispiece |
| Ger. | German |
| Gk. | Greek |
| GPO | Government Printing Office, Washington, D.C. |
| hist. | history, historian, historical |
| ibid. | *ibidem* 'in the same place,' i.e., in the cited title. Avoid using. Cite instead the author's last name and the page number. |
| i.e. | *id est* 'that is.' Preceded and followed by a comma. |
| illus. | illustrated (by), illustrator, illustration(s) |
| intro. (or introd.) | introduced by, introduction |
| ips | inches per second (used on labels of recording tapes) |
| It. | Italian |

| | |
|---|---|
| jour. | journal |
| L., Lat. | Latin |
| l., ll. | line(s). MLA style now uses "line" or "lines" instead of "l" or "ll." |
| lang., langs. | language(s) |
| LC, L. C. | Library of Congress. Typed with a space between when periods are used. |
| loc. cit. (not l.c.) | *loco citato* 'in the place (passage) cited.' Avoid using. Repeat the citation in shortened form. |
| MA, M.A. | Master of Arts. No space between. |
| mag. | magazine |
| ME | Middle English |
| ms, mss (or ms., mss.) | manuscript(s). Capitalized and followed by a period when referring to a specific manuscript. |
| MS, M.S. | Master of Science. No space between. |
| n., nn. | note(s) |
| narr., narrs. | narrated by, narrator(s) |
| NB, N.B. | *nota bene* 'take notice, mark well.' Not spaced. |
| n.d. | no date (in a book's imprint). No space between. |
| no., nos. | number(s) |
| n.p. | no place (of publication); no publisher. Not spaced. |
| n. pag. | no pagination. Space between. |
| OE | Old English |
| op. | opus (work) |
| op. cit | *opere citato* 'in the work cited.' Avoid using. Repeat citation in shortened form. |
| p., pp. | page(s). |
| par., pars. | paragraph(s) |
| passim | 'throughout the work, here and there' (as "84, 97, and passim") |
| PhD., Ph.D. | Doctor of Philosophy. No space between. |
| philos. | philosophical |
| pl., pls. | plate(s) |
| pref. | preface |
| prod., prods. | produced by, producer(s) |
| pseud. | pseudonym |
| pt., pts. | part(s) |
| pub., pubs. | published by, publication(s) |
| rept., repts. | reported by, report(s) |
| rev. | revised (by), revision; review, reviewed (by). Spell out "review," if there is any possibility of ambiguity. |
| rpm | revolutions per minute (used on recordings) |
| rpt. | reprinted (by), reprint |
| sc. | scene |
| sec., secs. | section(s) |
| ser. | series |
| sic | 'thus, so.' Put between square brackets when used to signal an editorial interpolation. |
| soc. | society |
| Sp. | Spanish |
| st., sts. | stanza(s) |
| St., Sts. | Saint(s) |

| | |
|---|---|
| supp., supps. | supplement(s) |
| Tech rep. | Technical report |
| TLS | typed letter signed |
| trans. (or tr.) | translated by, translator, translation |
| ts. | typescript. Cf. "ms." |
| v., vs. | versus 'against.' Cf. "v., vv." |
| v., vv. (or vs., vss.) | verse(s) |
| vol., vols. | volume(s) |

## 10g-2  The Bible and Shakespeare

Use the following abbreviations in notes and parenthetical references; do not use them in the text (except parenthetically).

### a.  The Bible

OLD TESTAMENT (OT)

| | | | |
|---|---|---|---|
| Gen. | Genesis | Eccl. | Ecclesiastes |
| Exod. | Exodus | Song. Sol. | Song of Solomon |
| Lev. | Leviticus | (also Cant.) | (also Canticles) |
| Num. | Numbers | Isa. | Isaiah |
| Deut. | Deuteronomy | Jer. | Jeremiah |
| Josh. | Joshua | Lam. | Lamentations |
| Judg. | Judges | Ezek. | Ezekiel |
| Ruth | Ruth | Dan. | Daniel |
| 1 Sam. | 1 Samuel | Hos. | Hosea |
| 2 Sam. | 2 Samuel | Joel | Joel |
| 1 Kings | 1 Kings | Amos | Amos |
| 2 Kings | 2 Kings | Obad. | Obadiah |
| 1 Chron. | 1 Chronicles | Jon. | Jonah |
| 2 Chron. | 2 Chronicles | Mic. | Micah |
| Ezra | Ezra | Nah. | Nahum |
| Neh. | Nehemiah | Hab. | Habakkuk |
| Esth. | Esther | Zeph. | Zephaniah |
| Job | Job | Hag. | Haggai |
| Ps. | Psalms | Zech. | Zechariah |
| Prov. | Proverbs | Mal. | Malachi |

SELECTED APOCRYPHAL AND DUETEROCANONICAL WORKS

| | | | |
|---|---|---|---|
| 1 Esd. | 1 Esdras | Bar. | Baruch |
| 2 Esd. | 2 Esdras | Song 3 | Song of the |
| Tob. | Tobit | Childr. | Three |
| Jth. | Judith | | Children |
| Esth. | Esther | Sus. | Susanna |
| (also Apocr.) | Apocrypha | Bel and Dr. | Bel and the |
| Wisd. Sol. | Wisdom of | | Dragon |
| (also Wisd.) | Solomon | Pray. Man. | Prayer of |
| | (also Wisdom) | | Manasseh |
| Ecclus. | Ecclesiasticus | 1 Macc. | 1 Maccabees |
| (also Sir.) | (also Sirach) | 2 Macc. | 2 Maccabees |

### NEW TESTAMENT (NT)

| | | | |
|---|---|---|---|
| Matt. | Matthew | 1 Tim. | 1 Timothy |
| Mark | Mark | 2 Tim. | 2 Timothy |
| Luke | Luke | Tit. | Titus |
| John | John | Philem. | Philemon |
| Acts | Acts | Heb. | Hebrews |
| Rom. | Romans | Jas. | James |
| 1 Cor. | 1 Corinthians | 1 Pet. | 1 Peter |
| 2 Cor. | 2 Corinthians | 2 Pet. | 2 Peter |
| Gal. | Galatians | 1 John | 1 John |
| Eph. | Ephesians | 2 John | 2 John |
| Phil. | Philippians | 3 John | 3 John |
| Col. | Colossians | Jude | Jude |
| 1 Thess. | 1 Thessalonians | Rev. (also | Revelation (also |
| 2 Thess. | 2 Thessalonians | Apoc.) | Apocalypse) |

### SELECTED APOCRYPHAL WORKS

| | | | |
|---|---|---|---|
| G. Thom. | Gospel of Thomas | G. Pet. | Gospel of Peter |
| G. Heb. | Gospel of the Hebrews | | |

## b. Shakespeare

| | | | |
|---|---|---|---|
| Ado | Much Ado about Nothing | MND | A Midsummer Night's Dream |
| Ant | Antony and Cleopatra | MV | The Merchant of Venice |
| AWW | All's Well That Ends Well | Oth. | Othello |
| AYL | As You Like It | Per. | Pericles |
| Cor. | Coriolanus | PhT | The Phoenix and the Turtle |
| Cym. | Cymbeline | PP | The Passionate Pilgrim |
| Err. | The Comedy of Errors | Q | Quarto ed. |
| F1 | First Folio ed. (1623) | R2 | Richard II |
| F2 | Second Folio ed. (1632) | R3 | Richard III |
| Ham. | Hamlet | Rom. | Romeo and Juliet |
| 1H4 | Henry IV, Part I | Shr. | The Taming of the Shrew |
| 2H4 | Henry IV, Part II | Son. | Sonnets |
| H5 | Henry V | TGV | The Two Gentlemen of Verona |
| 1H6 | Henry VI, Part I | Tim. | Timon of Athens |
| 2H6 | Henry VI, Part II | Tit. | Titus Andronicus |
| 3H6 | Henry VI, Part III | Tmp. | The Tempest |
| H8 | Henry VIII | TN | Twelfth Night |
| JC | Julius Caesar | TNK | The Two Noble Kinsmen |
| Jn. | King John | Tro. | Troilus and Cressida |
| LC | A Lover's Complaint | Ven. | Venus and Adonis |
| LLL | Love's Labour's Lost | Wiv. | The Merry Wives of Windsor |
| Lr. | King Lear | WT | The Winter's Tale |
| Luc. | The Rape of Lucrece | | |
| Mac. | Macbeth | | |
| MM | Measure for Measure | | |

# Eleven
## Sample Student Papers

**11a** Entire paper with parenthetical documentation in author-work style (MLA)

**11b** Excerpt from a paper with parenthetical documentation in author-year style (APA)

**11c** Excerpt from a paper with footnote documentation (traditional)

The following samples were researched and written by college freshmen. Except for a few minor corrections, they are reproduced as they were submitted. The accompanying marginal annotations clarify the format of the paper, explain specific problems, or draw attention to important aspects of research.

# 11a

## Entire student paper using the author-work style of documentation (MLA)

*Double space throughout the body of the outline.*

*The title, centered on the page, appears in the outline.*

*Place the thesis at the beginning of the outline, although it may not be the first sentence of the paper. The thesis in the outline may be worded more succinctly than in the paper.*

*The outline leaves out the details of the paper, mentioning only major points.*

i

} *1 inch margin*

Butch Mulcahey

Professor McCuen

English 101

13 January 1984

} *double space*

The Certainties of Hawthorne's Moral Ambiguity

} *double space*

in The Scarlett Letter

} *double space*

} *quadruple space*

Thesis:  Hawthorne's moral ambiguity suggests

certainties that transcend in importance

the ambiguity, which several critics claim

to be the novel's fault.

I.   There are matters of interpretation of

Hawthorne's concerns upon which most

critics agree.

A.   Most critics agree that Hawthorne

concerns himself with the consequences

of sin rather than with the sin itself.

B.   Hypocrisy is generally believed to be

what Hawthorne considered the most

200

*Use small
Roman
numerals for
paginating the
outline.*

ii

*Use standard
outline symbols.
For a full
discussion of
how to write the
outline, see 5b.*

grave consequence of sin.

C. A common interpretation is that
Hawthorne's moral seems to follow logically from his concern with the gravity
of hypocrisy.

II. Beyond this level of generally accepted interpretation, however, some critics suggest
that the value of the moral diminishes in
the presence of ambiguity in the novel.

A. Some argue that Hawthorne's definition
of sin itself is ambiguous and has at
best only a cloudy, tentative meaning.

B. Some, especially Jeffrey Duncan, suggest that Hawthorne's plea that men ''be
true'' is paradoxical.

C. Hyatt H. Waggoner questions whether
salvation is possible from Hawthorne's
proposed morality, observing the dark
and uncertain conclusion that Hester
and Dimmesdale seem to share.

III. Undoubtedly these ambiguities exist; however, they do not destroy the ''blossom'' of
wisdom that Hawthorne wishes to convey, but

iii

rather they enrich its meaning by implying

important certainties in life.

A. Hawthorne defines sin ambiguously be-

cause he wants to show the absolute rel-

ativity of it in this world.

B. Hawthorne also asserts his belief that

the existence of sin is certain.

*Neither the
introduction nor
the conclusion
carries a special
label.*

C. Finally, he implies in his ambiguity

the most important certainty that he

wishes to present, the certainty of

tragedy in life.

1

*The name of
the student,
professor, and
class, as well as
the date, are
repeated on the
title page of
the paper.*

Butch Mulcahey

Professor McCuen

English 101

13 January 1984

*The title is
centered (and
double spaced
if more than
one line).*

The Certainties of Hawthorne's Moral Ambiguity

in The Scarlet Letter

*A quotation
from a primary
source creates an
effective
opening.*

''Be true! Be True! Be True!  Show freely to the

world, if not your worst, yet some trait whereby the

worst may be inferred!''  Nathaniel Hawthorne (242)

impresses upon his readers this singular statement in

order to ''relieve the darkening close of a tale of

human frailty and sorrow'' (56).  The tale, of

course, is The Scarlet Letter, and the statement rep-

resents the ''sweet moral blossom'' which at the end

of the first chapter Hawthorne promises to present to

his readers.  He hopes that this ''moral blossom''

will project a brightening ray of wisdom into the

darkness of the fateful triangle of sin in which his

three main characters seem tragically entrapped.

Yet, despite Hawthorne's stated intention, several

critics suggest that his ''blossom'' lacks the sweet-

ness he wishes it to have, that his conclusion lacks

Mulcahey 2

moral value because of the ambiguity and paradox

found in the development of Hawthorne's view of

*An elevated
numeral
indicates
a content
note. Such
superscripts are
not used for
in-text
documentation.*

morality.[1]  And, of course, the critics observing

these ambiguities and paradoxes make valid points,

for such moral uncertainty undeniably exists in The

Scarlet Letter.  However, Hawthorne's moral ambigu-

ity is not the book's fault but its strength.  It will

be seen that Hawthorne's moral ambiguity actually en-

hances the wisdom, the ''blossom,'' which the reader

is to receive.  It does not confuse the meaning of

*The thesis is
placed in a
classical
position, at the
end of the first
paragraph.*

Hawthorne's conclusion, but rather it redefines and

enriches it by implying certainties concerning sin

which transcend in importance the ambiguities.

Amid the controversy concerning Hawthorne's

*A transitional
paragraph alerts
the reader to
what is
coming—
matters upon
which critics
agree.*

view of morality, there are nevertheless interpreta-

tions of his moral concerns upon which most critics

agree.

One observation accepted almost without debate

is that Hawthorne concerns himself with the conse-

quences of sin rather than the action of sin.  Several

critics assert that, regardless of its background,

the book obviously does not deal with the sin of adul-

tery.  Arlin Turner, for instance, draws attention to

*A Latin
expression is
underlined to
indicate italics.*

the fact that Hawthorne begins the novel in medias

res, long after Hester Prynne and Arthur Dimmesdale

*Note the in-text
citations to
"Works Cited."*

have committed the initial sin of passion (Turner

56). Apparently, then, Hawthorne wishes to deal

with the consequences of sin and to study them ex-

*A word referred
to as a word is
underlined to
indicate italics.*

clusively. As W. C. Brownell notes, the word adul-

tery does not even appear in the text of the novel

*Since the author
(Brownell) is
named, only the
page is cited
within
parentheses.*

(245). Brownell further suggests that the entire

book ultimately fails to support a study of original

sin. He comments, ''As a story of illicit love its

omissions are too great, its significance is not def-

*A direct
quotation is
smoothly
introduced by
"He comments."*

inite enough, its detail has not enough richness; the

successive scenes of which it is composed have not an

effective enough cohesion'' (246).

Certain critics of form indicate that the struc-

ture of the novel does support very well Hawthorne's

study in consequences. Gordon Roper considers the

entire progress of The Scarlet Letter to be divided

into four separate parts, in each of which a single

activating force affects three other forces in the

novel (49-52). The initial sin is seen simply as the

force which triggers the mechanism of the whole de-

velopment of the book. What results is a study in the

Mulcahey 4

reactions of the three main characters to this sin.

Another pattern observed by critic Roy Male is the

symmetrical approach of the characters to their ends,

as Hester Prynne becomes a repentant sinner, Dimmes-

dale a partially repentant sinner, and Chillingworth

an unrepentant sinner (91). In both of these pat-

terns, the presumption that Hawthorne places his ma-

jor emphasis on the effects of sin on the characters

is upheld.

*Coherence is maintained by reminding the reader of the continuing topic at hand—common agreement.*

There is also common agreement on what Hawthorne

considers the most grave consequence of sin. Although

interpretations of this consequence vary, Hawthorne

is generally thought to concentrate much of his con-

cern on the dangers of hypocrisy. Brownell inter-

prets the novel as an attempt to study predominantly

the problems resulting from concealment of sin, whereby

concealment itself is considered a serious sin (247).

And, of course, this form of hypocrisy pervades the

novel, as all three of Hawthorne's main characters

are continuously guilty of it. Hester is guilty be-

cause she refuses to reveal her partner in adultery;

Dimmesdale is guilty because he conceals both his

guilt in the adultery and his sin of concealment; and

*Coherence is achieved by repeating the phrase "is guilty because."*

Mulcahey 5

Chillingworth is guilty because he conceals both his
identity and his vengeful purpose.  More accurately,
however, Hawthorne's study of hypocrisy is seen as a
study of human perfidy and especially self-delusion.
Undoubtedly, Arthur Dimmesdale serves as the ultimate example of this type of hypocrisy.  Religious
and philosophical explanations would summarize

*A popular phrase is placed in quotation marks.*

Dimmesdale's dilemma as the ''skeptical predica-
ment.''  Dimmesdale assumes that flesh and spirit are
separate and different, that the sins of one are not
necessarily the sins of the other.  He lives a double
life, damning his flesh while pridefully glorifying
his spirit and maintaining his elevated ministerial
image in the Puritan society.  Consequently, he absolutely distorts his sense of which life is real, and
his life becomes totally false (Davidson 86).  He
loses his sense of his true humanity.  Here is seen,
then, why Hawthorne considered hypocrisy such a
dangerous sin.

The clarity of Hawthorne's extensive study of
hypocrisy emerges not only in Dimmesdale, whose hypocrisy is obvious, but also in Roger Chillingworth.
Chillingworth practices the most intense forms of

Mulcahey 6

hypocrisy.  He attempts to punish sin despite the

fact that he himself is not free from it.  He assumes

the role of Dimmesdale's presumably helpful physician

while, ironically, he knowingly inflicts the minis-

ter's harm (Turner 102).  He thus becomes the most

false of Hawthorne's characters, and he concludes the

story as a demon, a dehumanized mortal.  In this re-

spect, Hawthorne's concern with the dangers of hypoc-

risy is once again reflected.  As many critics have

indicated, this concern seems ever-present.

*Paraphrase
and personal
comment are
nicely
integrated.*

From these interpretations of Hawthorne's con-

cern with hypocrisy, his moral seems to follow logi-

cally.  ''Be true'' is obviously the morality he

prescribes for avoiding the terrible suffering of

Dimmesdale as well as that of the other characters

guilty of hypocritical sins.  ''Being true,'' as Roy

Male indicates, involves each character's direct con-

frontation of his own guilt (96).  Each character who

fulfills this requirement of Hawthorne's moral is be-

lieved to achieve salvation.  Hester, of course, must

embrace her guilt from the beginning of the novel.

*Bracketed words
help the reader
to understand
the quotation in
proper context.*

Her resulting ignominy is what makes her a heroine.

It causes her to ''[stand] erect, and [think],'' ques-

Mulcahey 7

tioning her punishment and the society which inflicts

it (Carl Van Doren 69–70). Her salvation is seen in

*Van Doren's first name is cited so he will not be confused with Mark Van Doren, who is cited later.*

her humbler spirit and her greater sympathy for

human fault as well as her increased generosity.

Dimmesdale appears to achieve his salvation in the

final scaffold scene, where he confronts and resists

Roger Chillingworth, the strong advocate of hypoc-

risy. In fact, his conclusion has been interpreted

*Since two of Waggoner's works appear in "Works Cited," a key word from the title appears here.*

to be almost Christlike (Waggoner, The Presence 66).

Pearl, who is Hawthorne's symbol of truth, reaches a

proportionately happy conclusion, becoming ''the

richest heiress of her day, in the New World'' (243).

From these observations, Hawthorne's view of morality

seems very beneficial, and indeed proves to be, with-

out further interpretation, the ''sweet moral blos-

som'' the reader anticipates.

*Here the student writer moves to negative criticism of the novel's ambiguity.*

Beyond this level of interpretation, however,

several critics suggest that the value of Hawthorne's

proposed morality diminishes because of his ambigu-

ity. They contend that his moral solution cannot

possibly be useful in the definite sense he wishes it

to be, because its meaning lacks certainty as a result

of the novel's atmosphere of ambiguity and paradox.

Mulcahey 8

Some argue that Hawthorne's concept of sin it-

*Here* sin *is referred to as a word.*

self is indefinite, that <u>sin</u> has at most only a

cloudy, tentative meaning in the novel.  Jeffrey

Duncan asserts that Hawthorne entertains at least two

possibilities about ''the essential nature'' of the

reality of sin and evil.  In one, sin is only ''com-

mitted in the flesh''; in the other, sin exists only

in the human mind——in thoughts——and ''sins of the

flesh'' only exist in the mind's interpretation of

*Direct quotation and paraphrase smoothly alternate, adding to the smooth flow of the paper.*

actions (61).  Duncan concludes of Hawthorne's pre-

sentation of sin that ''reality [hangs] in the bal-

ance, a moot point, indeterminable'' (61).  Thus it is

argued that Hawthorne's sin cannot be definitely per-

ceived, that what may be considered sin in one sense

may not be considered sin in another sense.  Arlin

Turner observes this ambiguity to be especially true

in the presentation of the sin of adultery:  ''The

transgression of Hester and Dimmesdale stands con-

demned by the laws of society but in an absolute sense

is condemned only mildly if at all by the author and

*Parenthetical documentation is placed inside the fourth period because the page citation is part of the context of the sentence.*

the reader . . .'' (Turner 59).  The adultery of Hes-

ter and Arthur seems acceptable in the context of

<u>The Scarlet Letter</u>, yet it is not condoned in a gener-

Mulcahey 9

al sense. According to this interpretation, the
gravity of this sin is uncertain and almost arbi-
trary. The obvious implication of these arguments is
that sin cannot be conquered if its true nature is
unknown.

In a similar argument, Hawthorne's plea that man
''be true'' is proven to be inherently and irreconcil-
ably paradoxical. Duncan indicates first of all that
Hawthorne does not explain to what one should be true
(Duncan 52). The perfect example of this ambiguity
occurs in chapter 18 of the novel, when Hester dis-
cards her scarlet ''A'' and proposes that she and
Dimmesdale flee from the Puritan community. As revealed in Pearl's disapproval of this act, Hawthorne
censures the idea, showing Hester as trying to ignore
the fact of her own sinfulness. Yet, as John Gerber
notes, she is true to the natural passion that she has
demonstrated throughout the book; therefore she does
not in essence commit what Hawthorne considers a sin
(107). Thus Hester can be considered a sinner or she
can be absolutely justified, regardless of her actions. Likewise, Roger Chillingworth, the undis-
puted antagonist of the novel, can be considered

Mulcahey 10

totally justified in his actions, for he is true to

his own antagonism throughout the novel.

Furthermore, Duncan contends that Dimmesdale's

final moment of truth, his apparent salvation through

confession, is ''perfectly ambiguous'' because of an

endless paradox in his ''being true.'' Duncan pro-

poses that the minister's confession may be inter-

preted in several different ways: (1) he may be false

in his confession in the sense that he confesses in

such a way as to appear to the Puritan community as

the Christlike saint which he is not; (2) his confes-

sion may be as sincere and true as common interpre-

tation contends; (3) he may be perfectly false in

confession, in which case he is perfectly true to him-

self (69-70). An endless cycle of paradox results,

which Duncan interprets to mean that Dimmesdale's

truth may be false and his falsity may in fact be

truth. Whether Dimmesdale gains his salvation from

his ''being true'' is therefore indefinite and ulti-

mately irreconcilable. Once more the usefulness of

Hawthorne's morality is questioned.

In one essay, Hyatt H. Waggoner questions

whether salvation ever comes about by Hawthorne's

Mulcahey 11

proposed morality, observing the dark and uncertain

conclusion which both Hester and Dimmesdale appear to

share.  He asserts that neither Hester nor Dimmesdale

achieves a glorious salvation:  ''. . . For Hester

there is no escape, only sublimation and self-

control.  For Dimmesdale there is only public confes-

sion of guilt and submission to a will he conceives as

higher than his own'' (The Presence 69).  Waggoner

further declares that the final images of the novel

are gloomy and pessimistic.  He suggests that the im-

agery of the final tombstone inscription ''ON A

FIELD, SABLE, THE LETTER A, GULES'' (Hawthorne 245)

implies all of the negativeness of Hawthorne's dual

symbols and none of the positiveness.  The scene, he

believes, is absolutely void of the relieving gleam

of hope which Hawthorne had promised, and death or

guilt seems to be all that is left to Hester and

Arthur in the end (The Presence 70).  ''Being true''

apparently has not brought them to a happier state

than they had experienced without ''being true.''

Thus, Waggoner concludes that Hawthorne does not suc-

ceed in lightening the dark close of his story.  He

notes that both Hawthorne and his wife wept miserably

*Three ellipsis
dots are used to
indicate a word
or words omitted
at the start of the
quotation.*

*Since the author
(Waggoner) is
mentioned twice
earlier in the
paragraph, only
an abbreviated
title is necessary.*

Mulcahey 12

when Hawthorne had read the conclusion aloud (<u>The
Presence</u> 72).  This reaction suggests to Waggoner
that even Hawthorne himself tended to feel that ambiguity of his moral, that he also had doubts concerning
the ultimate value of his ''moral blossom.''

These arguments have unanswerable validity.
Such ambiguity undeniably exists in <u>The Scarlet Let-</u>
<u>ter</u>, as Hawthorne's tears apparently attest.  In
fact, Hawthorne's ambiguity even serves as the cement
which bonds the entire novel together, allowing illu-
sions to assume a sense of reality and binding abstract ideas to materialistic symbols such as the
scarlet ''A.''  Contrary to what the critics cited
suggest, however, the ambiguity does not destroy the
true purpose of the story, nor does it confuse the
''blossom'' of wisdom which Hawthorne wishes to imply
to the reader.  Instead, it solidifies the certainties which Hawthorne had felt to be true throughout
his life.

In Waggoner's opinion, Hawthorne defines sin
ambiguously not because he doubted his own concept of
sin but because he wished to show the relativity it
assumes in this world.  He used ambiguity as an ex-

*The student
author now
leads the reader
back to his
original thesis.*

Mulcahey 13

pression of his own ''existentially oriented'' reli-

gious beliefs, and he based his view of life on his

*Key words from
Waggoner's
other work are
cited to avoid
confusion.*

own experience (''Art and Belief'' 67). Just as

Hawthorne's convictions depended on his own percep-

tion of life, the reality of the nature of sin in The

Scarlet Letter varies relative to the perception of

the characters of the novel. As John Gerber states,

*Words are added
in brackets to
clarify the
context.*

''Sin [in Hawthorne's novel] . . . is a violation of

only that which the sinner thinks he violates.'' The

inevitable conclusion of this statement is that a

uniform definition of sin cannot exist and indeed

is not supposed to exist in The Scarlet Letter.

Hawthorne is certain that sin is relative and depen-

dent on man himself. For instance, Hester Prynne

realizes that she has sinned against the Puritan

society, but she hardly views her adultery in the

sense that the Puritan community views it. She does

not consider it a breach of God's law, but a breach of

the law of order and Puritan orthodoxy (Gerber 108).

Although the society's and Hester's views are very

different, both nevertheless have a sense of reality

with respect to those who conceive them.[2] Hawthorne

is certain, then, that man's concept of sin is defi-

Mulcahey 14

nite only with respect to himself.

Thus Hawthorne's purpose is not to define sin
but to juxtapose his characters' relative concepts of
sin and let the reader observe the results.  R. W. B.
Lewis maintains that the novel is merely a showcase in
which the characters and the Puritan society are mea-
sured against each other (74).  It was therefore
Hawthorne's intention to have the entire effect of
the novel on the reader depend on the reader's deter-
mination of this measurement.  For instance, a reader
with a strong religious background might consider
adultery a serious sin, while on the other hand a
romantic might believe the act of passion to be totally justified.

Hawthorne does not intend to imply, however,
that sin does not really exist because it is merely a
formulation of each man's mind.  Strongly implicit in
The Scarlet Letter is that sin is inevitable despite
its relativity.  As an American writer who partially
refuted the ideas of Transcendentalism, Hawthorne was
certain that sin and evil were real enough so that they
could not be relinquished, as Ralph Waldo Emerson
had thought, by ''self-reliance'' or by simply im-

Mulcahey 15

*Van Doren's full
name is given to
avoid confusing
him with Carl
Van Doren,
cited earlier.*

agining that they did not exist (Mark Van Doren 137).

He saw the certainty of the existence of sin not as a

result of dogma, but as a direct implication of the

relativity of sin.  Men perceive sin with respect to

their own convictions, and therefore their percep-

tions are necessarily various.  And since men in-

teract with each other in a society, they must

perceive sin in each other and attempt to impress

their concepts of sin upon others.  Such is the case

with the Puritan society of Hawthorne's novel, of

which the adulterers are influenced members.  ''In

the minds of [Hawthorne's] characters, their sins are

absolute, for they have broken God's laws; and they

see themselves and their relations with people and

institutions about them in the light of that assump-

tion'' (Turner 57).  The main characters are con-

vinced that they are sinners, despite their ability

to believe otherwise.  That their sins depend on

their own relative perceptions does not make these

sins any less real to them.  Therefore, Hawthorne's

grand implication of sin's definite existence is

finally revealed.  Because he shows the nature of

sin's reality to vary from man to man, sin must always

Mulcahey 16

exist; for if a man does not see sin in himself, he must surely see it in others, and vice versa. In either case, the existence of sin will be definite.

And if the certainty of sin does not lie in man's perception of it, Hawthorne implies that evil must exist in the punishment of sin and the resulting suffering of his characters. If it is certain that one can justify Hester's adultery in her naturally passionate and wild nature, then surely the Puritan society has sinned against her by punishing her action. In this case, the sin committed is that of human injustice, which occurs ''because men fumbled in their understanding of justice'' (Mark Van Doren 138). In either sense, some form of sin has occurred, and Hawthorne shows evil and suffering to be tragically inevitable.

These ideas concerning human beings and their perceptions of sin imply the most important certainty which Hawthorne wishes finally to give to his reader. This is the certainty of tragedy in life. In his study of the consequences of sin, Hawthorne asserts a belief that ''retribution for sin is certain,'' and apparent in the entire progress of the novel is an

Mulcahey 17

assumed inevitability, a fatefulness surrounding

the destinies of the characters (Turner 58).

Chillingworth serves as the constant symbol, or in-

deed the mechanism, of this fatefulness.  It is he who

makes Hester and Arthur tragic victims of destiny.

*A colon precedes long quotations. The quotation is double spaced and indented 10 spaces. The final period is placed before the documentation parentheses. Double space above and below the quotation.*

This fact is clear in his statement to Hester in chap-

ter 14:

*} double space*

> It is not granted me to pardon.  I have no
>
> such power as thou tellest me of.  By thy
>
> first step awry thou didst plant the germ
>
> of evil; but since that moment, it has all
>
> been dark necessity. . . .  It is our
>
> fate.  Let the black flower blossom as
>
> it may. (167)

*double space*

*} double space*

It is also made definite by the entrapment of Hester,

Dimmesdale, and Chillingworth. For instance, the

plans of Hester and Dimmesdale to escape by boat are

spoiled by Chillingworth himself, who plans to board

the same ship.  All three characters are determinis-

tically tied to their destinies, and the occurrence

of tragedy in their conclusions is certain.

However, the certainty of tragedy in life that

Hawthorne wishes to demonstrate is ironically most

Mulcahey 18

apparent in the ambiguity of the moral itself.  The

inevitable tragedy implied by the ambiguity of the

moral exists in what Roy Male calls its ''eternal par-

adox.''  Man's knowledge, represented by the wisdom

of Hawthorne's final moral, may be ''insanity to

God,'' while celestial truth may likewise seem insane

in the social world (Male 94).  In this respect,

tragedy exists in the fact that man cannot be abso-

lutely sure of the nature of ultimate truth, that his

worldly perceptions do not reflect necessarily the

truths of the spirit.  The ambiguity of Hawthorne's

moral thus converts itself into an absolute cer-

tainty, the certainty that any of man's attempts to

solve the eternal problem of sin, including that of

Hawthorne, is unavoidably vested with tragic uncer-

tainty.  The weeping of Hawthorne which Waggoner

notes is not for his ambiguous moral but for the im-

pending tragedy which it implies.

The ''blossom'' which Hawthorne presents to the

reader therefore reveals its highest meaning.  It is

not represented by definite moral advice but by trag-

ic wisdom.  It is the sad knowledge that the reader

finally shares with Hester Prynne, the knowledge that

*The student
author moves
toward his
conclusion.*

220

Mulcahey 19

sin is ''a problem for which there is no solution in
life,'' the knowledge which makes ''the life of Hester
[increase], not [diminish] . . .'' (Mark Van Doren
132).  The ''blossom'' of wisdom serves for the reader
the same purpose that Pearl serves for Hester, reminding her of her guilt and sin and causing her to
''look with warm sympathy into the hearts of sinners''

*Once again
the thesis is
emphasized.*

(Turner 61).  Hawthorne's ''moral blossom'' therefore
does not lose its value or its sweetness.  It gives to
readers a renewed hope that although they cannot con-
quer the problem of sin altogether, they can still

*The paper has
come full circle,
beginning with
a reference to the
"moral blossom"
and ending
with this same
reference. The
final sentence is
a strong
conclusion.*

benefit from its tragedy.  At this point, the ''blossom'' is in full bloom.

Notes

*Content notes
are on a
separate page
entitled "Notes."*

¹ It is useful to compare Hawthorne's moral
ambiguity and paradox with that of Milton in Paradise
Lost.

*A reference to
another work for
comparison*

² Only in the forest (symbolizing a moral wil-
derness away from society) can Hester and Dimmesdale
escape the strict Puritan code and acknowledge their
bond.

*A note of further
explication*

Mulcahey 21

Works Cited

Brownell, W. C.  ''This New England Faust.''  The

Scarlet Letter: An Authoritative Text, Back-

grounds and Sources, Criticism.  Ed. Sculley

Bradley and others.  2nd ed.  New York: Norton,

1978.  291–293.

Davidson, Edward H.  ''Dimmesdale's Fall.''  Twentieth

Century Interpretations of The Scarlet Letter.

Ed. John C. Gerber.  Englewood Cliffs: Prentice,

1968.  82–105.

Duncan, Jeffrey L.  ''The Design of Hawthorne's Fab-

rications.''  The Yale Review 71 (Oct. 1981):

51–71.

Gerber, John C.  ''Form and Content in The Scarlet

Letter.''  The New England Quarterly 17 (1944):

25–55.

Hawthorne, Nathaniel.  The Scarlet Letter.  New York:

NAL, 1959.

Lewis, R. W. B.  ''The Return into Time: Hawthorne.''

Hawthorne: A Collection of Critical Essays.  Ed.

A. N. Kaul.  Englewood Cliffs: Prentice, 1966.

72–95.

Male, Roy R.  Hawthorne's Tragic Vision.  New York:

*"Works Cited"
must begin on
a new page.*

*The title of the
novel is not
underlined since
it is part of a title
that must be
underlined
(see 10b-3,
p. 190).*

*Citation of a
work within an
edited collection
(see 8b-2h,
p. 138).*

*Citation of a
journal article
(see 8b-4d,
p. 144).*

*Citation of
a book by a
single author
(see 8b-2a,
p. 136).*

Mulcahey 22

Norton, 1957.

Roper, Gordon. ''The Four Part Structure.'' Twentieth

Century Interpretations of The Scarlet Letter.

Ed. John C. Gerber. Englewood Cliffs: Prentice,

1968. 49–52.

Turner, Arlin. Nathaniel Hawthorne: An Introduction

and Interpretation. New York: Barnes, 1961.

Van Doren, Carl. The American Novel, 1789–1939. 2nd

ed. New York: Macmillan, 1940.

Van Doren, Mark. ''The Scarlet Letter.'' Hawthorne:

A Collection of Critical Essays. Ed. A. N.

Kaul. Englewood Cliffs: Prentice, 1966. 129–140.

Waggoner, Hyatt H. The Presence of Hawthorne. Baton

Rouge: Louisiana State UP, 1979.

---. ''Art and Belief.'' Twentieth Century Interpre-

tations of The Scarlet Letter. Ed. John C.

Gerber. Englewood Cliffs: Prentice, 1968.

67–72.

*Citation of a
book in its
second edition
(see 8b-2m,
p. 140).*

*The line
indicates a
repetition of
Hyatt H.
Waggoner as
author.*

# 11b

## Excerpt from a student paper using the author-year style of documentation (APA)

1

Kristin Townsend

Professor Cunningham } ⟩ *double*

Psychology        } ⟩ *space*

28 February 1984

} *double space*

More Funding for Autism?

} *quadruple space*

Autism is a syndrome of childhood characterized
by a lack of social relationships, limited communication abilities, persistently compulsive rituals, and
resistance to change (Paluszny, 1979). It is esti-
mated that of the almost ten million mentally or emo-
tionally ill children in the United States, over two
million are autistic (Greenfeld, 1979). Since the
origins of autism are uncertain and since clinicians
as well as researchers hold conflicting opinions
about this syndrome, much confusion has surrounded
it. The confusion stems directly from varying attempts
to uncover the origins of the disease, to probe its
effects, and to reach a consensus on how to treat it.

*Author and date
are placed
within
parentheses.*

Townsend 2

*The thesis is the last sentence of the opening paragraph.*

From the morass of arguments, however, one truth emerges with unyielding clarity: if the behavioral sciences, in cooperation with medicine, are ever to find the key to this mysterious disease and eventually to cure its victims, government funding will have to become far more generous in its support than it has been to date.

The knowledge presently available about childhood autism is meager and mostly still in the theoretical stage. A multitude of different voices offer opinions on what <u>may</u> cause this childhood syndrome.

*Since the author is mentioned, only the year and date appear within parentheses.*

According to Paluszny (1979, p. 53), the two most prevalent theories focus on the abnormalities of the psychological environment and on the structural or biochemical abnormalities of the child.

It was once commonly thought that autism resulted directly from the parents' psychological attitude toward their child. Researchers reasoned that certain highly intelligent and self-motivated people, who really did not want children, caused the child to retreat into himself. It was believed that the child could actually feel that he was unwanted and thus he withdrew into the autistic way of life. However,

Townsend 3

Bettelheim (1967) refuted this theory in his book The

Empty Fortress and claimed instead that infantile

autism stemmed from the infant's experiences during

three critical stages of life. According to

Bettelheim, the first stage occurs in the first

six months of life, during which time if a child is

unable to form social relationships because of disap-

pointment from parents, he withdraws into himself.

The next stage occurs during the six to nine months

period, when a child, if ignored when trying to reach

out to others, may retreat into himself. The third

and final stage is during the eighteen months to two

years period, when the child becomes aware that he

cannot master the world physically or intellectually

and again simply withdraws. During each of these

stages the child's desperate strivings to develop the

self have been blocked or interrupted; thus the child

becomes passive toward others and retreats into him-

self (Bettelheim, 1967, pp. 46-47).

*For easier
retrieval, the
paper provides
the pages
covered by this
summary of
Bettelheim's
ideas.*

Another popular but totally different view is

that autism is a structural or biochemical abnormal-

ity. Numerous studies have flooded research in this

area. One significant such study (Wing, 1976) found

Townsend 4

evidence of retardation in the autistic child's

height, weight, and bone age measurement. This study

explained that a maturation lag during the embryonic

development of the fetus contributed to the retarda-

tion and subsequent autism.

A new theory, presently being studied by Abraham

Weizman, an Israeli psychiatrist at the Geha

psychiatric hospital, is that a brain lesion may be at

fault. Bartusiak (1983) reports that Weizman reached

this conclusion after finding that autistic patients

were allergic to a brain protein. The allergic reac-

tion may be caused when a brain injury made the body

sensitive to its own nerve tissue (Bartusiak, p. 40).

Research on autism is greatly hampered by the

lack of clinical data on the children studied and by

the lack of repetition of experiments. Additionally,

there are many technical difficulties associated with

data contribution and analysis in both the psycho-

logical. . . .

*The date (in
parentheses)
follows the
author.*

*Titles of articles
are not set off by
quotation marks.*

*The volume,
underlined and
in Arabic
numberals,
precedes the
page numbers.*

*Titles of books
are underlined
but only the
initial letter is
capitalized.*

Townsend 5

Reference List

Bartusiak, M.  (1983).  Autism allergy.  Omni, 5,

35–42.

Bettelheim, B.  (1967).  The empty fortress.  New

York: Free Press.

Coffey, H. S., and Wiener, L. L.  (1967).  Group

treatment of autistic children.  Englewood

Cliffs, NJ: Prentice–Hall.

Graziano, A.  (1974).  Child without tomorrow.  New

York: Pergamon Press.

Greenfeld, J.  (1970).  A child called Noah.  New York:

Holt, Rinehart and Winston.

Paluszny, M.  (1970).  Autism.  New York: Syracuse

University Press.

Restak, R.  (1982).  Islands of genius.  Science, 3,

62–68.

Wing, L.  (1976).  Early childhood autism.  New York:

Pergamon Press.

# 11c

## Excerpt from a student paper using footnotes

1

Elaine Spray

Professor McCuen    } double space

English 101

21 June 1984

} double space

Rasputin's Other Side

} quadruple space

*The title is centered on the page.*

The name ''Rasputin'' commonly evokes an image of unbridled, mystical evil.  Few figures have fared as badly in the popular memory.  In the 1930s, Lionel Barrymore transfixed thousands of movie goers by portraying him as a devilish, licentious, mysteriously hypnotic fiend.  Hundreds of books published since his murder in 1916 unanimously agree on his subhumanity.  Reporting a libel trial involving one of his murderers, United Press International in 1965 casually labeled Rasputin as mad, filthy, licentious, semiliterate, fiendish, and lecherous.[1]  After six

} Quadruple space

[1] Dave Smith, ''Casting a Light on Rasputin's Shadow,'' <u>Los Angeles Times</u> 9 June 1977, pt. 4: 1.    } Single space

*An elevated numeral refers to footnote at bottom of page.*

*For proper footnote format, see Fig 7-2, p. 107.*

Spray 2

decades of being judged a demoniacal libertine,
Rasputin now deserves to be viewed from another point
of view——as a man who was intensely religious, who
passionately desired peace, and who was deeply devoted to his family and friends.

Who was this so-called horror incarnate, this
man named Rasputin?  It is said that on the night of
January 23, 1871, a great meteor seared a flaming path
across the skies of Western Siberia, hurtled in an arc
over the little village of Pokrovskoye and, at the
very moment that the meteor burned out, a seven-pound
boy was born to Anna Egorovina, the wife of Efim
Akovlevich, a Russian farmer.  The couple named the
boy, their second son, Grigori Efimovich Rasputin.

What was this second son, this Rasputin, really
like?  ''Supporters called him a spiritual leader and
claimed he had healing powers; detractors called him
a satyr and said his depraved faithful were merely in
awe of his sexual endowments.''[2]  By the time he was
lured to his death in the basement of a St. Petersburg
palace in 1916, he had aroused such intensities of

[2] Smith 10.

231

Spray 3

hatred and loyalty that the facts of his early life
had already become blurred and sensationalized. Was
it true that at sixteen he was already known in his
part of Siberia as an insatiable lecher whom peasant
girls found irresistible? Did he really have gifts
of second sight and prophecy that cast a glow of religious mysticism around him? Did he disappear from
his home for long intervals, wandering about Russia
and even to the Holy Land as a starets, a pilgrim of
God, who was simultaneously a drunkard and an insatiable womanizer? Was he really a member of the sec-
ret group known as the Khlysts, outlawed fanatics who
held frenzied rites in torch-lit forest glades that
ended with wild, naked dancing and savage sexual
orgies?[3] In these suppositions——all part of the
legend before Rasputin died——there is probably a ker-
nel of truth. Nevertheless, this remarkable man also
had another side, which has been entirely overlooked.

To begin with, Rasputin was a man of intense religious feelings. His love for Christianity bordered

[3] E. M. Halliday, ''Rasputin Reconsidered,''
Horizon 8.4 (1967): 83.

Spray 4

on an exuberant devotion.  Maria Rasputin writes of

her father's simple peasant faith:

*Long quotations
are introduced
by a colon,
double spaced,
and indented 10
spaces.
Double space
before and after
the long
quotation.*

> Entering his fourteenth year, my father
>
> passed into a new phase, his interest,
>
> which soon blossomed into a preoccupation,
>
> with religion.  Although he had not learned
>
> to read or write, skills he did not acquire
>
> until his later years in St. Petersburg, he
>
> possessed a remarkable memory and could
>
> quote whole passages of the Bible from hav-
>
> ing heard them read but once.[4]

Rasputin, moreover, taught a lofty, sublime sort

of Christianity at a time when numerous Russian

politicians were becoming suspicious of the Christian

religion.  Yet his teaching, made all the more simple

by his innate ability to explain abstruse theological

concepts in plain, comprehensible terms, was under-

stood by even the most common plowman.  Consequently,

as Christian Orthodoxy waned among those in power,

Rasputin was sought out more and more by the ordinary

---

[4] Maria Rasputin and Patte Barham, Rasputin: The
Man Behind the Myth (Englewood Cliffs: Prentice,
1977) 15.

Spray 5

man in the street.[5]

When Rasputin moved to St. Petersburg, he could often be found breakfasting with women followers and talking about God and the ''Mysterious resurrection.'' Suddenly, he would begin to hum softly to himself. Soon the voices around him would join in, swelling to a loud chorus. Then he would leap from his seat and dance around the room.[6] This religious demonstration was accepted as sincere by the Russian peasants, with whom dance had remained a rite of primitive religious activity, assuming the character of prayer.[7]

But a vital religion was not the only positive force in the life of Rasputin. He also expressed a passionate desire for peace and political harmony in Russia. For instance, he was deeply concerned about the Russian underdog. He had vague notions of turning over the landowners' land to the peasants, and the

[5] M. Rasputin 130.

[6] René Fülöp-Miller, Rasputin: The Holy Devil (New York: Garden City Pub., 1927) 268.

[7] Fülöp-Miller 267.

Spray 6

landowners' mansions to the educational system.  He

was genuinely concerned about the treatment of Jews

and other minorities.  His concern about the poor

people caused many to liken him. . . .

Spray 7

*"Works Cited"*
*appears on a*
*separate page.*

Works Cited

Fülöp–Miller, René.  Rasputin: The Holy Devil.  New

York: Garden City Pub., 1927.

Halliday, E. M.  ''Rasputin Reconsidered.''  Horizon

8.4 (1967):.81–87.

Massie, Robert K.  Nicholas and Alexandra.  New York:

Atheneum, 1972.

Pares, Bernard.  The Fall of the Russian Monarchy.

New York: Knopf, 1939.

Rasputin, Maria, and Patte Barham.  Rasputin: The Man

Behind the Myth.  Englewood Cliffs: Prentice,

1977.

Smith, Dave.  ''Casting a Light on Rasputin's Shad–

ow.''  Los Angeles Times 9 June 1977, pt. 4: 1,

10, 11.

# Appendix
# General and Specialized References

**A** A list of general references

**B** A list of specialized references

# A

## A list of general references

In the library, information on a topic is likely to be scattered throughout numerous books, magazines, journals, and newspapers, most of which are indexed by general references. Some of these references alphabetically index by author and subject the contents of magazines, journals, and newspapers; others similarly index the titles and contents of available books. The experienced researcher, therefore, usually begins a search for information by consulting the general references.

This section will systematically list the common general references and give a brief description of the information they provide. General references index information available on a variety of subjects; specialized references, which we will cover later, index information on specific subjects.

### A-1   Books that list other books

The best efforts of ambitious bibliographers cannot produce an exhaustive list of all books in print. Nevertheless, many important references catalog the publication of books. The following are the prime sources for information about existing books.

#### a.  Books currently in print

*Books in Print.* 6 vols. New York: Bowker, 1948–present. Published annually in October and updated by annual supplements in April. Also available on online database through Dialog Information Services, Inc., as are the other titles listed below.

*Paperbound Books in Print.* 3 vols. New York: Bowker, 1955–present. Published biannually in April and October.

*Publishers' Trade List Annual.* 5 vols. New York: Bowker, 1873–present. A compilation of yearly catalogs from almost all important publishers, arranged alphabetically by the publisher's name.

*Subject Guide to Books in Print.* 3 vols. New York: Bowker, 1957–present. Published annually and simultaneously with *Books in Print.* A companion volume to the three titles listed above.

#### b.  Bibliographies

*Bibliographic Index.* New York: Wilson, 1937–present. A subject list of bibliographies in English and foreign languages, published in paper issues in April and August and in an annual bound volume in December.

*Cumulative Book Index*. New York: Wilson, 1898–present. The *CBI*, an international bibliography of all books published anywhere in the world in English, is published each month, except August, in paper issues; there is also an annual bound cumulative volume.

The catalogs of national libraries come closer to achieving bibliographical universality than do any other listings. The most pertinent source for the purposes of most students is:

U.S. Library of Congress. *A Catalog of Books Represented by Library of Congress Printed Cards Issued to July 31, 1942*. 167 vols. Ann Arbor, Mich.: Edwards, 1942–46. Supplemented by catalogs covering 1942–54 and superseded by *An Author Index Representing Pre-1956 Holdings of American Libraries Reported to the National Union Catalog in the Library of Congress*. 16 vols. London: Mansell, 1981. Publications of all kinds are listed and represent the holdings of about 900 North American Research Libraries; and *National Union Catalog, Pre-1956 Imprints*. Past volumes of the *National Union Catalog*, as well as those currently being printed, are also available on microfiche.

For information on the existence of incunabula—books published before 1500—see:

Goff, Frederick R. *Incunabula in American Libraries: A Third Census of Fifteenth-Century Books Recorded in North American Collections*. New York: Bibliographical Soc. of America, 1964. Locates close to 50,000 copies of incunabula in America.

———. A supplement. New York: Bibliographical Society of America, 1972.

Lower-division students, although not likely to do research based on incunabula, should know that catalogs exist for them.

*c. Book industry journals*

*Publishers Weekly*. New York: Bowker, 1872–present. Weekly record of all books published in the United States. Semiannual issues announce books scheduled for publication.

*d. Books about book reviews*

*Book Review Digest*. New York: Wilson, 1905–present. Lists reviews and prints digests of reviews from 81 American, Canadian, and English periodicals.

*Book Review Index*. Detroit: Gale, 1965–present. Lists reviews from many more periodicals than *Book Review Digest*, but does not print excerpts of reviews.

## A-2   Books about periodicals and newspapers

Since its beginning in the eighteenth century, periodical literature—whether published weekly, monthly, seasonally, in serial form, or simply on a random basis—has become increasingly important for scholarly research, especially in any field where up-to-date knowledge is important. Millions of articles are published annually in periodicals, making a complete indexing of them nearly impossible. However, the following books about periodicals are especially useful:

### a.   Periodical and newspaper directories

These list the titles, addresses, and subscription prices, plus other valuable information, of periodicals and newspapers. Among the most useful are:

*Ayers' Directory of Newspapers and Periodicals.* Philadelphia: Ayers, 1880–present. An annual list of newspapers and periodicals currently published in the United States. The directory is organized by states and cities, and contains indexes.

*Editor and Publisher International Year Book.* New York: Editor and Publisher, 1920–present. Provides information on newspapers, advertising agencies, syndicates, and other aspects of journalism in the United States, Canada, and other countries.

*Standard Periodical Directory.* 8th ed. 1983–84. New York: Oxbridge, 1982. Issued annually, this directory is an exhaustive list of periodicals published in the United States and Canada; arranged by subjects.

*Ulrich's International Periodicals Directory.* 2 vols. New York: Bowker, 1932–present. Published annually. Supplemented by *Ulrich's Quarterly*, which provides continuous, up-to-date information on new titles, title changes, and cessations.

### b.   Union lists of periodicals and newspapers

Union lists catalog and record the collection of periodical and newspaper titles available in various libraries. The following are among the most prominent union lists:

*American Newspapers, 1821–1936: A Union List of Files Available in the United States and Canada.* New York: Wilson, 1937. Catalogs files of newspapers in nearly 6,000 libraries and private locations.

Brigham, Clarence S. *History and Bibliography of American Newspapers, 1690–1820.* 2 vols. Worcester: American Antiquarian Soc., 1947. The best list for anyone trying to find articles in old newspapers.

*New Serial Titles: A Union List of Serials Commencing Publication after Dec. 31, 1949*. Washington: U.S. Library of Congress, 1953–present. Keeps track of periodicals published after 1949.

*New Serial Titles, 1950–1970, Subject Guide*. 2 vols. New York: Bowker, 1975.

*Union List of Serials in Libraries of the United States and Canada*. 3d ed. 5 vols. New York: Wilson, 1956. First published in 1927, this list does an extraordinarily thorough job of locating files of periodicals in nearly a thousand libraries. It is supplemented by *New Serial Titles*, listed above.


*c. Indexes of periodicals and newspapers*

An index lists topics of magazine and newspaper articles alphabetically, giving each article's title and page number. William Poole, working with a group of dedicated librarians, compiled the first American index in 1802. His index is still in use, along with the following:

*Index of U.S. Government Publications*. Chicago: Infordata International, 1973–present.

*Index of the Times, 1906–present*. London: The Times, 1907–present. A thorough bimonthly index to the *London Times*.

*Magazine Index*. Menlo Park: Information Access Corp., 1977. This is a computer-output-microfilm index to more than 370 popular periodical titles, including all 185 titles indexed by the *Readers' Guide to Periodical Literature*. It is cumulated and updated each month on a roll of 16 mm. microfilm and provides easy access on a microfilm reader to a wealth of current periodical literature through subject, author, and title entries.

*National Newspaper Index*. Menlo Park: Information Access Co., 1979–present. An index to the *Christian Science Monitor, New York Times*, and *Wall Street Journal* produced on microfilm and continuously updated.

*News Bank, Inc.* New Canaan: 1982–present. An index to newspapers from over 100 cities in the United States. Articles on current topics of interest to students and other researchers are reproduced on microfiche each month, accompanied by a monthly printed index.

*Newspaper Index*. Wooster: Newspaper Indexing Center, Bell & Howell, 1972–present. Indexes articles in the *Chicago Tribune, Los Angeles Times, New Orleans Times-Picayune*, and *Washington Post*. Includes subject and author indexes.

*New York Times Index*. New York: The Times, 1913–present. A semimonthly and annual index to the daily issues of the *New York Times*.

*Poole's Index to Periodical Literature, 1802–1907.* 7 vols. Boston: Houghton, 1882–1907. This pioneer work indexes close to 600,000 articles in American and English periodicals. Contains a subject index only.

*Readers' Guide to Periodical Literature,* 1900–present. New York: Wilson, 1905–present. Published semimonthly (monthly in July and August) with quarterly and annual cumulations, this is by far the most popular periodical index, and has been widely used to research sources for thousands of freshman and graduate papers. Contains an author, subject, and title index to about 160 notable magazines in numerous fields.

*Social Sciences and Humanities Index.* New York: Wilson, 1965–present. Replaced *International Index.* New York: Wilson, 1907–1965. Since 1974, published separately as *Social Sciences Index* and *Humanities Index.* These two indexes are excellent guides to essays in scholarly journals such as *The New England Quarterly* or *Political Science Quarterly*; they both index articles by subject and author.

*On-line Access to Wilson Indexes*: The H. W. Wilson Company, publisher of *The Readers' Guide to Periodical Literature, General Science Index, Humanities Index, Social Sciences Index* and other periodical indexes, has announced on-line access to its subject indexes to be available in late fall of 1984. This access will provide the researcher with the ability to search and retrieve data quickly from these valuable index databases.

### A-3  Books about general knowledge: encyclopedias

The encyclopedia is the czar of general knowledge books, and a good place to begin research on almost any topic. While they seldom treat a topic in minute detail, encyclopedias are usually factual and current. Among the best are:

*Academic American Encyclopedia.* 21 vols. Danbury: Grolier, 1983. This new entry in the encyclopedia field emphasizes brevity and clearness in short articles, as well as current coverage, over the long, detailed, and scholarly articles found in its well-established competitors.

*Collier's Encyclopedia.* 24 vols. New York: Macmillan, 1983. Emphasizes modern subjects, but also contains information that supplements high school and college courses. Aims at covering every major area in simplified terms. Includes an index volume.

*Columbia Encyclopedia.* 1983 ed. New York: Columbia UP, 1983. An excellent one-volume encyclopedia.

*Encyclopaedia Britannica.* 15th ed. 30 vols. Chicago: Encyclopaedia Britannica, 1983. The latest and most up-to-date of the multivolume general encyclopedias. Published originally in England, it retains a British flavor. It is the oldest and most distinguished of the encyclopedias, emphasizing both old and new areas of knowledge. The newest edition comes with elaborate index volumes that synopsize information on various topics.

*Encyclopedia Americana.* 30 vols. Danbury: Grolier, 1983. A scholarly encyclopedia consisting mainly of short entries, with complex subjects treated in longer articles. Excellent coverage of science and technology. Includes an index volume.

*The Lincoln Library of Essential Information.* Columbus: Frontier Press, 1982–present. Available in one or two volumes. Revised with every printing to remain current. Divided into twelve areas of knowledge that are subdivided into sections. Contains numerous charts, graphs, and tables. Includes an index.

*The Random House Encyclopedia.* New rev. ed. New York: Random, 1983. The emphasis is on color illustrations in this one-volume encyclopedia.

## A-4 Books about words: dictionaries

Dictionaries were originally invented to list equivalent words in two languages, as an aid in translating from one language to another. Sumerian clay tablets listed Sumerian words beside their Semitic-Assyrian equivalents. By the seventeenth century, *dictionary* had come to mean a book that explained the etymology, pronunciation, meaning, and correct usage of words. Nathan Bailey's *Universal Etymological English Dictionary,* published in 1721, was the first comprehensive dictionary in English.

Modern dictionaries provide information about the meaning, derivation, spelling, and syllabication of words, and about linguistic study, synonyms, antonyms, rhymes, slang, colloquialisms, dialect, and usage. Unabridged dictionaries contain complete information about words; abridged dictionaries condense their information so as to be more portable.

### a. General dictionaries

*The American Heritage Dictionary.* Ed. William Morris. 2nd college ed. Boston: Houghton: 1982. The distinguishing feature of this dictionary is that it was written in conjunction with a usage panel and a long list of consultants in specialized areas. It is greatly praised for its excellent photography and illustrations.

*Oxford American Dictionary.* Comp. Eugene Ehrlich et al. Oxford: Oxford University Press, 1980.

*Oxford English Dictionary.* 13 vols. Oxford: Clarendon, 1888–1933. A monumental work that presents the historical development of each word in the English language since 1150, illustrating correct usage with varied quotations. An updated version has been in preparation since 1972.

―――. A Supplement to the *Oxford English Dictionary*. Ed. R. W. Burchfield. Oxford: Clarendon, 1972–.

*The Random House College Dictionary*. Rev. ed. Ed. in chief, Jess Stein. New York: Random, 1982.

*The Random House Dictionary of the English Language*. Ed. in chief, Jess Stein. Unabridged ed. New York: Random, 1981.

*Webster's New World Dictionary of the American Language*. 2d college ed. Ed. in chief, David B. Guralnik. New York: Simon, 1982.

*Webster's Ninth New Collegiate Dictionary*. Springfield: Merriam, 1983.

*Webster's Third New International Dictionary of the English Language*. 3d ed. Springfield: Merriam, 1961.


## b. Specialized dictionaries

Craigie, William A., and James R. Hulbert. *Dictionary of American English on Historical Principles*. 4 vols. Chicago: U of Chicago P, 1936–44. A valuable work for anyone interested in how English developed during Colonial times. Indicates which words originated in America and which in other English-speaking countries. Excludes dialect and slang.

Partridge, Eric. *A Dictionary of Slang and Unconventional English*. 7th ed. New York: Macmillan, 1970. Published as two volumes in one book, this is a comprehensive treatment of both old and current slang.

Wentworth, Harold, and Stuart B. Flexner. *Dictionary of American Slang*. 2nd supplemented ed. New York: Crowell, 1975. A comprehensive listing of current American slang, including taboo words and expressions.


## c. Dictionaries of synonyms and antonyms

Dictionaries of synonyms and antonyms list the equivalents and opposites of words. Among the best-known are the following:

Lewis, Norman. *The New Roget's Thesaurus of the English Language in Dictionary Form*. New York: Putnam's, 1978.

Roget, Peter M. *Roget's International Thesaurus*. 4th ed. New York: Crowell, 1977. This is the modern edition of a work first published in 1852. It is the most popular of all thesauruses.

*Roget's II: The New Thesaurus*, by the editors of the American Heritage Dictionary. Boston: Houghton, 1980.

Urdang, Lawrence. *A Basic Dictionary of Synonyms and Antonyms*. New York: Lodestar, 1979.

*Webster's New Dictionary of Synonyms*. Springfield: Merriam, 1978. Illustrates usage with quotations from old as well as new authors.

## A-5  Books about places

Reference books on places come in two forms: atlases and gazetteers.

### a.  Atlases

An atlas is a bound collection of maps, sometimes amplified by charts, tables, and plates, that provide information about the people, culture, and economy of the countries covered. Among the most comprehensive and useful atlases are the following:

*Hammond Standard World Atlas: Latest and Most Authentic Geographical and Statistical Information*. Deluxe ed. Maplewood: Hammond, 1983.

*Maps on File*. Ed. Lester A. Sobel. New York: Facts on File, 1981. A loose-leaf service.

National Geographic Society. Cartographic Division. *National Geographic Atlas of the World*. 5th ed. Washington: National Geographic Soc., 1981. Maps are arranged according to region and are accompanied by brief gazetteer information.

*The Prentice-Hall Great International Atlas*. Englewood Cliffs: Prentice, 1981.

Rand McNally & Company. *Commercial Atlas and Marketing Guide*. 114th ed. Chicago: Rand, 1983.

———. *The New International Atlas*. Chicago: Rand, 1982.

*The Times Atlas of the Oceans*. Ed. Alastair Couper. New York: Van Nostrand, 1983.

### b.  Gazetteers

A gazetteer is a geographical dictionary or index that gives basic information about the most important regions, cities, and natural features of the countries of the world. The pronunciation and even syllabication of names are often included with this information. A gazetteer is consulted when a researcher wants information about the legal or political status of a country, its location, and its most important features. The best general gazetteers are:

*The International Geographic Encyclopedia & Atlas.* Boston: Houghton, 1979.

Stamp, Dudley, and Audrey N. Clarke. *A Glossary of Geographical Terms.* 3rd ed. New York: Longman, 1979.

*Webster's New Geographical Dictionary.* Rev. ed. Springfield: Merriam, 1980. Locates and identifies about 47,000 countries, regions, cities, and geographical features. Based on 1970 census figures.

### A-6 Books about people

Biographical reference books are classifiable under four primary headings: (a) general biography about deceased persons, (b) general biography about living persons, (c) national biography about deceased persons, and (d) national biography about living persons.

*a. General biography about deceased persons*

*Chambers's Biographical Dictionary.* Ed. J. O. Thorne. Rev. ed. New York: St. Martin's, 1977. Gives close to 10,000 sketches of famous people of the past.

*The McGraw-Hill Encyclopedia of World Biography.* 12 vols. New York: McGraw, 1973. Geared to high school and college students, this work is a compilation of 5,000 biographies of individuals famous throughout history. Each entry includes a bibliography. An index is also provided.

*New Century Cyclopedia of Names.* Rev ed. 3 vols. New York: Appleton, 1954. Identifies all kinds of important proper names, including the names of persons, places, events, and characters from literature and opera.

Slocum, Robert B. *Biographical Dictionaries and Related Works.* Detroit: Gale, 1967. (Supplement, 1972; 2nd supplement, 1978). This work lists all major biographical works—over 8,000 titles. An excellent place to begin finding biographies. International in scope.

*Webster's Biographical Dictionary.* Springfield: Merriam, 1980. A dictionary of the names of noteworthy persons, with pronunciations and concise biographies. Covers heads of state and other high officials.

*b. General biography about living persons*

*Biographical Books, 1950–1980.* New York: Bowker, 1980.

*Biography and Genealogy Master Index*. 2nd ed. Detroit: Gale, 1980.

—————. 1981–82 supplement. 3 vols. Detroit: Gale, 1982.

—————. 1983 supplement. 2 vols. Detroit: Gale, 1983.

*International Who's Who*. London: Europe, 1935–present. Issued annually. Provides sketches of important people all over the world.

*Who's Who in the World*. 6th ed. Chicago: Marquis, 1983.

## c. National biography of deceased persons (American and British)

*Appleton's Cyclopedia of American Biography*. 7 vols. New York: Appleton, 1887–1900. Contains full-length articles, often illustrated with portraits and autographs of the biographee. Includes people from Mexico and South America.

*Concise Dictionary of American Biography*. 3rd ed., complete to 1960. New York: Scribner's, 1980. A one-volume edition of the large set.

*Dictionary of American Biography*. 21 vols. New York: Scribner's, 1928–37. A 1944–73 supplement in 3 vols. This is considered the most scholarly of all American biographical dictionaries. An abbreviated edition is available which provides in one volume all the essential facts contained in the larger work.

*Dictionary of American Biography*. Supplements. New York: Scribner's, 1944–present.

*Dictionary of National Biography*. 22 vols. London: Smith, Elder, 1908–09. Supplements 1–7, 7 vols. London: Smith, Elder, 1912–71. Condensed edition: *The Concise Dictionary of National Biography from the Beginnings to 1950*. 2 vols. London: Oxford UP, 1948–61. The large edition provides rounded-out sketches of notable inhabitants (now deceased) of Great Britain and the colonies from the earliest historical period to contemporary times. The small edition contains abstracts of the large edition.

*Dictionary of National Biography*. Supplements. New York: Macmillan, 1912–present.

*The Dictionary of National Biography. The Concise Dictionary*. 2 vols. London: Oxford UP, 1982–present.

*Encyclopedia of American Biography*. Ed. John A. Garraty. New York: Harper, 1974.

*Notable American Women, 1607–1950: A Biographical Dictionary*. Ed. Edward T. James. Cambridge: Belknap Press of Harvard University,

1971. One of the best scholarly biographies to focus on the work of the prominent women in America.

*Notable American Women—The Modern Period: A Biographical Dictionary.* Ed. Barbara Sicherman et al. Cambridge: Belknap Press of Harvard University, 1980.

*Who Was Who.* 1897/1915–. New York: St. Martin's, 1920–present. A companion volume to *Who's Who.*

*Who Was Who in America.* 1897/1942–. Chicago: Marquis, 1943–present. A companion volume of *Who's Who in America.*

### d.  *National biography about living persons (American and British)*

*National Cyclopaedia of American Biography.* 59 vols. New York: White, 1892–present. A monumental work that presents a complete political, social, commercial, and industrial history in the form of sketches of individuals, deceased and living, who helped shape America.

*Who's Who.* London: Black, 1849–present. Annual. Contains excellent biographical sketches of prominent people living in Great Britain and its commonwealth.

*Who's Who in America.* Chicago: Marquis, 1899–present. Editions come out biennially. Identifies people of special prominence in all lines of work. Supplemented by *Who's Who in the East, Who's Who in the Midwest, Who's Who in the South and Southwest,* and *Who's Who in the West*—all issued by the Marquis Company.

*Who's Who of American Women.* Chicago: Marquis, 1958–present. Biennial. A dictionary identifying American women who have made a name for themselves in various fields.

Many countries and professions now publish "Who's Who" rosters. Examples are:

> *Prominent Personalities in the USSR*
> *Who's Who in Australia*
> *Who's Who in China*
> *Who's Who in France*
> *Who's Who in Germany*
> *Who's Who in Italy*
> *Who's Who in the U.A.R. and the Near East*
>
> *Who's Who in American Art*
> *Who's Who in American Politics*
> *Who's Who in Engineering*
> *Who's Who in Finance and Industry*
> *Who's Who in Government*

*Who's Who in Music*
*Who's Who in Soviet Social Sciences, Humanities, Art and Government*

Ask your librarian about other areas in which a "Who's Who" roster is published. There are too many to include here.

### e. Indexes to biographical material

Two general and most useful indexes to biographical material in books and magazines need to be mentioned.

*Biography Almanac: A Comprehensive Reference Guide to More Than 23,000 Famous and Infamous Newsmakers from Biblical Times to the Present*. Ed. Susan L. Stetler. 2nd ed. Detroit: Gale, 1983. Supplements are issued between editions.

*Biography Index*. New York: Wilson, 1974–present. Issued quarterly with annual and triennial cumulations. This work is a guide to articles and books written about all kinds of persons, living and dead.

### A-7 Books about government publications

The work of government bureaucracy is reflected in government publications—in speeches, annual reports, transcripts of hearings, statistical charts, regulations, and research results. Government publications—issued at public expense by thousands of federal, state, and local agencies—are available to the general public. The United States Government Printing Office (GPO), an independent body of the legislative branch of government, is the chief government printer. Distribution of materials is supervised by the Superintendent of Public Documents, from whom government publications may be ordered. The most important references that list government publications are:

Ames, John G. *Comprehensive Index to the Publications of the United States Government, 1881–1893*. 2 vols. Washington: GPO, 1905. This work will help a researcher locate government information by subject or title. Covers a decade of post-Civil War times.

*Guide to U.S. Government Publications* (microform). McLean: Documents Index, 1981–present.

Poore, Benjamin P. *A Descriptive Catalogue of the Government Publications of the United States, September 5, 1774–March 4, 1881*. Washington: GPO, 1885. A 1,392-page compilation, invaluable to the student of early U.S. history.

U.S. Superintendent of Documents. *Catalog of the Public Documents of Congress and of All Departments of the Government of the United States for the Period March 4, 1893–December 31, 1940*. 25 vols. Washington: GPO,

1896–1945. A comprehensive summary of materials published before 1945.

————. *Checklist of United States Public Documents, 1789–1909.* 3rd ed. Washington: GPO, 1911. Covers 120 years of government printing.

————. *Monthly Catalog of United States Government Publications.* Washington: GPO, 1895–present. A monthly catalog, arranged by departments, that provides up-to-date listings of publications from all governmental agencies. Includes subject indexes.

————. *U.S. Government Books; Publications for Sale by the U.S. Government Printing Office.* Washington: GPO, 1982–present. Published quarterly. A catalog of almost 1,000 popular government publications arranged by subject. Replaces the GPO's *Price Lists.*

In addition to these catalogs, the GPO offers a subscription service on microfiche titled *Publications Reference File.* The *PRF* lists all publications and subscriptions currently for sale by the GPO. The *PRF* is also available online through Dialog Information Retrieval Service.

Several guides exist that orient the novice to the vast number of government publications. Among the best are the following:

Congressional Information Service. *Directory of Government Documents: Collections of Librarians.* 3rd ed. Washington: 1981.

*Government Reference Books.* Littleton: Libraries Unlimited, 1970–Present. Biennial.

Morehead, Joe. *Introduction to United States Public Documents.* 3rd ed. Littleton: Libraries Unlimited, 1983.

U.S. Library of Congress. *Monthly Checklist of State Publications.* Washington: GPO, 1910–present. Keeps track of all state government publications received by the Library of Congress.

Foreign countries have their own government printing offices, catalogs, and indexes.

### A-8 Books about nonbooks

In recent years nonbooks have become a necessary and distinctive part of library collections. Materials stored on microform, film, and sound recordings is often valuable to researchers.

*a. General guides*

*Educators Guide.* Series. Randolph: Educators Progress Service. Includes guides to free films, filmstrips, and tapes.

*Media Review Digest*. Ann Arbor: Pierian, 1973–present. An annual guide to reviews and descriptions of nonbook material.

National Information Center for Educational Media. *NICEM Media Indexes*. Los Angeles: National Information Center, University of Southern California.

*The Video Source Book*. 5th ed. Syosset: National Video Clearinghouse, 1979–present.

### b. Indexes of microforms

Bell & Howell, Micro Photo Division. *Publications on Microfiche*. Wooster: Bell & Howell. Revised annually.

*Dissertation Abstracts International*. Ann Arbor: Xerox University Microfilms, 1969–present. Issued monthly, this index lists and provides copies of dissertations produced in all major American universities.

*Guide to Microforms in Print*. Westport: Microform Review, 1978–present. Annual.

Microfilming Corporation of America. *Catalog*. Sanford: Microfilming Corporation of America. Revised annually. Includes oral history collections.

*Serials in Microform*. Ann Arbor: UMI. Revised annually.

U.S. Library of Congress. Union Catalog Division. *Newspapers on Microfilm*. Washington: 1948–67. Superseded by: U.S. Library of Congress. Catalog Publication Division. *Newspapers in Microform: United States* and *Newspapers in Microform: Foreign Countries*. Washington: 1972–present.

### c. Guides to films

*The American Film Institute Catalog of Motion Pictures: Feature Films, 1921–1930*. 2 vols. Ed. Kenneth W. Munden. New York: Bowker, 1971.

*The American Film Institute Catalog of Motion Pictures: Feature Films, 1961–1970*. 2 vols. Ed. Richard Krafsur. New York: Bowker, 1976.

*American Folklore Films and Videotapes: A Catalog*. Comp. Center for Southern Folklore. 2 vols. New York: Bowker, 1982.

*Educational Film Locator of the University Film Centers and R. R. Bowker*. 2nd ed. New York: Bowker, 1980.

*Film Programmer's Guide to 16 mm. Rentals*. Ed. Kathleen Weaver. 3rd ed. Albany: Reel Research, 1980.

Media Referral Service. *The Film File, 1983–84*. Minneapolis: Media Referral Service, 1983. A reference and selection guide to over 20,000 films and videocassettes available from over 100 U.S. and Canadian producers and distributors.

Limbacher, James L. *Feature Films on 8 mm., 16mm., and Videotape: A Directory of Feature Films Available for Rental, Sale, and Lease in the United States and Canada*. 7th ed. New York: Bowker, 1982.

National Information Center for Educational Media. *Index to 16 mm. Educational Films*. 4 vols. New York: McGraw, 1977. Lists films recorded since 1958 in the Master Data Bank at the University of Southern California.

U.S. Library of Congress. *Library of Congress Catalog—Motion Pictures and Filmstrips, 1953–1957, 1958–1962, 1963–1967, 1968–1972*. Ann Arbor: Edwards, 1958–1973. Superseded by *Films and Other Materials for Projection*. Washington: 1974–present.

Film catalogs are available from many colleges and universities, such as the following:
    Indiana University
    Kent State University
    Pennsylvania State University
    UCLA
    University of Illinois
    University of Iowa
    University of Minnesota
    University of Southern California

### d.  Guides to sound recordings: music

*American Music Recordings: a Discography of 20th Century U.S. Composers*. Ed. Carol J. Oja. New York: Inst. for Studies in American Music, Brooklyn College, City University of New York, 1982.

Cohn, Arthur. *Recorded Classical Music: A Critical Guide to Compositions and Performances*. New York: Schirmer, 1981.

Gray, Michael. *Bibliography of Discographies*. 3 vols. New York: Bowker, 1977–1983.

Rodgers and Hammerstein Archives of Recorded Sound. *Dictionary Catalog of the Rodgers and Hammerstein Archives of Recorded Sound*. 15 vols. Boston: Hall, 1981.

Rust, Brian, *Jazz Records, 1897–1942: Fourth Revised and Enlarged Edition*. 2 vols. New Rochelle: Arlington, 1978.

*Schwann Record and Tape Guide*. Boston: Schwann, 1973–present. Monthly.

U.S. Library of Congress. *Library of Congress Catalog—Music and Phonorecords, 1953–72.* Washington: Library of Congress, 1953–1972. Superseded by: *Music, Books on Music, and Sound Recordings.* Washington: Library of Congress, 1973–present.

*e. Guides to sound recordings: speeches, readings, and oral history*

Columbia University. Oral History Research Office. *The Oral History Collection of Columbia University.* Ed. Elizabeth Mason and Louis M. Starr. New York, 1979.

*Dictionary of Oral History Programs in the United States.* Ed. Patsy A. Cook. Sanford: N.C.: Microfilming Corp. of America, 1982.

Hoffman, Herbert H., and Rita L. Hoffman. *International Index to Recorded Poetry.* New York: Wilson, 1984.

U.S. Library of Congress. General Reference and Bibliography Division. *Literary Recordings: A Checklist of the Archive of Recorded Poetry and Literature in the Library of Congress.* Washington: Library of Congress, 1966.

# B

## A list of specialized references

A specialized reference classifies and indexes information about a specific subject. Depending on the complexity of your topic, you may or may not have to consult a specialized reference. Numerous such references exist, covering virtually all subjects. A complete listing of all the specialized references on popular subjects such as history and literature, for instance, would easily fill an entire book.

Specialized references are listed here in alphabetical order by subject, and are restricted to those most likely to be useful in student research.

### B-1   Art

*American Art Dictionary.* New York: Bowker, 1952–present. Revised biennially. Gives information about museums and other art organizations in the United States and Canada.

Appel, Marsha C. *Illustration Index.* 4th ed. Metuchen: Scarecrow, 1980.

*Art Books, 1876–1949.* New York: Bowker, 1981. A bibliography of more than 20,000 books in the fine and applied arts.

*Art Books, 1950–1979.* New York: Bowker, 1980. A bibliography of more than 36,000 books on the visual arts.

*Art Index.* New York: Wilson, 1929–present. Provides an index to archeology, architecture, history of art, fine arts, industrial design, interior decorating, landscape design, photography, and other subjects connected with art.

*Encyclopedia of World Art.* 15 vols. New York: McGraw, 1959–68. Supplement. New York: McGraw, 1983.

*Fine and Applied Arts Terms Index.* Ed. Laurence Urdang. Detroit: Gale, 1983.

Kleinbauer, W. Eugene, and Thomas P. Slavens. *Research Guide to the History of Western Art.* Chicago: American Library Assn., 1982.

*Larousse Dictionary of Painters.* New York: Larousse, 1981.

*Macmillan Encyclopedia of Architects.* Ed. in chief, Adolph K. Placzek. 4 vols. New York: Free Press, 1982.

Osborne, Harold, ed. *The Oxford Companion to Art.* Oxford: Clarendon, 1970. An excellent source for the stduent who wants to become familiar with the fundamentals of art and art history.

*Oxford Companion to Twentieth Century Art.* Ed. Harold Osborne. Oxford: Oxford UP, 1981.

*The Pelican History of Art.* Baltimore: Penguin, 1953–present. In progress. When completed, this 50-volume expansive work will cover all aspects of art—ancient, medieval, and modern. Includes architecture.

*Print Index: A Guide to Reproductions.* Comp. Pamela J. Parry and Kathe Chipman. Westport: Greenwood, 1983.

*The Random House Library of Painting and Sculpture.* Gen. ed., David Piper. 4 vols. New York: Random, 1981.

ART JOURNALS

> *Art Bulletin*
> *Art in America*
> *Art International*
> *Artforum*
> *Studio International*

## B-2  Business and economics

*AMA Management Handbook.* William K. Fallo, ed. 2nd ed. New York: American Management Assn., 1983.

Auld, Douglas, et al. *The American Dictionary of Economics.* New York: Facts on File, 1983.

Banki, Ivan S. *Dictionary of Administration and Management*. Los Angeles: Systems Research Institute, 1981.

*The Basic Business Library: Core Resources*. Ed. Bernard S. Schlessinger. Phoenix: Oryx, 1983.

Berenyi, John. *The Modern American Business Dictionary, Including an Appendix of Business Slang*. New York: Quill, 1982.

*Business Firms Master Index*. Ed. Donna Wood. Detroit: Gale, 1983–present.

*Business Periodicals Index*. New York: Wilson, 1959–present.

*Economic Handbook of the World*. Ed. Arthur S. Banks et al. New York: McGraw-Hill, 1981.

*Economics Information Resources Directory*. Detroit: Gale, 1984–present.

*Encyclopedia of American Economic History: Studies of the Principal Movements and Ideas*. Ed. Glenn Porter. 3 vols. New York: Scribner's, 1980.

*Encyclopedia of Banking and Finance*. Ed. F. K. Garcia. 8th ed. Boston: Bankers Publishing, 1983.

*Encyclopedia of Business Information Sources*. 5th ed. Ed. Paul Wasserman et al. Detroit: Gale, 1983.

*Encyclopedia of Economics*. Ed. in chief, Douglas Greenwald. New York: McGraw, 1982.

*Encyclopedia of Investments*. Ed. Marshall E. Blume and Jack P. Friedman. Boston: Warren, 1982.

*Encyclopedia of Management*. Ed. Carl Heyel, 3rd ed. New York: Van Nostrand, 1982.

*Moody's Handbook of Common Stocks*. New York: Moody's, 1965–present.

Nemmers, Edwin E. *Dictionary of Economics and Business*. 4th ed. Totowa: Rothman, 1978.

Rosenberg, Jerry M. *Dictionary of Banking and Finance*. New York: Wiley, 1982.

Shapiro, Irving J. *Dictionary of Marketing Terms*. 4th ed. Totowa: Littlefield, 1981.

*Standard & Poor's Register of Corporations, Directors, and Executives*. New York: Standard & Poor's, 1975–present.

*Thomas Register of American Manufacturers and Thomas Register Catalog File*. New York: Thomas, 190?–present.

U.S. Bureau of Labor Statistics. *Handbook of Labor Statistics*. Washington: GPO, 1926–present.

*World Directory of Multinational Enterprises*. 2nd ed. 3 vols. New York: Macmillan, 1982–1983.

BUSINESS AND ECONOMICS JOURNALS AND NEWSPAPERS

> *Administrative Management*
> *American Economic Review*
> *Barron's; National Business and Financial Weekly*
> *Business Week*
> *Dun's Business Month*
> *Forbes*
> *Fortune*
> *Harvard Business Review*
> *Los Angeles Business Journal*
> *Monthly Labor Review*
> *Nation's Business*
> *Wall Street Journal*

## B-3 Dance

*American Dance Directory*. New York: Assoc. of American Dance Companies, 1980–present.

Balanchine, George, and Francis Mason. *Balanchine's Complete Stories of the Great Ballets*. New York: Doubleday, 1977.

*Bibliographic Guide to Dance*. Boston: Hall, 1975–present.

Grant, Gail. *Technical Manual and Dictionary of Classical Ballet*. 3rd rev. ed. New York: Dover, 1982.

Kersley, Leo, and Janet Sinclair. *A Dictionary of Ballet Terms*. New York: Da Capo, 1979.

Koegler, Horst. *The Concise Oxford Dictionary of Ballet*. 2nd ed. New York: Oxford UP, 1982.

*The Lively Arts Information Directory: A Guide to the Fields of Music, Dance, Theatre, Film, Radio and Television, for the United States and Canada*. Ed. Steven R. Wasserman. Detroit: Gale, 1982.

DANCE JOURNALS

> *Ballet News*
> *Ballet Review*
> *Dancemagazine*
> *Dance Research Journal*

## B-4 Ecology

*Air Pollution Abstracts*. Research Triangle Park: Air Pollution Technical Information Center of the Environmental Protection Agency, 1970–present. Issued quarterly, these abstracts from periodicals, books, and reports cover the entire field of air pollution and air standards.

*California Environmental Directory: A Guide to Organizations and Resources*. Claremont: Center for California Public Affairs, 1977–present.

Counihan, Martin. *A Dictionary of Energy*. Boston: Routledge, 1981.

Dorf, Richard C. *The Energy Factbook*. New York: McGraw, 1981.

*Energy Bibliography and Index*. Comp. Texas A&M University Libraries. 4 vols. Houston: Gulf Pub. Co., 1979–81.

*Environment Abstracts*. New York: Environment Information Center, 1971–present.

*Environment Abstracts Annual*. New York: Environment Information Center, 1980–present.

*Environment Index*. New York: Environment Information Center, 1971–present.

*Environment Information Access*. New York: Environment Information Center, 1971–present. Issued monthly, this handbook is a guide to information from periodicals, reports, government hearings, and conferences dealing with environmental problems or facts.

Gottlieb, Richard, ed. *The Solar Energy Directory*. New York: Wilson, 1982.

Hunt, V. Daniel. *Solar Energy Dictionary*. New York: Industrial, 1982.

Kut, David. *Dictionary of Applied Energy Conservation*. New York: Nichols, 1982.

*McGraw-Hill Encyclopedia of Energy*. 2nd ed. Ed. Sybil P. Parker. New York: McGraw, 1981.

*Pollution Abstracts*. Washington: Cambridge Scientific Abstracts, 1970–present.

Schultz, Marilyn S., and Vivian L. Kasen. *Encyclopedia of Community Planning and Environmental Protection*. New York: Facts on File, 1983.

*Solar Energy Handbook*. Ed. in chief, Jan F. Kreider. New York: McGraw, 1981.

*SYNERJY: A Dictionary of Energy Alternatives*. New York: SYNERJY, 1974–present. Semiannual; July issues are cumulative for one year.

Tver, David F. *Dictionary of Dangerous Pollutants, Ecology, and Environment.* New York: Industrial, 1981.

Weber, R. David. *Energy Information Guide.* Santa Barbara: ABC-Clio, 1982–83.

*World Dictionary of Energy Information.* Comp. Cambridge Information and Research Services; ed. Christopher Swain and Andrew Buckley. New York: Facts on File, 1981–present.

ECOLOGY JOURNALS

*Conservationist*
*Environment*
*Environmental Ethics*
*International Wildlife*
*Sierra Club Bulletin*
*Solar Age*

## B-5   Education

*An Annotated Bibliography of ERIC Bibliographies, 1966–1980.* Comp. Joseph G. Drazan. Westport: Greenwood, 1982.

Beach, Mark. *A Subject Bibliography of the History of American Higher Education.* Westport: 1984.

*Bibliographic Guide to Education.* Boston: Hall, 1978–present. Published annually.

*The College Blue Book.* New York: Macmillan, 1923–present.

*Current Index to Journals in Education.* Phoenix: Oryx, 1969–present.

Dejnozka, Edward L., and David E. Kapel. *American Educator's Encyclopedia.* Westport: Greenwood, 1982.

*Directory of American Scholars: A Biographical Directory.* New York: Bowker, 1942–present.

*Education Abstracts.* 16 vols. Fulton: Education Clearing House, 1936–present. Contains abstracts of most of the important essays in the field of education.

*Education Index.* New York: Wilson, 1929–present.

*Education Literature, 1907–1932.* 12 vols. New York: Garland, 1979.

*Encyclopedia of Educational Research.* 5th ed. 4 vols. New York: Free Press, 1982.

*International Yearbook of Education.* Paris: UNESCO, 1948–present.

Rowntree, Derek. *A Dictionary of Education*. Totowa: Barnes, 1981.

U.S. Office of Education. *Bibliography of Research Studies in Education, 1926–1940*. 4 vols. Detroit: Gale, 1974.

*Yearbook of Higher Education*. Chicago: Marquis, 1969–present.

EDUCATION JOURNALS

> *American Educational Research Journal*
> *American Journal of Education*
> *Change*
> *Chronicle of Higher Education*
> *Educational Computer Magazine*
> *Journal of Educational Research*
> *Journal of Higher Education*
> *Phi Delta Kappan*

## B-6   Ethnic studies

*a. General*

*Harvard Encyclopedia of American Ethnic Groups*. Cambridge: Belknap Press of Harvard University, 1980.

Lankevich, George J. *Ethnic America, 1978–1980: Updating the Ethnic Chronology Series*. Dobbs Ferry: Oceana, 1981.

ETHNIC STUDIES (GENERAL) JOURNALS

> *Ethnic and Racial Studies*
> *Ethnic Forum*
> *Journal of Ethnic Studies*

*b. American Indian Studies*

Brumble, H. David, III. *An Annotated Bibliography of American Indian and Eskimo Autobiographies*. Lincoln: U of Nebraska P, 1981.

Dockstader, Frederick J. *Great North American Indians: Profiles in Life and Leadership*. New York: Van Nostrand, 1977.

Hirschfelder, Arlene B., et al. *Guide to Research on North American Indians*. Chicago: American Library Assn., 1983.

AMERICAN INDIAN JOURNALS

> *Akwesasne Notes*
> *American Indian Culture and Research Journal*
> *Amerian Indian Quarterly*

*c. Asian American Studies*

Chen, Jack. *The Chinese of America.* New York: Harper: 1980.

Melendy, Henry Brett. *Asians in America: Filipinos, Koreans, and East Indians.* New York: Hippocrene, 1981.

Montero, Darrel. *Vietnamese Americans: Patterns of Resettlement and Socioeconomic Adaptation in the United States.* Boulder: Westview, 1979.

Wilson, Robert A., and Bill Hosokawa. *East to America: A History of the Japanese in the United States.* New York: Quill, 1980.

ASIAN AMERICAN JOURNALS

*Amerasia Journal*
*Bridge*
*East Wind*
*Jade*


*d. Black American Studies*

*Bibliographic Guide to Black Studies.* Boston: Hall, 1975–present.

*Dictionary of American Negro Biography.* Ed. Rayford W. Logan and Michael R. Winston. New York: Norton, 1982.

*Encyclopedia of Black America.* Ed. W. Augustus Low. New York: McGraw, 1981.

Hughes, Langston, et al. *A Pictorial History of Black Americans.* 5th rev. ed. New York: Crown, 1983.

*In Black and White: A Guide to Magazine Articles, Newspaper Articles, and Books Concerning More than 15,000 Black Individuals and Groups.* 3rd ed. 2 vols. Ed. Mary M. Spradling. Detroit: Gale, 1980.

*Index to Periodicals By and About Blacks.* Boston: Hall, 1950–present.

Matney, William C. *America's Black Population: A Statistical View, 1970–1982.* Washington: U.S. Dept. of Commerce, Bureau of the Census, 1983.

Newman, Richard. *Black Index: Afro-Americans in Selected Periodicals, 1907–1949.* New York: Garland, 1981.

Ploski, Harry A., and James Williams, comps. and eds. *The Negro Almanac: A Reference Work on the Afro-American.* 4th ed. New York: Wiley, 1983.

*Who's Who Among Black Americans.* Northbrook: Who's Who Among Black Americans, 1976–present.

BLACK AMERICAN JOURNALS

> *Ebony*
> *Journal of Black Studies*
> *Journal of Negro History*
> *Phylon*

## e. Hispanic American Studies

Foster, David W., ed. *Sourcebook of Hispanic Culture in the United States*. Chicago: American Library Assn., 1983.

*Hispanic American Periodicals Index*. Los Angeles: UCLA Latin American Center Publications, 1974–present.

*Hispanics in the United States: A New Social Agenda*. Ed. Pastora San Juan Cafferty and William McCready. New Brunswick: Transaction, 1984.

Meier, Matt S., and Feliciano Rivera. *Dictionary of Mexican American History*. Westport: Greenwood, 1981.

Newton, Frank, et al. *Hispanic Mental Health Research: A Reference Guide*. Berkeley: U of California P, 1982. Updates are available on-line through the Spanish Speaking Mental Health Research Center, UCLA.

*¿Quien Sabe?: A Preliminary List of Chicano Reference Materials*. Comp. and ed. Francisco Garcia-Ayvens et al. Los Angeles: Chicago Studies Research Center Publications, University of California, 1981.

HISPANIC AMERICAN JOURNALS

> *Agenda: A Journal of Hispanic Issues*
> *Aztlan*
> *Hispanic Link Weekly Report*

### B-7 High Technology

This term encompasses the dynamic and fast-changing areas of computers, computer-aided design and manufacture, electronics, robotics, and artificial intelligence.

*Advances in Automation and Robotics: Theory and Application*. Ed. George N. Sardis. Greenwich; JAI, 1984–present.

*Advances in Computer-Aided Engineering Design*. Ed. Alberto Sangiovanni-Vincentelli. Greenwich: JAI, 1984–present.

Besant, C. B. *Computer-aided Design and Manufacture*. New York: Wiley, 1983.

*Bowker/Bantam 1984 Complete Sourcebook of Personal Computing.* New York: Bowker/Bantam, 1983.

*Computer Literature Index.* Phoenix: Applied Computer Research, 1971–present.

*Dictionary of Computing.* General ed.: Valerie Illingworth. Oxford: Oxford UP, 1983.

*Electronics Engineers' Handbook.* Ed. in chief, Donald G. Fink. 2nd ed. New York: McGraw, 1982.

Feigenbaum, Edward A., and Pamela McCordnek. *The Fifth Generation: Artificial Intelligence and Japan's Challenge to the World.* Reading: Addison, 1983.

Graham, John. *Dictionary of Telecommunications.* New York: Facts on File, 1983.

Grayson, M., ed. *Encyclopedia of Semiconductor Technology.* New York: Wiley, 1983.

Juvinall, Robert C. *Fundamentals of Machine Component Design.* New York: Wiley, 1983.

*McGraw-Hill Computer Handbook.* Ed. in chief, Harry Helins. New York: McGraw, 1983.

*McGraw-Hill Encyclopedia of Electronics and Computers.* Ed. in chief, Sybil P. Parker. New York: McGraw, 1983.

Markus, John. *Modern Electronics Circuits Reference Manual.* New York: McGraw, 1980.

Ralston, Anthony, ed. *Encyclopedia of Computer Science and Engineering.* 2nd ed. New York: Van Nostrand, 1983.

*Robotics and Automation Today: A Guide to Information Sources.* New York: Bowker, 1984.

Rosenberg, J. M. *Dictionary of Computers, Data Processing and Telecommunications.* New York: Wiley, 1983.

*Solar Index: The Guide to Alternate Energy Periodicals.* Denver, 1981–present.

HIGH TECHNOLOGY JOURNALS

*Artificial Intelligence*
*Byte*
*Computers and People*
*Datamation*

*High Technology*
*Kiloband*
*Microcomputing*
*Robotics Age*

## B-8   History

*a. World history*

*Annual Register of World Events: A Review of the Year.* London: Longmans, 1758–present.

Boorstin, Daniel J. *The Discoverers: A History of Man's Search to Know His World and Himself.* New York: Random, 1983.

*Cambridge Ancient History.* 3rd ed. London: Cambridge UP, 1970–present.

*Cambridge Mediaeval History.* Planned by J. B. Bury; ed. H. M. Gwatkin and J. P. Whitney. 2nd ed. Cambridge: Cambridge UP, 1975–present.

*Dictionary of the Middle Ages.* New York: Scribner's, 1982.

Durant, Will and Ariel. *The Story of Civilization.* 11 vols. New York: Simon, 1935–1975. A monumental work of enduring worth, written in an extremely readable style.

Garraty, John, and Peter Gay, eds. *The Columbia History of the World.* New York: Dorset, 1981.

*Historical Abstracts: Bibliography of the World's Periodical Literature, 1775 to present.* Santa Barbara: ABC-Clio, 1955–present.

*Magill's History Annual: Book of 19––.* Englewood Cliffs: Salem, 1983–present.

*The New Cambridge Modern History.* 14 vols. Cambridge: Cambridge UP, 1957–79.

*Rand McNally Historical Atlas of the World.* General ed., R. I. Moore. Chicago: Rand, 1981.

*World Almanac Dictionary of Dates.* Ed. Laurence Urdang. New York: Longman, 1982.

WORLD HISTORY JOURNALS

*Current History*
*History Today*
*Journal of Modern History*
*Journal of the History of Ideas*

## b. American history

*Album of American History.* Rev. ed. 3 vols. New York: Scribner's, 1969. *Supplement I, 1968–1983.* New York: Scribner's, 1984.

*America: History and Life.* Santa Barbara: ABC-Clio, 1964–present. A periodical index for U.S. and Canadian history.

*The Annals of America.* 20 vols. Chicago: Encyclopaedia Britannica, 1968–74.

*Atlas of American History.* Rev. ed. Ed. Kenneth T. Jackson. New York: Scribner's, 1978.

*The Civil War Almanac.* Exec. ed., John S. Bowman. New York: Facts on File, 1983.

Commager, Henry S. *Documents of American History.* 8th ed. New York: Appleton, 1968. A collection of the most famous documents relating to American history from 1492 to contemporary times.

*Dictionary of American History.* Rev. ed. 8 vols. New York: Scribner's, 1976.

*Encyclopedia of American History.* 6th ed. Ed. Richard B. Morris. New York: Harper, 1982.

Johnson, Thomas H. *The Oxford Companion to American History.* Oxford: Oxford UP, 1966. Contains nearly 5,000 brief summaries of significant events, places, and people in American history.

Kane, Joseph N. *Facts About the Presidents.* 4th ed. New York: Wilson, 1981.

Kane, Joseph N. *Famous First Facts.* 4th ed. New York: Wilson, 1981.

*Liberty's Women.* Ed. Robert McHenry. Springfield: Merriam, 1980.

*The Presidents: A Reference History.* Ed. Henry F. Graff, New York: Scribner's, 1984.

*Writings on American History, 1981–82: A Subject Bibliography of Articles.* Ed. Cecilia J. Dadian. Washington: American Historical Assn., 1983.

AMERICAN HISTORY JOURNALS

*American Historical Review*
*American History Illustrated*
*Journal of American History*

## B-9  Literature

## a. General

*Abstracts of English Studies.* Urbana: National Council of Teachers of English, 1958–present.

Bartlett, John. *Familiar Quotations*. 15th ed. Ed. Emily M. Beck. Boston: Little, 1980.

*Columbia Dictionary of Modern European Literature*. 2nd ed. Gen. eds., Jean-Albert Bede and William B. Edgerton. New York: Columbia UP, 1980.

*Contemporary Authors: The International Bio-Bibliographical Guide to Current Authors and Their Works*. Detroit: Gale, 1962–present.

*Contemporary Literary Criticism*. Detroit: Gale, 1973–present.

*Dictionary of Literary Biography*. Editorial director, Matthew J. Bruccoli. Detroit: Gale, 1978–present.

*Encyclopedia of World Literature in the 20th Century*. 2nd rev. ed. 4 vols. Ed. Leonard G. Klein. Detroit: Gale, 1981–present.

*Essay and General Literature Index*. New York: Wilson, 1934–present.

*Fiction Catalog*. 10th ed. New York: Wilson, 1980. An annotated bibliography of over 5,000 fiction works. Supplemented by four annual paperbound issues (1981–1984).

*Fiction, 1876–1982: A Bibliography of United States Editions*. New York: Bowker, 1983.

*Granger's Index to Poetry*. 7th ed. New York: Columbia UP, 1982.

Grant, Michael. *Greek and Latin Authors: 800 B.C.–A.D. 1000*. New York: Wilson, 1980.

Holman, C. Hugh. *A Handbook to Literature*. 4th ed. Indianapolis: Bobbs, 1980.

Kuntz, Joseph M., and Nancy C. Martinez. *Poetry Explication: A Checklist of Interpretation Since 1925 of British and American Poems, Past and Present*. Boston: Hall, 1980.

*McGraw-Hill Encyclopedia of World Drama: An International Reference Work in 5 Volumes*. Ed. in chief, Stanley Hochman. 2nd ed. 5 vols. New York: McGraw, 1984.

*Magill's Bibliography of Literary Criticism. Selected Sources for the Study of More Than 2,500 Outstanding Works of Western Literature*. Ed. Frank N. Magill. 4 vols. Englewood Cliffs: Salem Press, 1979.

Modern Language Association of America. *MLA International Bibliography of Books and Articles on the Modern Languages and Literatures*. New York: 1921–present.

*The Oxford Companion to the Theatre*. 4th ed. Ed. Phyllis Hartnoll. Fair Lawn: Oxford UP, 1984.

*Play Index*. New York: Wilson, 1953–1983. Thousands of plays published in the last 34 years are indexed in a series of six volumes; the first volume covers the years 1949–1952.

Vinson, James, ed. *Contemporary Dramatics*. 3rd ed. New York: St. Martin's, 1982.

Wakeman, John, ed. *World Authors: 1950–1970*. New York: Wilson, 1975.

## b. American literature

*American Literary Scholarship: An Annual*. Durham, N.C.: Duke UP, 1963– present.

*American Women Writers: A Critical Reference Guide from Colonial Times to the Present*. Ed. Lina Mainiero. 4 vols. New York: Ungar, 1979–82.

*Bibliography of American Literature*. Comp. Jacob Blanck for the Bibliographical Society of America. New Haven: Yale UP, 1955–.

Dickinson, A. T., Jr. *American Historical Fiction*. 4th ed. Metuchen: Scarecrow, 1981.

Gerhardstein, Virginia B. *Dickinson's American Historical Fiction*. 4th ed. Metuchen: Scarecrow, 1981.

Hart, James D. *The Oxford Companion to American Literature*. 5th ed. New York: Oxford UP, 1983.

Karl, Frederick R. *American Fictions 1940/1980: A Comprehensive History and Critical Evaluation*. New York: Harper, 1983.

*Literary History of the United States*. Ed. Robert E. Spiller et al. 4th ed., rev. 2 vols. New York: Macmillan, 1974.

*Modern American Literature*. Comp. and ed. Dorothy Nyren et al. 4th ed. 4 vols. New York: Ungar, 1969–76.

## c. British literature

*Annals of English Literature, 1475–1950: the Principal Publications of Each Year*. 2nd ed. Oxford: Clarendon, 1961.

*British Writers*. Gen. ed., Ian Scott-Kilvert. 8 vols. New York: Scribner's, 1979–1983.

*The Cambridge Guide to English Literature*. Comp. Michael Stapleton. Cambridge: Cambridge UP, 1983.

*Cambridge History of English Literature*. 15 vols. Cambridge: Cambridge UP, 1919–30. Considered the most authoritative history of English literature. The volumes represent a collaboration by specialists, and cover all aspects of English literary history from its beginnings to the twentieth century. The work is updated by: Sampson, George. *Concise Cambridge History of English Literature*. 3rd ed. Cambridge: Cambridge UP, 1970.

*English Novel Explication. Supplement*. Hamden: Shoestring, 1976–present. Supplements *English Novel Explication: Criticism to 1972*. Comp. Helen H. Palmer and Anne J. Dyson.

Evans, Gareth L., and Barbara. *The Shakespeare Companion*. New York: Scribner's, 1978.

Gillie, Christopher. *A Companion to British Literature*. Detroit: Gale, 1980.

*Modern British Literature*. Comp. and ed. Ruth Z. Templeton et al. 4 vols. New York: Ungar, 1966–75. A part of the Library of Literary Criticism series.

*The New Cambridge Bibliography of English Literature*. Ed. George Watson. 5 vols. Cambridge: Cambridge UP, 1969–77.

*Oxford Companion to English Literature*. Comp. and ed. Sir Paul Harvey. 4th ed., rev. by Dorothy Eagle. Oxford: Clarendon, 1967.

*Oxford History of English Literature*. Oxford: Clarendon, 1945–present.

LITERATURE JOURNALS

> *American Literature*
> *Journal of Modern Literature*
> *Modern Fiction*
> *PMLA*
> *Speculum*
> *World Literature Today*

## B-10 Music

*ASCAP Biographical Dictionary*. Comp. for the American Society of Composers, Authors and Publishers by Jaques Cattell Press. 4th ed. New York: Bowker, 1980.

Bordman, Gerald. *American Musical Theatre: A Chronicle*. New York: Oxford UP, 1978.

Burbank, Richard. *Twentieth Century Music*. New York: Facts on File, 1983.

Cohen, Aaron I. *International Encyclopedia of Women Composers*. New York: Bowker, 1981.

*Dictionary of Music*. Ed. Alan Isaacs and Elizabeth Martin. New York: Facts on File, 1983.

Ewen, David, comp. and ed. *Great Composers: 1300–1900*. New York: Wilson, 1983.

Hamilton, Clive U. *The Great Symphonies*. New York: Facts on File, 1983.

*Music Index*. Detroit: Information Service, 1949–present. An important periodical index.

*The Musician's Guide: The Directory of the World of Music*. New York: Music Information Service, 1954–present.

*The New Grove Dictionary of Music and Musicians*. Ed. Stanley Sadie. 20 vols. London: Macmillan, 1980. A comprehensive reference source on all aspects of music since 1450.

*New Kobbe's Complete Opera Book*. Ed. and rev. the Earl of Harewood. New York: Putnam's, 1976.

*The New Oxford Companion to Music*. 2 vols. Gen. ed.: Denis Arnold. New York: Oxford University Press, 1983.

*New Oxford History of Music*. Ed. J. A. Westrup et al. 10 vols. New York: Oxford University Press, 1954–present.

*Popular Music: An Annotated Index of American Popular Songs*. 8 vols. Ed. Nat Shapiro and Bruce Pollock. New York: Adrian Press, 1964–present.

*Resources of American Music History: A Directory of Source Materials from Colonial Times to World War II*. D. W. Krumme et al. Urbana: U of Illinois P, 1981.

Salem, James M. *A Guide to Critical Reviews, Part 2: The Musical, 1909–1974*. 2nd ed. Metuchen: Scarecrow, 1976.

MUSIC JOURNALS

> *High Fidelity*
> *Music Journal*
> *Musical Quarterly*
> *Opera News*

## B-11 Mythology/Classics

Bell, Robert S. *Dictionary of Classical Mythology: Symbols, Attributes, and Associations*. Santa Barbara: ABC-Clio, 1982.

*Brewer's Dictionary of Phrase and Fable*. Rev. ed. Ed. Ivor H. Evans. London: Cassell, 1981.

*Bulfinch's Mythology*. New York: Avenel, 1978.

Campbell, Joseph. *Historical Atlas of World Mythology*. Vol 1. San Francisco: Harper & Row, 1983–. Other volumes in preparation.

Cotterell, Arthur. *A Dictionary of World Mythology*. 1st American ed. New York: Putnam's, 1980.

Frazer, Sir James. *The Golden Bough*. 1981 ed. New York: Avenel, 1981.

Gwinup, Thomas, and Fidelia Dickinson. *Greek and Roman Authors: A Checklist of Criticism*. 2nd ed. Metuchen: Scarecrow, 1982.

Hamilton, Edith. *Mythology*. Boston: Little, 1942.

*The Oxford Classical Dictionary*. 2nd ed. Ed. N. G. Hammond and H. H. Scullard. Oxford: Oxford UP, 1970.

Stassinopoulous, Arianna, and Roloff Beny. *The Gods of Greece*. New York: Abrams, 1983.

MYTHOLOGY/CLASSICS JOURNALS

> *Classical Bulletin*
> *Classical Journal*
> *Classical Quarterly*
> *Greece and Rome*

## B-12  Philosophy

Copleston, Frederick. *History of Philosophy*. 9 vols. Westminster: Newman Bookshop, 1946–75.

De George, Richard T. *The Philosopher's Guide: To Sources, Research Tools, Professional Life, and Related Fields*. Lawrence: Regents Press of Kansas, 1980.

*The Encyclopedia of Philosophy*. Ed. in chief: Paul Edwards. 8 vols in 4. Rpt. New York: Macmillan, 1972.

*Handbook of World Philosophy: Contemporary Developments Since 1945*. Westport: Greenwood, 1980.

*Philosopher's Index: An International Index to Philosophical Periodicals*. Bowling Green: Bowling Green University, 1967–present.

Reese, William L. *Dictionary of Philosophy and Religion: Eastern and Western Thought*. Atlantic Highlands: Humanities, 1980.

Tice, Terrence N., and Thomas P. Slavens. *Research Guide to Philosophy*. Chicago: American Library Assn., 1983.

*World Philosophy: Essay-Reviews of 225 Major Works*. Ed. Frank N. Magill. 5 vols. Englewood Cliffs, Salem, 1982.

PHILOSOPHY JOURNALS
> *Ethics*
> *International Philosophical Quarterly*
> *Journal of Philosophy*
> *Mind*

## B-13  Psychology

*Annual Review of Psychology.* Stanford: Annual Reviews, 1950–present.

Campbell, Robert J. *Psychiatric Dictionary.* 5th ed. New York: Oxford UP, 1981.

*Child Development Abstracts and Bibliography.* Chicago: U of Chicago P, 1927–present.

*The Encyclopedic Dictionary of Psychology.* Ed. Rom Harre and Roger Lamb. Cambridge: MIT Press, 1983.

*Longman Dictionary of Psychology and Psychiatry.* Ed. in chief, Robert M. Goldenson. New York: Longman, 1983.

*Mental Measurements Yearbook.* Highland Park: Gryphon, 1938–present.

*Psychoanalysis, Psychology, and Literature: A Bibliography.* Ed. Norman Kiell. 2nd ed. 2 vols. Metuchen: Scarecrow, 1982.

*Psychological Abstracts.* Washington: American Psychological Assn., 1927–present.

*Tests in Print III: An Index to Tests, Test Reviews, and the Literature on Specific Tests.* Ed. James V. Mitchell, Jr. Lincoln: U of Nebraska P, 1983.

PSYCHOLOGY JOURNALS

> *American Journal of Psychiatry*
> *American Psychologist*
> *Behavioral Science*
> *Journal of Abnormal Psychology*
> *Journal of Applied Psychology*
> *Journal of Comparative and Physiological Psychology*
> *Journal of Social Psychology*
> *Psychological Bulletin*
> *Psychology of Women Quarterly*

## B-14  Religion

Brunkow, Robert deV., ed. *Religion and Society in North America: An Annotated Bibliography.* Santa Barbara: ABC-Clio, 1983.

Dell, David J., et al. *Guide to Hindu Religion.* Boston: Hall, 1981.

**B**

*Eerdmans' Handbook to the World's Religions*. Consulting eds., R. Pierce Beaver et al. Grand Rapids: Eerdmans, 1982.

*Encyclopaedia Judaica*. 16 vols. New York: Macmillan, 1972. Offers comprehensive information on all aspects of Judaism in the twentieth century.

Hardon, John A. *Modern Catholic Dictionary*. New York: Doubleday, 1980.

*The International Standard Bible Encyclopedia*. Rev. ed. Gen. ed., Geoffrey W. Bromley. Grand Rapids: Eerdmans, 1979–present.

Mead, Frank S. *Handbook of Denominations in the United States*. New 7th ed. Nashville: Abingdon, 1980.

Melton, J. Gordon. *The Encyclopedia of American Religions*. 2 vols. Wilmington: McGrath, 1978.

*New Catholic Encyclopedia*. 17 vols. New York: McGraw, 1967–79.

*Oxford Dictionary of the Christian Church*. 2nd ed. Ed. F. L. Cross and E. A. Livingstone. London: Oxford UP, 1974.

*Religion Index One: Peridicals*. Chicago: American Theological Library Assn., 1949–present.

Reynolds, Frank E., et al. *Guide to Buddhist Religion*. Boston: Hall, 1981.

Runes, Dagobert D. *Dictionary of Judaism*. Secaucus: Citadel, 1981.

*Sacred Books of the East*. 50 vols. Ed. Max Muller. Livingston: Orient Book Distributors, 1977–80.

Stutley, Margaret and James. *Harper's Dictionary of Hinduism: Its Mythology, Folklore, Philosophy, Literature, and History*. 1st U.S. ed. San Francisco: Harper, 1984.

*Who's Who in Religion*. Chicago: Marquis Who's Who, 1975/76–present.

Wilson, John F., and Thomas P. Slavens. *Research Guide to Religious Studies*. Chicago: American Library Assn., 1982.

*Yearbook of American and Canadian Churches*. Nashville: Abingdon, 1973–present.

RELIGION JOURNALS

*America*
*Christian Century*
*Christianity Today*
*Journal of Biblical Literature*
*Journal of Jewish Studies*

*Journal of Religion*
*Journal of the American Academy of Religion*
*Theology Today*

## B-15 Science

*Album of Science.* Gen. ed., I. B. Cohen. New York: Scribner's, 1978–present.

*American Men and Women of Science.* 15th ed. 7 vols. New York: Bowker, 1982. This database is now available for on-line searching through Dialog Information Services, Inc., and Bibliographic Retrieval Services, Inc.

*Annual Review of Information Science and Technology.* New York: Wiley, 1966–present. An annual review of developments in science and technology.

*Dictionary of Scientific Biography.* Ed. in chief, Charles C. Gillispie. 8 vols. New York: Scribner's, 1970–1981.

*Dictionary of the History of Science.* Ed. and introd. William F. Bynum et al. Princeton: Princeton UP, 1981.

*General Science Index.* New York: Wilson, 1978–present. A periodical index to scientific information in 87 English-language periodicals.

*McGraw-Hill Dictionary of Scientific and Technical Terms.* Ed. in chief, Sybil P. Parker. 3rd ed. New York: McGraw, 1984.

*McGraw-Hill Encyclopedia of Science and Technology.* 5th ed. 15 vols. New York: McGraw, 1982.

*McGraw-Hill Modern Scientists and Engineers.* 3 vols. New York: McGraw, 1980.

*McGraw-Hill Yearbook of Science and Technology.* New York: McGraw, 1962–present. Supplements to the *McGraw-Hill Encyclopedia of Science and Technology.*

*Pure and Applied Science Books.* 6 vols. New York: Bowker, 1982. A comprehensive bibliography of more than 220,000 books in science and technology.

*The Weather Almanac.* Ed. James A. Ruffner and Frank E. Bair. 3rd ed. Detroit: Gale, 1981.

*Van Nostrand's Scientific Encyclopedia.* 6th ed. 2 vols. Ed. Douglas M. Considine. New York: Van Nostrand, 1983.

SCIENCE JOURNALS

*American Scientist*
*Bulletin of the Atomic Scientists*
*Nature*
*New Scientist*
*Science*
*Science 84*
*Scientific American*

## B-16   Social sciences

Andrews, Frank M., et al. *A Guide for Selecting Statistical Techniques for Analyzing Social Science Data.* 2nd ed. Ann Arbor: Inst. for Soc. Res., University of Michigan, 1981.

*Contemporary Issues Criticism.* Ed. Dedria Bryfonski. Detroit: Gale, 1982–present.

*Encyclopaedia of the Social Sciences.* 8 vols. New York: Macmillan, 1937.

International Committee for Social Science Information and Documentation. *International Bibliography of the Social Sciences: Sociology.* New York: Methuen, 1983.

*International Encyclopedia of Population.* Ed. John A. Ross. 2 vols. New York: Free Press, 1982.

*International Encyclopedia of the Social Sciences.* 17 vols. New York: Macmillan, 1968. *Biographical Supplement.* New York: Macmillan, 1979.

*A New Dictionary of the Social Sciences.* Ed. G. Duncan Mitchell. 2nd ed. Hawthorne: Aldine, 1980.

*Public Affairs Information Service Bulletin.* New York: Public Affairs Info. Serv., 1905–present.

*Social Sciences Citation Index.* Philadelphia: Inst. for Scientific Information, 1973–present.

*Social Sciences Index.* New York: Wilson, 1974–present. An important periodical index.

*Sociological Abstracts.* San Diego: Sociological Abstracts, 1953–present.

SOCIAL SCIENCE JOURNALS

*American Behavioral Scientist*
*American Journal of Sociology*
*International Social Sciences Journal*
*Journal of Social Issues*

*Social Forces*
*Social Research*
*Society*

## B-17  Women

Borenstein, Audrey. *Older Women in 20th-Century America: A Selected Annotated Bibliography*. New York: Garland, 1982.

Fishburn, Katherine. *Women in Popular Culture: A Reference Guide*. Westport: Greenwood, 1982.

*The Index/Directory of Women's Media*. Washington, DC: Women's Inst. for Freedom of the Press, 1975–present.

*The International Dictionary of Women's Biography*. Comp. and ed. Jennifer S. Uglow. New York: Continuum, 1982.

James, Edward T., and Janet W., eds. *Notable American Women, 1607–1950: A Biographical Dictionary*. 3 vols. Cambridge: Belknap Press of Harvard University, 1971. Begins with an introductory survey of the history of women in America, then presents signed articles analyzing the lives of American women who have made notable contributions in various fields.

McGlen, Nancy E., and Karen O'Connor. *Women's Rights; The Struggle for Equality in the Nineteenth and Twentieth Centuries*. New York: Praeger, 1983. A history of the women's movement since 1848. Also provides a synthesis of the literature from recent years.

*Who's Who of American Women*. Chicago: Marquis 1970/71–present.

*Women Studies Abstracts*. Honeoye: Rush, 1972–present.

*The Women's Annual: The Year in Review*. Boston: Hall, 1980–present.

*Women's History Sources: A Guide to Archives and Manuscript Collections in the United States*. 2 vols. Ed. Andrea Hinding in association with the University of Minnesota. New York: Bowker, 1980.

WOMEN'S STUDIES JOURNALS

*Feminist Studies*
*International Journal of Women's Studies*
*New Directions for Women*
*Resources for Feminist Research*
*Signs*
*Women's Studies*

# Index